SERPENT
of
LIGHT

SERPENT
of
LIGHT

The Movement of the Earth's Kundalini
and the Rise of the Female Light,
1949 to 2013

Drunvalo Melchizedek

WEISERBOOKS
San Francisco, CA / Newburyport, MA

First published in 2007 by
Red Wheel/Weiser, LLC
With offices at:
500 Third Street, Suite 230
San Francisco, CA 94107
www.redwheelweiser.com

ISBN: 978-1-57863-401-9

Library of Congress Cataloging-in-Publication Data available upon request

Typeset in ITC Legacy Serif.
Cover photograph © Nikada33/iStockphoto

Printed in Canada
TCP
10 9 8 7

To our ancestors who still live within our hearts, and who someday will again walk with us into the future.

CONTENTS

INTRODUCTION

Life is amazing! Every 13,000 years on Earth a sacred and secret event takes place that changes everything, an event that changes the very course of history. And at this moment, this rare event is occurring, but only a few people know. And most of those who do know have kept it quiet and hidden until now.

What I am speaking about is the Earth's Kundalini. Connected to the center of the Earth is an energy that appears and behaves much like a snake as it moves, similar to the way Kundalini energy moves in the human body.

It is this energy that gives rise to the spiritual seekers everywhere on Earth—not only in the ashrams, kankas, and monasteries of the world, but also even in ordinary life and ordinary people who, in their own way, are seeking God. The Earth's Kundalini is the secret energy that is connected to the hearts of all of mankind.

The Earth's Kundalini is always attached to a single location on the surface of the Earth and stays there for a period of about 13,000 years. But then it moves to a new location for the next 13,000 years, based upon cycles of time, or what we call the Precession of the Equinox. And when it moves, our idea of what "spiritual" means changes. It transforms according to the new energies of the future cycle, leading us into a higher spiritual path.

The bigger picture is this. The Kundalini has two poles, and one is in the exact center of the Earth. The other is located on the surface somewhere and anywhere in the world. It is the consciousness of the Earth herself that decides where it is to be.

And there is a pulse of exactly 12,920 years when the polarity of the Earth's Kundalini changes to the opposite pole, and it simultaneously changes location on the surface of the Earth. This new location not only rapidly wakes up the people living near this sacred point on the Earth, but also it sends a frequency into the electromagnetic grids surrounding the Earth. This, in turn, affects those consciousness grids in ways that are determined by the Earth's DNA. We grow according to a set plan and design.

To the few that know of this event and what is occurring all around us, a wisdom is transferred, and a peaceful state of being becomes their inheritance, for they know the awesome truth. In the midst of chaos, war, starvation, plagues, environmental crisis, and moral breakdown that we are all experiencing here on Earth today at the end of this cycle, they understand the transition and know no fear. This fearless state is the secret key to the transformation that, for millions of years, has always followed this sacred cosmic event.

On one level, this means that spiritually the female will now have her turn to lead mankind (womankind) into the New Light. And eventually, this female spiritual light will permeate the entire range of human experience from female leaders in business and religion to female heads of state. By 2012–2013 this female spiritual light will become so strong as to become obvious to all who live on this dear planet and will continue to grow for thousands of years.

For many of you, none of this will probably make any sense until you read chapters two and three. Chapter two is the Cosmic Knowledge of what is actually occurring in nature and the stars and how it relates to this new cycle of light. Chapter three is the history of what the ancient cultures understood about this sacred event up to this present time. This prepares you for the content of this book.

Beginning with chapter four will be the stories of my personal experience and involvement with this Serpent of Light and the hundreds of indigenous tribes and cultures that have secretly helped guide this spiritual energy from Tibet to its new home in South America. Coming out of Tibet into India, it then moved in a snake-like manner to almost every country in the world until it reached Chile, the new home of the Earth's Kundalini, the new "Tibet."

What has occurred in the world along this path that the Earth's Kundalini has taken is almost unbelievable. People from different cultures and countries all cooperating together "as though" they were coordinated by a higher power simply for the good of human life. And without this spiritual assistance, I believe, humanity will be unable to evolve to the next level of consciousness, crucial to our very survival.

For me, the call to this way of life was so strong that I felt like I had no choice. It simply began to happen all around me as I followed my inner guidance.

But I am not the only one. There are tens of thousands of people, mostly indigenous people, who have been led by a deep inner guidance, from 1949 to the present, to help to bring this unyielding White Snake to its new location high up in the Andes Mountains in Chile, where it now finally resides. Not only is this a shift of spiritual power from the male to the female, but it is also a spiritual power shift from Tibet and India to Chile and Peru. The Light of the World that has been nurtured and expanded with the Tibetan and Indian cultures is now completed. Its new reign has just begun in Chile and Peru, and soon it will affect the hearts of all mankind.

These are my personal stories as I have followed my inner guidance helping bring balance to a troubled world. My training has been to stay connected with Mother Earth and Father Sky within a secret place within my heart. It is very simple. Once one is connected to the Divine Mother and Father in this way, life becomes one miracle after another. Never could anyone plan these kinds of stories. They are conceived from outside myself in the nature that surrounds us. Some of these stories break the laws of physics, but not the laws of our Mother.

Like I said, Life is amazing!

CHAPTER ONE

THE OPENING

In 1971 two softly glowing spheres of light, one a bright green and the other an ultraviolet color, entered into the room where I was meditating and identified themselves by saying, "We are not separate from you. We are you."

From that moment on, my heart opened to new possibilities of life and has continued to open wider each day. Sure, I have the same everyday problems as everyone else. I have a wife and kids. I have to pay the bills and give much of my energy to my responsibilities as a father, but these beings that call themselves angels and appear as beautiful spheres of light have kept me connected to the inner Light within my heart, and that Light has always led me through the outer circumstances in ways that are hard to believe from the viewpoint of a spectator observing by the sidelines.

And know for certain, this same inner Light is within your heart also. No one is special in the eyes of God. We are all exactly the same, for there is only One Spirit that moves through absolutely everything and everyone.

It is the simple Truth of reality as spoken by St. Thomas in his Gospel of the Christ, "God is all around you and within you." It is easy in this modern world, with the images of television and the

Internet flooding the mind, to forget the Truth of our reality. Just look at the moon—I mean really look at the moon—and it is easy to sense the incredibleness of our existence. So the Truth is still the Truth no matter how much man distorts it.

From 1972 until 1994 I studied with these spheres of light a subject that the world has named sacred geometry, which showed me, for certain, that all of creation was created by a single pattern, the Flower of Life. This gave me the proof that my mind needed to understand that there is only One Consciousness in this One Universe, and this undeniable proof let my mind surrender to my heart. Finally, life begins in a simple way, in what could be called the original way.

To let you know a little bit more about myself, I offer the following. I graduated from the University of California at Berkeley with a degree in fine arts, and a minor in physics and mathematics. I have studied human consciousness with over seventy spiritual teachers from all over the world and from almost every religion and discipline. My first book, *The Ancient Secret of the Flower of Life: Volume I*, was published in 1998, and *Volume II* in 2000. Within a few short years these books were in many languages all over the world and on every continent, reaching out to over 100 countries.

A school on teaching the Mer-Ka-Ba meditation, the human light body, coming from the instructions of the second volume, emerged in 1994 (before the books were printed) and soon led to the creation of schools in over sixty countries, with over 150 trained teachers.

By 2004 a new book, *Living in the Heart*, was published. This work opened up new information about human consciousness that was, and still is, hardly known by the world's population, as it has been kept secret by almost all of the world's spiritual and religious teachings. This book also has spread worldwide.

Slowly, I have been responding to requests and invitations to teach this knowledge in seminars and workshops, lectures, magazine articles, Web sites, and on radio and television, and I have, at present, visited and taught in over fifty-some countries.

The knowing of this story about the Serpent of Light has come to me slowly—in pieces at the beginning, but more quickly in the last

Figure 1: Flower of Life

five years. At first I didn't understand the full significance of what was being presented to me. Not until just after the turn of the millennium did I begin to truly understand all that was happening to me and to this energy now called the Serpent of Light, as it was named hundreds of thousands of years ago. (In the Orient it was simultaneously called, "The Great White Snake.")

When you read these stories, stay within your heart, not your mind, for your mind will never understand how people can coordinate themselves over thousands of years and how complex human events can realize themselves without any human planning. But your heart will know. Within your heart is all knowledge and all wisdom.

For sure your heart will know the Truth and hopefully will respond.

I am using my life stories to give you inspiration to help you find the same place that is in both of our hearts. When you are in your heart, nothing needs to be done to bring change; it will happen automatically and with grace. But to reach your heart, as every indigenous tribe I know has told me, you must first remember your Divine Mother. If you remember this first great understanding of all indigenous people on Earth, then the inner meaning of what is given within will appear. Your Mother is alive and very much conscious—extremely conscious, beyond what twenty-first-century industrialized man understands.

Earth is not a rock; she has a name and a personality in the cosmos. And believe me, she knows your name. And it is her spirit, the spirit of Mother Earth, that is behind each one of these stories. It is She who created these stories that, woven with thousands of other stories from other men and women worldwide, will surely lead to an entire transformation of humanity. When you finish these stories, how could you not know how much your Mother loves you? And in gratitude, how could you not offer your service to your Mother's needs?

Ceremony

And finally, the awesome significance of ceremony. Mankind long ago lived not from the mind, but the heart. It was dreaming that created the world, but now it is thinking that is shaping our way of life. The old way has tremendous power that most of us have long forgotten, and, as you will see in these stories, it is possible that unless we remember the old way, we may be faced with an imbalance that will not resolve itself until we do.

From the day that Adam and Eve were created, taking care of the "gardens" was their inherent purpose. And as humanity slowly developed over hundreds of thousands of years, this initial purpose has never changed or faltered.

Taking care of Mother Earth eventually crystallized into what is now recognized as ceremony. And ceremony to all primitive and indigenous cultures over the entire world has always been understood to hold the essence of a tribe's responsibilities to their ancestors, of course, in their hearts all the way back to the first man and woman.

In my tribe, the Taos, a ceremony was held every year on September 30, a day that was given the name "San Geranamo Day." The Taos believed that this ceremony was absolutely necessary to be completed or the Earth would literally spin off of its axis and all would be lost for all people on the planet. People would come from all over the world to watch the "Indians" climb this incredibly high pole, a 100-foot-high tree stripped of all its branches and buried in the earth about eight feet, so that it stood vertical in the way it grew. From hanging ropes, four Indians would attempt to climb this pole and through this ceremony give the Earth another year to round the sun.

It was a beautiful and dangerous ceremony that pulled people from all over the world to this pueblo, but did they really believe that if the Indians didn't climb this pole that all would be lost? Hardly. Perhaps one or two. But most of the world believes that indigenous ceremony is superstition and something that has no grounding in science. To the Indians (Native Americans), however, this is the truth of their reality. They believe it in every cell of their bodies.

Mankind has moved away from the heart of the world to the logic of the mind, and their belief is in the chemist, the physicist, and the mathematician. Science has proven to them that all this ancient belief in ceremony is simply ignorance.

And yet modern man has created, with its great science, which it is certain is the ultimate "truth," a world on the brink of total destruction in less than two hundred years and perhaps only a few years left to exist if something drastic is not done. Whereas ancient man, with its silly ceremonies, managed to sustain itself for millions of years. Perhaps if we wish to survive at all, we should consider this ancient wisdom, at least to understand, even with our logical mind, how it is possible that ceremony actually can create a world in balance.

As a Native American in a white body, I have followed the indigenous ways, as they have shown me the secret to creation. It is not the mind that is so brilliant, but the light of the world that comes from the heart. Creation always begins in the heart, and then it is transferred to the mind. We have forgotten our essence, and if we do not remember it very soon, our great technological mind will lead us into a world of massive pain and worldwide destruction. A world without heart is a mechanical world separating itself from the Reality.

What follows are stories of remembering our intimate interconnection with God and the creation process. My stories are given to you so that you also will remember and return into the harmony and flow of the Universe.

Love is the answer to every question—even the questions of the mind.

CHAPTER TWO

Ancient Cosmology 101 and Modern Changes

In order for you to hear these stories that will follow with understanding, so that everything makes sense, there is a bit of cosmology that must be understood. This cosmology, the underlying landscape of what is being presented in these pages, is based primarily upon the Precession of the Equinox and the cycles of change that are associated with it.

The Precession of the Equinox

You may believe you know what the Precession of the Equinox is and what it means, but please, there is something extraordinary about this cycle that you probably have not heard. As far as I know, it has never been written about before, but kept only in oral traditions by indigenous tribes and cultures around the world. This is called the Serpent of Light.

In the simplest terms, the Precession of the Equinox itself (hereafter referred to as simply POE) is merely a wobble in the Earth's axis. It's a wobble, or revolution, that requires a little less than 26,000 years to complete. To be exact, this period of one revolution is 25,920 years. If the axis of the Earth were a pencil, the circle drawn from one of the ends would appear as below.

(Additional wobbles exist within the POE and are discussed in *The Ancient Secret of the Flower of Life: Volume I*. It is the primary POE we're now concerned with in this story.)

As the wobble of the Earth's axis slowly turns in a circle, it eventually points to and passes through all twelve of the heavenly constellations, one after another. This means that the POE points to or "enters" a new constellation about every 2,160 years. In other words, there are twelve divisions in the POE, each division representing a different constellation and a considerably different type of energy. Most ancient civilizations were aware of the POE and of these twelve divisions of the night sky—even the oldest civilization known to us, the Sumerians, which existed about 6,000 years ago.

It is interesting to note that astronomically and mathematically speaking, it takes 2,160 years of continuous observation of the night sky to become aware that there even is this wobble in the Earth's axis. From an archeological point of view, before the Sumerians, we humans were thought to be hairy barbarians who lacked the intelligence and discipline required to observe and record the night sky for such a long period of time. Yet the Sumerians knew exactly of the POE from the very beginning of their civilization.

It is an archeological bewilderment to scientists who have studied this matter, but it is true. From ancient Sumerian cities that were buried deep under the earth, thousands of clay tablets have been discovered in recent times. Written in the first and oldest known human language—ancient Cuneiform—these tablets go back to the beginning of the Sumerian civilization and fully describe the POE in great and exact detail. The ancient Sumerians possessed this cosmic knowledge even though it is impossible by the understanding of history that we now hold.

How can this be? In my first two books, *The Ancient Secret of the Flower of Life: Volume I* and *Volume II*, I have offered a possible answer, but I'm not going to go into this information now, as it is not pertinent to this story.

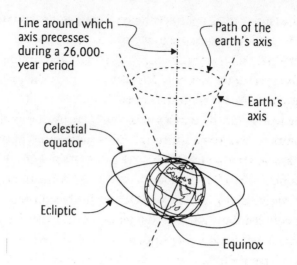

Figure 2: Drawing of POE

The Tibetans and the Hindus also recorded the movements of the POE from ancient times. Both cultures placed vast importance on each of the twelve divisions and referred to the divisions as "Yugas," or "periods of time," giving each Yuga a different characteristic that they believed affected all of mankind during that specific Yuga. Remember, each Yuga also represented a different constellation and would therefore be an integral part of astrology.

We have all heard that we are moving into the Age of Aquarius. This is true. On December 21, 2012, the axis of the Earth will be on the edge of this constellation, and, for the first time in 12,920 years, it will also be moving toward the center of the galaxy instead of away from it. For the next 2,160 years, the axis of the Earth will be moving through the constellation of Aquarius. But there is so much more about this phenomenon that generally is not known and will actually affect your life as you live and breathe and fulfill your destiny.

Modern Astrology

Today the vast majority of the Earth's population doesn't really believe in astrology. It's looked on as something of an old wives' tale, primarily identified with the birthday of an individual and the star patterns at the moment of birth, but it has not always been this way.

Astrology has been adopted in human consciousness since the beginning of civilization to understand and predict various aspects of the future. But its main use was not for personal consideration. In ancient times, as with Babylonia and Assyria, going back into Egypt 6,200 years ago, the interpretation of the movement and the patterns of the stars and planets was used to assist the public welfare and the person of the king, because his person was linked to the public's survival. It was not until the occupation of Egypt by Alexander the Great in 332 B.C. that individual "horoscopic astrology" first appeared.

The Earth's closest star, the sun, is a major part of astrology. The sun also affects our weather, places our satellites and our worldwide communications network in jeopardy when there are solar flares, and even affects the Earth's magnetic fields. Without the radiation from the sun, there would be no life whatsoever on this planet. Earth would simply be a rock floating through space.

The moon moves the Earth's oceans and creates the tides. It also deeply influences our weather, affects biological mating and birthing patterns of life-forms all over the Earth, and even influences human emotions, as police blotters in any major city prove. There are more crimes the day before, the day of, and the day after the full moon than at any other time. This crime rate is not just a coincidence. People become more emotional during the full moon and consequently do things that they normally would not do without the influence of the moon.

So to say that the heavens have no effect on people or the Earth is rather ignorant and not scientifically true.

Since there are influences such as those just described, would there be an influence if the Earth herself were facing in a different direction relative to the entire heavens? According to the ancient civilizations, yes; we change every time the axis of the Earth rotates into a new position and a new constellation. In fact, according to ancient beliefs, everything on Earth changes.

The Serpent of Light

The Kundalini of the Earth changes locations on the surface of the Earth at two very specific points on the POE. It is not the apogee, the farthest point from the center of the galaxy, nor the perigee, the closest point, that we are interested in. Rather, it is the points when the *direction of the axis* of the Earth begins to point toward the center of the galaxy and when it begins to point away from the center. On Dec 21, 2012, the axis begins pointing to the center of the galaxy, and the Kundalini of the Earth begins to change locations on the surface of the Earth.

Life is organic and is not always perfect and mathematical, since most of life is based upon the Fibonacci Series (0, 1, 1, 2, 3, 5, 8, 13, etc.), which only approximates the Golden Mean. In other words, Dec 21, 2012, is the mathematical date when this occurs, but in fact this shift of the Kundalini has already happened in 2002. But on an elliptical cycle of 25,920 years, ten years is almost perfect and very organic. Still the actual major impact on human consciousness is only beginning and will not be reached until sometime in the immediate future. What a great time to be alive!

At both of these points, the Earth's Kundalini actually moves from one fixed location on the surface of the Earth to another. So as the Earth finds itself in the cycle where the axis faces away from the center of the galaxy, the Earth's base energy, coming from its center, moves to a new location on its surface. The result is a huge and distinctly new change in spiritual understanding and practice filtering down eventually to ordinary everyday life in the streets.

The impact for the geographical location that the Kundalini just left and the new location to which it just moved to is also enormous. For the place it just left, the spiritual energy is now gone, and it will probably never return. For the place it just moved to, a new, revitalized spiritual energy seems to have appeared out of nowhere and dramatically affects the people who live in that area. They, in turn, affect the entire world with their newfound wisdom and light.

Kundalini Energy

What is the Earth's Kundalini? It probably would best be explained from a human perspective, because the Earth and the human body are almost identical energetically. Not only is the Earth's Kundalini energy very similar to a human being's, but also even such massive energy fields as the Mer-Ka-Ba field of the planet and the human Mer-Ka-Ba field (the Light Body) are exactly the same except for proportional size. Every electromagnetic geometrical field within the Mer-Ka-Ba field of the Earth is exactly identical to every human being on Earth.

For humans, there are five possible energy streams that originate at the base of the spine. Each one has a different purpose for different stages of human development. One of these is sexual energy, and this one most of us are familiar with. We know what it is like when we have an orgasm, and we can feel this sexual energy rising up our spines. But there are four more energy streams, and one of these is called the Kundalini. Most people experience Kundalini in sequence after the sexual orgasm, but not always; a few people experience the Kundalini first. When this Kundalini energy rises up our spines, it changes our way of "seeing" or interpreting the world around us depending on where it moves within the human energy system.

Kundalini energy feels somewhat like sexual energy in that it is a very strong, uncontrollable energy rising up our spine. But whereas sexual energy is related to the creation process, Kundalini energy is related to our spiritual growth process. Eventually, after we have experienced the sexual and the Kundalini energy, we will slowly, over time, experience the other three energy streams, though this experience may not occur in this lifetime. (I'm not going to expand upon these other three energy streams now, as they are not part of these stories.)

At this moment in history, it will be the Kundalini of the Earth that is moving and changing locations, beginning a new vibration. This energy shift will affect every last person on Earth. This Earth Kundalini energy is called the *Serpent of Light*.

A Dramatic Side Note

To better understand the significance of the point on the POE that we will reach on December 21, 2012, consider the following scientific facts.

Thirteen thousand years ago, at the mememt (or close to it) when the axis of the Earth began to point away from the center of the galaxy, the entire Earth's north pole changed positions from Hudson Bay (they believe) to where it is now at the North Pole. A complete polar-axis shift relative to the surface of the Earth occurred and has been scientifically recorded.

And 13,000 years before that—26,000 years ago—when we were at the very point on the POE cycle where we are now, the axis of the Earth also dramatically shifted. Some scientists are considering the possibility of another pole shift, based on what happened the last two times the Earth was at these points on the POE. Nature moves in cycles.

Another reason many scientists are concerned is that in both of the physical pole shifts mentioned above, the magnetic field of the Earth also shifted prior to the actual pole shift. And at this moment, the magnetics of the Earth are the most unstable they have been in 13,000 years. It has been scientifically noted that about 2,000 years ago, the Earth's magnetic field began to gradually weaken. Then suddenly, about 500 years ago, the Earth's magnetic field began to weaken sharply.

About thirty-five to forty years ago, the Earth's magnetic field began to demonstrate anomalies, which were reflected in the migration patterns of birds and animals that depended on the magnetic field to guide them. For the first time, migrating bird and animals were getting lost, because the magnetic field had either changed direction or was not present at all.

In about 1997, the magnetic field began to grow unstable—so much so that it was becoming dangerous to land airplanes on automatic pilot. Too many deviations from true north were occurring. So all of the airport magnetic maps of the world had to be changed to bring them up to date with reality. (You can easily check this as truth.)

In 2005, the world's geological scientists began to talk about the incredible magnetic anomalies being recorded worldwide. They suggested that some time in the near future the Earth may experience a *reversal* of its magnetic poles, with the North Pole becoming the South Pole and visa versa. This scientific global communication lasted eleven days before the Earth's governments shut the communication down. In 2006, the same scientists became even more excited by the extreme nature of magnetic anomalies, predicting that this reversal of the poles could happen any time now. Their conversation was shut down again, this time after only five days.

The stories you are about to read are based upon this cosmic information. They are true stories, though they may seem incredible by modern beliefs, and are given to you to inspire you to perceive the possibility of a beautiful future outside of the darkness cycle that seems to be invading this world. I'm asking you to not look at the darkness, but to turn your attention to the Light.

Pure guidance is within you.

Life may appear as a mysterious journey, but from within the heart it is child's play.

CHAPTER THREE

THE SERPENT OF LIGHT AND THE GREAT WHITE PYRAMID OF TIBET

As science has recorded, about 16,000 years ago, three great pieces of an asteroid struck the Atlantic Ocean off the coast of what is now the state of Georgia in the United States. The Atlantian priesthood knew the end was near for their great country.

Plato named this lost continent Atlantis 2,000 years ago and spoke elegantly about its culture and its beauty, but most modern archeologists still consider Atlantis only a legend. With all the searching and exploration conducted over the years to prove its existence, nothing conclusive has ever been determined, for when Atlantis disappeared below the waves of the Atlantic Ocean, it took all evidence with it to the ocean floor.

So this is history that cannot be proven at this time. But in the future, hopefully it will be. Edgar Cayce, the Sleeping Prophet, said in the 1920s that Atlantis would rise out of the Atlantic Ocean near Bimini before the year 1970, and it very well could have. In January 1970, *Life* magazine reported that many small islands, originating on the ocean floor, over a mile deep in the Atlantic Ocean near Bimini, broke the surface in December 1969. Many of them were resubmerged, but some of them are still there today. Was Cayce's prediction correct? Time will tell.

Cayce made over 12,000 predictions about the time prior to 1970, and only one of these predictions turned out not to be true—a simple one relating to a twin brother for whom he made a diagnosis.

The Spiritual Light of the World, the Earth's Kundalini, a snake-like energy coiled deep inside the Earth, had resided inside this ancient continent for thousands of years. It was this spiritual energy that had caused other cultures to come to Atlantis from all over the world to seek enlightenment, much in the same way that modern seekers travel from around the world to India and Tibet.

This huge asteroid streaming in from the heavens actually preceded the end of Atlantis by three thousand years, but was the physical reason for the demise of Atlantis. The Kundalini of Mother Earth, the Serpent of Light, would soon begin to move to a new location to bring balance to what would rapidly become a new world. A new world perhaps, but this impact would mean the sinking and death of Atlantis.

Always remember, there are no mistakes. Everything that happens, happens for reasons that affect all life everywhere and with sheer precision.

The inner priesthood of the ancient continent of Atlantis, the Nakkal Brotherhood, knew from their inner knowing exactly where the Serpent of Light would move to and settle, coiling like a snake down inside the Earth to hibernate for another long cycle of 13,000 years, and that by changing positions on the surface of the Earth, it would would change the way humans interpret life. The Nakkal Brotherhood knew they would have to leave Atlantis and move to where the Serpent of Light would find its new home.

They also knew that wherever the Light of the World settled, the people of that region would become the great spiritual teachers of the planet. It has always been that way, for this Light affected people who live near where it was coiled and naturally brought them into a state of enlightenment, depending upon their ability to receive it. The people of this new region would begin to awaken and remember their intimate connection with all life everywhere and with God. Eventually they would even remember the sacred place within their hearts where God resides and where all of creation began. And their remembering, they would become spiritual lights to the rest of humanity simply by their very being.

So the Nakkal Brotherhood began to make plans to leave their beloved country of Atlantis and follow the source of their understanding. They had no choice. They made their plans and prepared to leave almost two hundred years before Atlantis finally sank deep into the ocean, before they found themselves in chaos. Eventually, the Nakkals followed the Great White Serpent of the Earth's Kundalini to a remote area high in the Himalayan mountains located in the western region in what is today called Tibet.

When Atlantis finally did sink, about 13,000 years ago, the outer priesthood (not the inner Nakkals) of Atlantis quickly left in elaborate ships. They were forced to evacuate as the earthquakes, volcanoes, and sinking land and onrushing water never ceased. They didn't travel far. The outer priesthood went to the shores of what is now the Yucatan in Mexico, and today are known as the Maya. We know this is true not only because the Maya say so, but also because of an ancient stone document found by archeologists in the Yucatan; called the Troano Document, it is now located in the British Museum. Estimated to be at least 3,500 years old, it was translated by the historian Augustus Le Plongeon and describes in detail the sinking of Atlantis.

The calendar that the Maya now hold was originally created during the time that Atlantis was alive and well, and was actually hand-carried to the Yucatan by the priesthood in their escape from certain death.

This outer priesthood is alive in present-day Mayan men such as Hunbatz Men, a Mayan priest and shaman. He was the one elected by the secret elders in the 1980s to be the spokesman for the outer world. Now he has been replaced by a humble man named Don Pedro Pablo, also elected by the Maya elders. Even deeper into the Mayan culture we find Don Alejandro Cinlo Perez Oxlaj, one who holds the original information back to the very beginning of his culture. Don Alejandro is now the president of the High Mayan Council of over

400 elders from Mexico, Belize, and Guatemala. Time will unfold the depth of his knowledge and wisdom.

The Great White Pyramid

The Nakkals, the inner priesthood of Atlantis, arrived in Tibet with tremendous difficulty, to begin construction of one of the world's greatest pyramids. This pyramid they constructed is made of solid white stones and appears today as though it was created in modern times, for it is still in perfect condition. It appears brand new.

The purpose of this Great White Pyramid was both to mark the exact location of the Earth's Kundalini energy and to focus that energy for the benefit of mankind. It created an area of energy stretching for vast distances, and the people who lived within this area would undergo special changes in their minds, bodies, and hearts. Some would change more than others, but with training, the changes were inevitable. This influence on the people resulted in great spiritual teachers whose enlightenment reached to the rest of the world. Tibet, parts of China, India, and Nepal became the new center for the Light of the World (although at the time of the construction of this pyramid, none of these countries were born yet).

Almost 6,000 years went by after Atlantis sank into the ocean before the human race began to remember who it really was and civilization once more began to flourish. During all of these thousands of years the Nakkals remained with the Great White Pyramid to protect it and to thrive with its enlightening energy. Eventually, the Nakkals actually seeded the Tibetan race, extending themselves into modern times.

Slowly the influence of the Serpent of Light began to give birth to great souls such as Lao Tzu, who wrote the Tao Te Ching—the Way of Life—one of the greatest works ever created. And, of course, the I-Ching, probably the most amazing book ever written, came from this region. The Buddha lived within this area of influence, creating Buddhism, a world religion that, more than any other religion, in my personal experience, has a deeper understanding of the human

energy fields and consciousness dimensions beyond normal awareness. Tibetan Buddhism is the only religion left that remembers the
Mer-Ka-Ba, the human light body and, even more importantly, what
it means and how to create and use it. (The Mer-Ka-Ba is the human
energy field that extends out beyond the body about twenty-seven to
thirty feet spherically in all directions.) Many great men and women
(but mostly men during this male part of the cycle) emerged from
this area simply because the White Serpent was coiled inside the
Earth under this Great White Pyramid built by the ancient Nakkal
Brotherhood.

But soon all of this would change one more time.

The modern-day Maya knew, by their amazing calendar, the most
accurate calendar that humanity has ever created, that a special time
was approaching. Like the great sun rising to reveal the morning sky
and the beauty of the living world, something tremendous within
the Earth was beginning to move, and it would reveal something
fantastic long lost to the human soul. Deep inside the Mother's belly
an ancient energy began to slowly move from side to side, much
as a snake glides across the land. This snakelike energy began to
awaken and feel an intense need to find a new home and a new way
to express life as the constellation of Aquarius slowly begins to yield
its influence.

Every 12,920 years this urge is undeniable!

China Invades Tibet and the Serpent of Light Begins to Move

The Panchen Lama, the second highest ranking lama after the Dalai
Lama, then only eleven years old, asked China in 1949 to "unify the
motherland," meaning to bring Tibet back into China's domain.
China's communist leader, Mao Tse-tung, responded by announcing
China's intention to "liberate Tibet from foreign imperialists."

In 1949, China invaded Tibet.

The world was still tired and sickened by all the killing and pain
of World War II, which had only ended four years before. The British,
who declared to the United Nations that they had an "interest in the

maintenance of Tibetan autonomy," had neither the heart nor the means to resist the Chinese, and would not support the Tibetans or come to their defense.

In 1959, after the Tibetan uprising at Lhasa and its savage suppression by the Chinese, the Dalai Lama fled to India for refuge, followed by a wave of thousands of Tibetan refugees pouring over the border.

At this very moment, after a 13,000-year rest, the Serpent of Light began to slide out of the Nakkal's Great White Pyramid and onto the surface of the Earth. Slowly at first, but then faster and faster, this Kundalini energy started moving through Tibet. Then, in a single day, it left the country along with the Dalai Lama and moved into India. It was almost as if the Dalai Lama invoked the Serpent to leave Tibet.

But this movement of the Serpent of Light into India was only the beginning of a very long, long earthly journey that would eventually transverse most of the planet, just as had happened when it left ancient Atlantis to arrive high up in the Tibetan mountains 13,000 years before.

The Grand Meeting

On the other side of the world, the Mayan elders from all areas of Mexico, Belize, and Guatemala, called for a grand meeting of all Mayan tribes. It was the first time such a meeting had ever been called in modern times, and it was a truly tremendous event.

This meeting was brought into being because the Mayan calendar clearly showed that the Serpent of Light was going to move in 1959 and that it would eventually require the assistance of the indigenous peoples of North and South America.

The Mayan elders met to hold a ceremony together because of what the Mayan calendar was prophesying: the end of a grand cycle and the beginning of a new cycle and a new world—a world where the entire heavens would be opened up to humanity, and we would be free to explore our natural environment of space, time, and dimension beyond the Earth. The prophecy had predicted a time of a wonderful peace and spiritual growth. The beginning of this new cycle was predicted by the Guatemala Maya to be February 19, 2013.

Why not December 21, 2012, as predicted by the moment of the change of the POE into Aquarius? Sorry, I can't tell you. This question you will have to ask the Guatemala Maya themselves, as they are the only ones who really understand why this two-month discrepancy exists.

Like the Nakkal Brotherhood before them, the Maya held this enormous meeting to share their knowledge and prophecy, so that they would be prepared as a culture to properly perform their cosmic responsibility in the guidance and marking of the movement of this eternal Serpent of Light. During this meeting it was discovered that the lowland Maya, those living in Mexico and Belize, had lost—to time and to the Spanish conquistadors—almost all of their knowledge and prophecy and that their living legacy had all but disappeared. But to the relief of Mother Earth, the legacy was not dead. It was still alive and well in Guatemala. There, high up in the mountains, near the beautiful ancient city of Tikal, the Mayan elders, most over a hundred years old, still held the knowledge and prophecies that had been brought from Atlantis 13,000 years before.

So the elders of Guatemala handed the lowland Maya "fifteen books." The lowland Maya were told to study and learn this knowledge and that they would be given more books in the future. In this way, the return of the Mayan calendar, knowledge, and prophecy was initiated.

The outer world at this time knew nothing of this exchange, nor did they care. Materialism was the way of the world.

Industrial Man Intervenes

With the best of intentions, certain explorers of knowledge, such as Jose Arguelles and others, began to study the Mayan calendar with the belief and understanding that the Maya of Mexico held their knowledge intact, when, in fact, they did not. Their knowledge was limited by an incomplete infusion from the Guatemalan Maya. And so many books have been written about the Mayan calendar, which cannot really be made complete and accurate until the Guatemala Maya finish returning their knowledge to the lowland Maya.

According to the Guatemalan Maya, there are still five more "books" for the lowland Maya to read and understand, and it is the sixteenth book, *The Book of the Insects and the Fixed Stars*, that determines the beginning and ending of cosmic cycles. This is the reason that the date of December 21, 2012, was never really understood, and the date of February 19, 2013, was never known.

The Serpent of Light Searches for Its New Home

The Serpent of Light followed the Dalai Lama into India, but it did not stop there. It continued to move, gradually making its way across every region of the Earth's surface.

This movement continued for about ten years, from 1959 to sometime in the late 1960s. Finally, near the end of its worldwide journey, the Kundalini energy of Mother Earth moved down from Canada, into the United States, into Mexico, Belize, and Guatemala, and then deeper into Central America.

When it reached Panama, something incredible happened that most indigenous tribes, with the exception of the Maya, didn't expect. When the Serpent of Light reached the Panama Canal, it could not pass. The Panama Canal was the largest Earth geomancy ever performed in the world. It literally and energetically separated two continents from each other, and it forcefully prevented this Kundalini energy from crossing into South America.

The Kundalini energy of the Earth became constipated and blocked. Many believe the stopping of the Serpent of Light was the source of the problems of war and strife within Colombia and other nearby countries. The Earth Kundalini could not cross the canal, creating a huge energetic imbalance. (This same kind of thing can happen in an individual person. As the Kundalini rises up a person's spine, if a chakra is blocked, the Kundalini energy cannot continue to rise, though it will continue to try. This can cause pain, sickness, and even the death of the person if the condition is not resolved.) It presented a real problem to the indigenous people of the world that would not be solved for many years.

No one, except the Maya, knew what to do.

Peru Responds to the New Cycle

Meanwhile, high in the mountains of Peru, a fully enlightened man named Oscar Ichazo and twelve men that surrounded him like Jesus, were prepared to act upon the completion of this Earth Kundalini energy and to ready the world for the coming new age. They expected the Serpent of Light to be settled high in the northern mountains in Chile before the end of the sixties and that at that time their work could be initiated.

So Oscar and one of these great twelve men, Claudio Naranjo, traveled to the United States in the mid-sixties to present to the industrial world an ancient form of knowledge based upon something that was not understood at that time, sacred geometry, which Oscar called *Arica*.

Claudio also prepared to present another form of knowledge based upon the work of the great Russian Sufi Gurdjieff. This knowledge came from what is called the Enneagram, a system of knowledge that ties human transformation to sound and music. Claudio was about to present a little-known aspect of this knowledge by which the human personality could be broken down into twenty-seven forms. His purpose in doing this was simple: to give the industrial world a tool with which they could get off the wheel of "ego types" and enter the higher world of enlightenment. Doing so, he believed, would begin to change the entire world by bringing us out of this materialistic life we lead, so we could enter into the higher chakras and extended human potential.

But all of this ended only a few years after it began. On a single day, Oscar stopped the school that he had begun and that had spread all across the United States, and he returned to Peru. Why? Simple—

the Serpent of Light was blocked, its completion was not on time (at least not as interpreted by most of the indigenous world), and no one knew when it would be completed. The Maya, of course, knew exactly what the problem was, exactly how to correct it, and even when it would be corrected. But they were being silent and waiting.

The Ceremony of the Eagle and the Condor

The Maya knew that this problem could not be solved until the Ceremony of the Eagle and the Condor was performed. The Mayan calendar said so. They also knew that it was going to take more human energy than was contained within just Central and South America to move the flowing stream of power of the great Serpent of Light. They needed the energy and cooperation of North America. And this ceremony would reunite North America, the Eagle, and South America, the Condor, so that they could work as one to help this Earth Kundalini energy move to its final destination.

Many tribes, including white people imitating native people, thought that they could perform this ceremony, and so several times the Ceremony of the Eagle and the Condor was performed. What wasn't understood was that this ceremony had to wait until a specific day in the future and that it could only be performed by the Maya.

On February 19, 2001, just as the Mayan calendar predicted, the Maya and about two hundred other indigenous tribes of North, Central, and South America, came together in Guatemala, and the real Ceremony of the Eagle and the Condor took place. It's all documented in a beautiful film called *The White Road: Visions of the Indigenous People of the Americas*.

When the ceremony was complete, finally something could be done to help the Serpent of Light find its resting place, where it would coil deep in the Earth for the next 13,000 years and present the entire world with new spiritual knowledge and energy that would be necessary for the human race to continue.

The Two Great Birds Fly as One

Later that year, 2001, tribes from all over the Americas, including the Eskimo, the Hopi, and many other tribes in the United States, the Maya, of course, and over 500 tribes from both continents, began to work together for one united purpose: to assist the Great White Snake to pass the Panama Canal and complete its journey.

I was asked by the Maya to help, because I am also part of a North American tribe—the Taos Pueblo of New Mexico—in my roots. Three days were designated, which I remember to be in September 2001, for every tribe and person in their own way to work for this one common goal. Indigenous tribes on both continents, working together on the same day, began ceremonies everywhere.

I remember that I took off from all work for those three days and went into meditation. In my tradition, the Mer-Ka-Ba, the human Light Body, is the method of choice, and so I placed a living Mer-Ka-Ba field over the Panama Canal and went into a deep meditation, using everything I knew to help move this Earth Kundalini over the canal.

The first and second day it seemed like nothing happened. I could feel the tremendous energy of so many dedicated people working as one, but I could not perceive any change with the Serpent. It was beginning to feel to me that perhaps we were failing, but I kept my doubts from entering my being and continued to meditate.

Late on the third day, I felt it happen. At first it was a small energy flow, like a tiny leak in a dam, but the energy kept widening and becoming more powerful. At last, the Serpent of Light broke free and began to energetically move side to side as it did when it was moving around the world. It entered Columbia with great power and determination and continued into South America, moving everywhere, into every region and country.

The whole indigenous world breathed a sign of relief, and cries of joy filled the air from two continents. The two great birds flying together as One had made this miracle happen. The Maya knew it would happen, for it had been prophesied in their sacred calendar;

but calendar or no calendar, when it happened in real life, it was exciting. Now it comes down to human experience and deep emotions.

Simultaneously, high in the Andes Mountains in northern Chile, 112 tribes sat in a huge circle, waiting for the Serpent of Light to arrive. The exact place had already been predicted by the Maya, and the tribes circled this spot, chanting and dancing, making this ceremony the most important human event in thousands of years. They also helped make this tiny piece of earth the holiest region on the surface of the planet.

These pure men and women continued to perform ceremony until many months later, when the Serpent of Light finally slithered home and entered its sacred resting place in the Earth. It is a place that will transform the area of Chile and Peru into a new Tibet and India, a place where great teachers will be born—teachers who will be brilliant lights to the world, just as those in Tibet and India have been.

My own part in this continuing saga was just beginning. There was much more that had to be completed, and I had no premonition of the coming changes in my life. Mother Earth was about to enlist me into the Rainbow Tribe of liberation and enlightenment. A part of my life was about to unfold in ways I could never have imagined.

What else is there to do but to be of service?

CHAPTER FOUR

THE NAKKAL PYRAMID

I woke up one morning in 1985 high up in the dry New Mexico desert, about 8,500 feet above sea level. The gray-green sagebrush expanded over the horizon in all directions like a vast ocean, except to the east where the awesome Sangre de Cristo (the Blood of Christ) Mountains stretched to the sky. The snow still lingering on the peaks on this early summer day was not unusual. Sometimes the snow would not leave these mountains all year long. To the west, hidden from view, lay the deep canyon of the Rio Grande River, secretly winding its way through this part of the desert where hardly any human beings have ever been. To the north, twenty miles from my home, stood the second largest freestanding mountain in the world, Ute Mountain.

It was on Ute Mountain that the U.S. Cavalry tried to eliminate the Ute Indians in the 1800s. Because they tried to defend themselves against the terrible injustice the U.S. government was dishing out to them, the Ute were considered dangerous and needed to be destroyed.

The cavalry chased the Ute for hundreds of miles until they reached Ute Mountain, which was named much later in their honor. The Ute and the cavalry knew there was no water on Ute Mountain, but in desperation the Ute climbed the mountain to hide. The cavalry circled the mountain and waited. In truth, they were not certain that's where the Ute had gone, but the cavalry waited, believing that with no water, if the Utes were up there, they would have to come down.

As the story goes, the Ute prayed to Mother Earth to give them water, for they knew that without it they would either die on the mountain or be forced to go down where the cavalry would kill them all—men, women, and children. They would become extinct.

And Mother Earth, who was living in the hearts of the Ute, responded. A spring of water gushed from the mountain, nourishing their bodies and saving their lives.

About three months later, the U.S. Cavalry decided that the Ute must not have climbed up the mountain in the first place and abandoned their search. The Ute are alive today because of this mountain and its miracle, the energy of which pervaded the entire valley where I was living in 1985.

I lay there thinking that something seemed different or special this morning, but had no reason to say why. The feeling stayed with me all day.

I was part of a group of men and women running an esoteric school called the Nakkal Mystery School. The name came from the angels, who never really told us the reason for it. I knew the Nakkals were the ancient priesthood from Atlantis, but other than that I had no idea. I simply accepted the name because of the suggestion from a higher source.

Our compound rested on roughly twenty acres with literally millions of uninhabited acres surrounding us. We had two adobe houses, a natural garden, a small apartment space, a work area and garage, a very beautiful adobe conference center with twenty-five-foot high ceilings and built in the shape of a pentagon, and, most important, a beautiful underground prayer room called a kiva. The school was perfect for teaching and learning.

Being completely isolated from civilization made our job much easier, as there was no one around to judge our work or actions, which would have seemed strange to some of our present-day culture. For example, every new moon we would hold a Native American sweat lodge with an enormous fire to heat the rocks. About forty people would fast from food for at least one day before the sweat, and we would drum and chant for hours, calling on the name of the Mother and the presence of Great Spirit, moving into our hearts and waiting for the rocks to become red-orange with life.

When the moment was right, we would enter into the underground kiva in complete darkness, with humility and without clothes, as was the native tradition, and with absolute sacredness to be with the Mother. It was like being in her womb. Prana, void, earth, water, fire, air—all six elements of creation and nature were present at once in this ceremony.

That afternoon I heard someone yell out a robust "Wow!" and I found myself running to see what it was. The sun was going down in another thirty minutes perhaps, and it was softly raining up against the mountains directly to the east.

The "wow!" was apparent. Framing the Sangre de Cristo Mountains was the most incredible rainbow I have ever seen in my life—ever. There was not one rainbow, but three—one rainbow inside another rainbow inside another rainbow. Brilliant, brilliant colors vibrated like they were electrically charged. I was speechless.

As I stood watching this miracle, the same feeling came over me that I felt when I woke up that morning. Somehow this day was special. But nothing showed itself as different than that of any other day except this amazing rainbow. Nevertheless, the feeling would not go away.

The very next morning a white, unmarked van pulled into our conference center. Since we were hidden from the public and so remote, it was unusual for anyone to find us when there wasn't a workshop taking place.

A group of four young men in their thirties piled out of the van and walked straight to the conference room where I stood in a small side kitchen making breakfast. One of them opened the front door, looked in at me, and asked, "Do you know where we can find a man named Drunvalo?"

Figure 3: Flower of Life

I told him who I was, and he got right to the point. "Have you ever seen this design before?" He held up a drawing of the Flower of Life. The nineteen circles were as familiar to me as my own hand.

I had first discovered this design on a 6,000-year-old Egyptian wall and since then had found it all over the world, in India, England, Ireland, Turkey, Israel, Poland, Switzerland, Greece, China, Japan, Mexico, and in about fifty other countries, almost always in ancient places. And we are still finding it in new countries each year. But most significantly to this story, as you will see, I had also found it in Tibet.

Since I had been teaching about this design since 1984, these men had found out about me and wanted to know what it meant.

I asked them, at this point, why they were so interested in the Flower of Life. They all sat down around me and began to tell me a long, long story of the discovery of a very unusual pyramid in Tibet that their exploration team had discovered a few months before. What they had to say was prodigious.

It's been so long that I have forgotten their names, but the one that seemed to be their leader or spokesman became excited and began to speak with authority. He pulled out maps and photographs and laid them all over the tabletop, flattened them out and looked me in my eyes.

He told me about the first exploration team that tried to reach this Tibetan pyramid, but spoke about how they just were not prepared for the trek. It took six months to reach this pyramid, which was high up in the western Himalayan mountains. There were no clear maps, as hardly anyone had ever been in that area, and they had underestimated how long it would take to reach this spot.

To further complicate matters, this pyramid was all white and was covered with snow for the entire year except for about two to three weeks, so a team would have to perfectly time their arrival in order to actually be able to find and hopefully to enter the structure.

He said that the first team made it all the way to the edge of the mountains where they could look down at this magnificent pyramid in the valley below, but were unable to continue or the whole team would have died. They simply did not have enough supplies for the extra time and were forced to return. This was, I believe, in the early 1980s. But only a few years later these men sitting around my table had tried one more time.

This time they were better prepared and had arrived at this Tibetan pyramid just as it was completely exposed for their exploration. They were amazed to find that, unlike the Great Pyramid in Egypt, it was not sealed. It had a single opening that allowed the team to enter unobstructed.

Over the next two days, they told me their story of finding the pyramid, which they called the Great White Pyramid. They explained how it appeared and how there were no markings, writing, hieroglyphs, or anything whatsoever on the surface or walls of the pyramid, inside or outside, except a single primary image high up on a central wall inside the main room. It was the image of the Flower of Life. This was why they had searched for me and found me in the middle of an isolated desert.

They wanted me to speak about what the Flower of Life meant. They were hoping I would lead them to whoever built this pyramid, for they had no idea.

I could not explain what the Flower of Life "really meant" in an hour or two. This is why they stayed two days. It is the creation pattern for the entire universe and everything in it, including all living creatures. It's even the creation pattern for aspects of the universe that are not considered things or matter, such as emotions and feelings. But I did my best, giving them a mini Flower of Life workshop, minus all the ceremonies, prayer circles, meandering stories, and, of course, the Native American sweat lodge.

These men talked about their incredible luck of being the first human beings to actually touch this unusual pyramid. They said that no other pyramid was known to exist anywhere near this one, which was completely isolated in an inaccessible region of the Himalayan mountains. They kept talking about how strange it was for such a pyramid to be located where no civilization has ever been.

The feeling from the day before of something special occurring had not left me. I knew this information was significant, but really, I didn't know at that time how significant.

When they left the Nakkal Mystery School, filled with excitement, the photographs they had showed me of this amazing pyramid kept coming back to me over and over again. I could almost taste why this was important, but still, nothing would come to my mind.

Finally, a couple of days later, I was in meditation, and the two angels appeared in my inner vision and said, "This pyramid is called the Nakkal Pyramid. We know you don't understand now, but in time, you will. In the future, all will be revealed to you."

But why the "Nakkal Pyramid"? And why the Nakkal Mystery School? At that time all I knew was that the Nakkals were the high priesthood from Atlantis. I didn't know they had anything to do with Tibet.

There was so much I didn't know. But I trusted the angels and kept them in my heart. When they would speak to me, I always felt like a little child trying to understand the world around me, sometimes bewildered, sometimes excited, but mostly amazed by life and how the angels so gently introduced knowledge to my simple understanding.

In time the Nakkal Mystery School was disbanded, as all such schools are, but the memory of this exploration team and the pyramid they found would not leave me. And in time, the angels did tell me the entire history, which I will share with you as we continue.

The Serpent of Light had now left its home, the Nakkal Pyramid, and was moving freely to find a new home and eventually a new pyramid, and the Unity Consciousness Grid above the Earth was growing close to completion. By 1989–1990, four years after I first learned of the pyramid, the grid had grown to its first level of Unity, but the Serpent of Light would still be searching for its place in the Earth, appearing out of phase with the Cosmic DNA.

But one must always remember, Life is perfect.

CHAPTER FIVE

THE BALANCING OF THE FEMALE ASPECT OF THE UNITY CONSCIOUSNESS GRID

Psychic abilities are not considered important in most spiritual traditions, but nevertheless, one must pass through this area of human consciousness to get to the other side. During my time at the Nakkal Mystery School, through the direction of the angels, I was taught psychic abilities on various levels.

But, be aware that the way of the mind, psychic ability, is also considered dangerous by many spiritual traditions, because a person can achieve very high levels of psychic phenomenon and still retain their ego. One must proceed with caution, but one must proceed. It is a necessary step to spiritual enlightenment.

As students we began with simple things like seeing auras. Auras are the electromagnetic colors that extend from the body in an egg-shaped energy envelope. They can be seen by scientific instruments and computers, but they can also be seen by human consciousness, when it is trained.

Basically, from the shoulders up, auras are mostly your thoughts. From the shoulders to about the knees, they are mostly your emotions and feelings. Body diseases will cause color to come from affected parts of the body, usually in geometrical shapes, and the shapes and colors change as the person's illness gets better or worse.

Seeing auras leads to reading auras, which means knowing what the colors mean. This leads to knowing what people are thinking and feeling with their emotions. And all of this begins to take one over the subtle bridge from thinking that you are an individual and that the outer world is separate from you to realizing that there is only One Consciousness and anything can be known and experienced. There are no secrets in the One Universe.

During this time of teaching, I began to find that I could communicate with people over long distances. I don't mean communicate as you would on a telephone, but more like on a video-phone—except I would be speaking telepathically and know everything that was behind the words.

My first psychic experience on a telepathic level occurred back in 1971. It was with an Eastern Indian woman named Bupi Naopendara, who appeared to me by means of a bright point of light, like a tiny sun, that would seem to come out of nothing. Usually a few feet directly in front of me, the tiny sun would expand, become dimmer, then change into an oval shape about four feet across and three feet high. The center of the oval would open up as the tiny sun expanded, and in the middle of this oval would be a window that I could see through into another location. Through this window I could see and speak to Bupi as if we were standing in the same room. I could see not only her, but also anyone else she would introduce to me. Sometimes even her dog would walk by. This communication with Bupi went on every day for about a year and a half.

So I knew this aspect of the *Siddhis* (Hindu for "psychic powers") even before I began to study at the Nakkal Mystery School. Even so, when our story begins in 1985, I considered myself a beginner.

The whole experience of psychic study was exciting most of the time—sometimes a little scary, but mostly mind-blowing. And just as I was beginning to become a little comfortable with these unusual ideas, my inner guides pushed me out into the world to be used, perhaps tested, by Mother Earth. I really didn't know very much. But apparently, there were certain things I could do for the Ascended

Masters and guides that would help the world's consciousness and healing.

Now, who are these inner and outer guides? This is a little difficult to explain, so bear with me. The two spheres of light or angels were the one thread that held the entire tapestry together, but there were many mentors; most were alive, but some were not. And most of the teachers who were alive in 1985 have now, in 2007, moved to higher levels of being. These days I am pretty much left alone, except for the angels, who continue to guide the course of my life.

Almost all of these teachers were in one way or another connected with the Great White Brotherhood and the Ascended Masters. These are simply people, like you and me, who have spiritually gone ahead of most of humanity and are living typically on other dimensions of Earth's consciousness. Both the Great White Brotherhood and the Ascended Masters have people within their orders that experience and directly affect this third-dimensional Earth, such as St. Germain and Thoth.

As of this moment, I have had perhaps ninety major teachers from every major religion, and most of the spiritual disciplines in the world. However, I'm not saying that I'm a great student. I'm a slow learner, and consider myself rather lazy. Really, I'm sure you could have done better. I have made so many mistakes learning and remembering my connection to All Life everywhere. But I can say that I did the best I could, and if I have learned anything it is that Life is perfect, whole and complete, lacking nothing.

The Beams of Light, the Unity Consciousness Grid, and the Serpent of Light

When I traveled in the Yucatan in about 1987, something happened that was intimately connected to the Nakkal Pyramid and that helped me to become greatly more conscious. It was when I was shown by the Maya something they call the Beams of Light, which are generated from the pineal. These Beams of Light appear around the human head only when a person is spiritually healthy. It is believed by my mentors and guides that this step in consciousness is absolutely necessary in order for someone to *consciously* begin the ascension process.

These Beams of Light are the connection between the mind and the heart, and their appearance is a huge step toward remembering our true connection to the Creator. In order to fully connect to the energy of the Serpent of Light on the highest levels one must have their Beams of Light functioning, at least on a minimal level. They are too complex to explain in a book like this one, but in the future I will write a book on this level of understanding. If you want an explanation now, it is taught in my global workshops, where I can show you this information personally.

Thoth

One of my inner mentors, often referred to as Thoth, the Scribe of Egypt, appeared to me several years before the Nakkal Pyramid was discovered. Thoth was assigned to me by the angels to study with for a period of time, and there is no doubt that his experience and wisdom have been paramount to my understanding.

In 1985 Thoth said to me, "There is an out-of-balance situation with the Unity Consciousness Grid around the Earth, specifically in the female aspect. We need your help, and at the same time this experience will help you grow spiritually. Will you accept?"

Well, first of all, what is the Unity Consciousness Grid? This is information that is generally not known by most people, though it is known by most of the more powerful governments. There are electromagnetic fields that are geometrical in shape and that surround and completely contain the Earth. There are millions of them, and they appear from space as a glow of light around the Earth. Every single living species of every living thing, even if it is a bug, has—in fact, must have—a grid of energy that surrounds the Earth in order for it to exist.

Humans are no different, and there are three grids associated with human consciousness. The first one is connected to certain indigenous peoples around the world, who are the oldest people alive, such as the Aboriginals in Australia. The second is geometrically based on triangles, and it is the grid that allows our specific (good and evil) human consciousness on Earth. The third is the Unity Consciousness Grid, based on the pentagonal dodecahedron interconnected to the icosahedron, which is the new grid for the consciousness that is now evolving on Earth. Without this Unity Consciousness Grid, humanity would be doomed to the material world until we eventually completely destroy ourselves. Without this Unity Consciousness Grid, humanity would never be able to ascend into the higher level of consciousness, and so its importance is obvious.

It was the United States that discovered the second grid, and it was Russia that discovered the Unity Consciousness Grid.

The Unity Consciousness Grid has been "under construction" for about 13,200 years, since just before "the Fall"—the fall in consciousness—that the Bible speaks about. And ever since the Fall, Life has been attempting to restore this all-important grid, so that humanity can get back to the stage of evolution it was on before the Fall. On one level, it is all pretty simple.

There are three energetic parts to this grid: the male, located in Egypt; the female, located on a huge circular area centered in the Yucatan in Mexico; and the child, or neutral, part, located in Tibet. It was the female part that was not completely balanced and needed attention. And it is this female part of the Unity Consciousness Grid that is the focus of the story to follow.

It will help to understand that this Unity Consciousness Grid and the Serpent of Light are deeply interconnected. The Unity Consciousness Grid is the pattern that holds and allows human consciousness on a specific level just past our present human good-and-evil consciousness; the Kundalini, or the Serpent of Light, is the energy that guides humanity to find and access this Unity Consciousness Grid. Without this new specific vibration coming from the Serpent of Light, humanity would be lost and never find its way into higher consciousness. Great Spirit has provided everything we need—perfectly.

But there are very few people actually directly connected to and expressing this Unity Consciousness. There have to be at least two or it would not exist. In truth there are at least 8,000 Ascended Masters who use this grid to be conscious. I personally believe that many more people are making the transformation over to Unity Consciousness as I write these words.

But, most important for most human beings, this is the consciousness grid that we, as a human race, are about to shift to in the immediate future. Ascension is not necessarily leaving the Earth, as some suggest—it is a change in consciousness, or a change in how one interprets the One Reality.

The Eight Temples and the Eight Crystals

I had to answer Thoth. Would I accept his assignment? Sheepishly, I said, "Yes, I'll help. But I don't really know what to do."

"Don't worry, Drunvalo, simply follow your heart. The procedures are always the same."

"Okay, exactly what is it you would like me to do?"

Without hesitation, Thoth said, "We need you to go to eight Mayan temples in Mexico and Guatemala and plant a crystal at each temple in a specific place. The location of each crystal must be absolutely perfectly placed within a few nanometers, or it will not function, and everything you are attempting to do will fail.

"We will show you where to plant the first four crystals, but you must discover for yourself where the last four crystals are to go. Only your heart can help you complete this task."

On the next day I was given the names of the eight crystals, told that they should be of a very high quality, and told to go purchase them that very day. I hurried out to a crystal store I was familiar with and discovered that this was not a cheap purchase. Money was very tight for me at that time, but there was nothing I could do about it. I bought them.

Back home, I laid them out on a dark blue cloth and went into meditation again. I was told that now I had to go to Katrina Raphael's house, who was a close friend of mine at the time, and ask her to tell me which temple each crystal should go to. This seemed so silly to me, and to this day I don't know why I had to go ask Katrina. Couldn't Thoth just tell me?

Since Katrina and I were both living in Taos, New Mexico, it was easy. I drove over to see her. But this was not an ordinary day for Katrina. She is a crystal expert who was writing her first book, called *Crystal Enlightenment*, on her special knowledge, and her publisher had demanded that the manuscript be turned in by 5 p.m. that day. So when I showed up at her door, she said, "Go away, Drunvalo, not today. I'm way too busy to talk."

I raised the index finger of my left hand, and said, "Katrina, I just need about five minutes, please."

"Drunvalo, please, I'm so behind today. Another time." But I was told to make sure I received the information of where the crystals went *today*. So I insisted, and she said, "Okay, five minutes, not a second more."

Quickly, I explained about the eight temples and the eight crystals and handed her the list as it was given to me. She read it in about three seconds, opened the blue cloth with the eight crystals in it, and, without thinking at all, pointed to each temple and announced a crystal to match, each in less than eight seconds.

"Okay, goodbye, Drunvalo, I must work."

"Okay, okay," I mumbled, "Just let me write down what you told me."

Looking back on this experience, I know it was truly greatness that inspired Katrina to choose which crystal went with each temple. As I traveled from temple to temple, each crystal she selected was always exactly the color of the primary color and/or energy of that temple. I still don't see why they didn't just tell me this in the first place. I was learning trust, I guess.

While this trip to Mexico and Guatemala was unfolding, having something to do with psychic phenomena and the grid above the Earth, another part of the story also became engaged. For this part, I'll have to go back to the beginning.

The Taos Pueblo

In my last and only other life on Earth, from 1850–1890, I lived as a medicine woman in a small pueblo tribe in New Mexico called the Taos Pueblo. I can remember every minute of this life, which is a story in itself, but not a necessary one to be told here.

What is important is that my father at that time was the chief of the tribe, and my mother was considered by the Taos to be a great soul. In this life today, my mother from the tribe is my older sister, Nita Page, and my father from the tribe is my sister's kid, Ken Page. I'm now his uncle, though there is only four years difference in our age. (My sister is sixteen years older than I am.)

In this lifetime, every year, for more than forty years, a strong and purely holy man named Juan Concha, the spiritual leader of the Taos tribe in 1985, traveled to my sister's home in California to make sure that Nita, Ken, and I never forgot our roots. In truth, the tribe had work for us to do in the future and didn't want to lose track of us.

The Three Bears Wake Up

My sister woke up first, long ago, in the early 1960s. The tribe took her in, confirmed who she was, and began a special training program created just for her. There were twelve tribes within the one Taos tribe, and each smaller tribe had its own kiva and its own spiritual way. Nita was trained in the Crystal-Fetish Tribe and taken into its kiva deep inside the Earth to begin her training. This was extremely unusual, since only males are normally ever allowed into the kivas. But because of who she was, they made an exception and trained her in the old ways.

I was the second to awaken, in 1971, when the two spheres of light, the angels, appeared to me, but it was not until 1980 that the angels asked me to go to Taos to begin my training with the tribe. I assumed that when I arrived there, the tribe would come rushing out with open arms and take me in, but that is not how it happened.

I announced that I was there to begin my remembering, and they just looked at me and said, "Go into the town and wait. We will come for you when the time is right."

Two years later, after I had almost forgotten why I came there, Jimmy Reyna, my mentor to be, arrived at my home and asked me to come to a tribal ceremony. It was the beginning of a twelve-year training program, where much of what I have learned on spiritual levels was taught to me.

I spent a great deal of time with Juan Concha's sister, Cradle Flower, who showed me the inner workings of the tribe's way of using crystals, fetishes, and dreaming to create realities. Though I learned this directly from the tribe, it was in ordinary life that I had to realize the power. It was crossing the bridge between the two worlds, the two ways, which are so different, that I had to master.

My sister and I waited for years for Ken to awaken. We kept thinking that it would be any day, but nothing ever happened. Ken had grown up in the Catholic tradition, but money was his god. He had become very wealthy with shopping centers, boat marinas, restaurants, automobile dealerships, and on and on. I think it is safe to say that Ken was a multimillionaire with materialism at the very core of his world.

Years went by. Both Nita and I began to give up on Ken ever waking up. Finally, I admit, I put him on hold, and I moved back to New Mexico from Colorado, where I was living at the time, to continue my life. After many more years, I had almost forgotten about him since we were living in two parallel worlds. Then one day in 1983–1984, a year or two before the Nakkal Pyramid was discovered, Ken had an experience.

You see, Ken had no idea about the kind of subjects that we are talking about here. He was living a life based completely on the material things one owned and walked around within. The only part of life that mattered to him was the kind of car he drove, the name brand of the suit he wore, or the address where he lived. The spiritual side of life had entirely eluded him. Psychic abilities? Ken didn't believe in any of these weird possibilities. In fact, if someone were to float an object around the room, he would instantly believe this was from the devil. Purely Catholic.

But on this day, Ken's life changed forever. Ken was asked to a party—wine and cheese and everyone standing around talking about themselves. But Mother Earth had decided it was time for Ken to begin to awaken.

A young woman approached Ken and asked him if he would like to have a "reading." He said to her, "You want to read me a book?"

She sat him down and laid out the Tarot cards and began to give him a reading, his first one in his entire life. I guess you would call it his virgin reading.

She began to tell him things that only he knew. Not just one or two things, but many deep hidden past experiences down to exact details. His mind was being blown. No one, especially a stranger, had ever told him things about himself in the way this young lady was doing. This was altering his concept of life.

By the end of the reading, Ken was wide open to anything she said. For him a miracle was taking place. Leaning forward, she pointed a finger directly at his third eye, lowered her voice, and said, "Ken, you have an uncle living in New Mexico, and you need to go visit him. He has something to teach you. You should stay three days with him."

That was the last straw. Ken knew that I was living in New Mexico, but he was beyond trying to figure out how this girl knew. He left the party, and the next morning called his mom to get my phone number. This was something he could not just walk away from. It was too powerful, and his curiosity about what it was that I would teach him was exploding like a supernova.

Reunion

I was living with my girlfriend at that time in an old Spanish community near Taos. Our house was primitive: a little adobe home with two rooms and no real bathroom. We both were artists, painting on canvas scenes mostly Southwestern in nature in order to put food on the table. I had a degree in art and a passion for art. It never seems to leave me for long. Though my surroundings were minimal, I was very happy where I lived.

One day I got a phone call from Ken. I hadn't spoken to him in almost ten years, as I said, and our lives had definitely moved in divergent directions. Ken told me about the reading with the young lady and asked if he could come and see me "for three days."

"Of course, Ken, I would love to see you."

About a week later he pulled up to my humble home in a new black Lincoln Town Car. It was incredibly out of place in this old poor Spanish community. He stepped out of the car wearing a three-piece suit and special sunglasses that change to clear when you move out of the sun.

I answered the door. Instead of saying hello, he peered inside, scanning the room, then looked at me and said, "You live here?" He couldn't believe, coming from his lifestyle, that I would actually live in a house like this.

What could I say? "Ken, I know it is simple, but I find life beautiful. Come on in."

He walked over to a chair, wiped off dust with disgust, and sat down. He looked directly into my eyes and said, "So you know about the reading, but what you don't know is that she said that you have something to teach me and that it would take three days. So what is it?"

"Slow down, Ken, I have no idea what I'm supposed to teach you, if anything. If you will wait here for a few minutes, I'll be back and perhaps I can answer you."

I went into the back room where I had made a place for meditation. I sat down and went into an altered state of consciousness very quickly, as I had been trained. There in my inner vision were the two angels. I asked them what they wanted me to do. "Show Ken everything you know about crystals," they told me. And they disappeared.

I stood up and thought about this for a moment. I had been studying crystals for many years and was even giving crystal workshops to help support myself. (The art and painting was not enough, for sure.) If I were to teach Ken everything I knew about crystals, it would take every bit of those three days.

I reentered the room where Ken was sitting.

"Well, do you know what you're going to teach me?" Ken asked.

Straightforwardly, as Ken would have it, I answered, "Yes, it seems that I am to teach you everything I know about crystals."

Ken's eyes bulged out of their sockets, and his face looked shocked. "Rocks! You're going to teach me about rocks. This is ridiculous! Rocks aren't going to help me."

"Ken, crystals are a little more than rocks." I began to explain how crystals are actually alive and conscious, something that I realize is outside of normal consciousness, but not outside of science. I showed him the periodic table of the elements, which I had posted on one of my walls. I showed him how carbon, the sixth element, is associated with all organic chemistry and everything that is normally considered to be alive. But directly below it, one octave below, is the element of silicon, the primary element of quartz crystal and 80 percent of the crust of the Earth.

I explained to him that science in the 1950s discovered that silicon displayed the same exact principles of life as carbon did, and that today science understands how carbon and silicon are the only two elements known that create life. Science has now found life-forms deep in the ocean that are alive, conscious, and reproductive, whose bodies are made up of 100 percent silicon, with no carbon whatsoever. And so when you speak of crystals, you should understand they are aware of far more than what we humans give them credit for.

Crystals are able to receive and send both human thoughts and emotions. This was discovered by Marcel Vogel, a world-renown scientist who holds over 200 patents, including one for the floppy disc for computers, while he was working at Bell Labs. It makes sense when you realize that the first radio in the world was a "crystal set." You simply placed a quartz crystal on a table, touched a wire to the crystal somewhere on it and you could hear the radio signal through the speakers. The crystal was picking up the electromagnetic signal in the radio band of frequencies.

But human thoughts are also found in the electromagnetic range of frequencies. Thoughts are very, very long wavelengths compared to radio waves, but except for the length of their wavelength, they are exactly the same. So why wouldn't a crystal be able to pick up your thoughts?

Ken, had never, ever, thought of this before. "So you mean that a crystal can know what you are thinking?"

"Yes. But Ken, it is far more than that. How do you think computers work? Computers are nothing but crystals, and without crystals, computers would not exist. It is the living nature of a crystal that allows computers to do what they do. Do you understand?

"Natural crystals can hold a 'program,' which means a thought pattern, and continue to replay that thought pattern for eternity unless someone erases the program. A properly programmed crystal can change and influence vast areas in the human world."

This was how Ken and I began to exchange ideas about crystals. Our discussion went on for three days until I felt that Ken had a pretty good idea of how crystals worked with human consciousness. On the fourth day, Ken gave me a big hug and went back to his world a slightly changed man. At least I believe he understood that a crystal was more than a rock.

CHAPTER SIX

The Balancing of the Female Grid Around the Earth
The Yucatan and the Eight Temples, Part One

Juan Concha Walks In

When Ken drove away, I wasn't sure I would ever see him again. There had been ten years in between now and the last time we had seen each other. But now, hopefully, the distance between us appeared to be changing.

About two weeks later Ken gave me a call, so excited he could hardly talk. Voice trembling, he said that he had been staying at the Hilton Hotel in Walnut Creek, California, and as he was checking out he noticed a crystal display in the lobby. They were selling fantastic crystals to the public.

With a little knowledge of crystals, Ken had noticed an enormous generator quartz crystal that was of superior condition, and he purchased it. A generator crystal will focus your own energy and use it in ways that depend upon your intention. This crystal was about ten inches long and a couple of inches wide. It potentially held great power if used correctly.

As he was driving home to the other side of the mountains by the ocean, Ken held the quartz generator in his left hand and the steering wheel in his right. He was on a freeway moving about sixty-five miles per hour, when a car zoomed past, cut into his lane, and began to spin wildly out of control in front of him. Ken had no choice but to swerve into the oncoming traffic to avoid hitting this car.

He said the next thing he remembered was heading directly into a woman's oncoming automobile. They were both moving at high speed and were about twenty feet apart. Ken could see the woman screaming, her arms up to protect her face.

But then he seemed to lose consciousness, and the next thing he knew he was back in the proper lane moving at about fifteen miles per hour. There was nothing in front of him. He looked into his rearview mirror and could see many cars piling up in multiple accidents about a quarter mile behind him. But he was safe, without a scratch.

He could explain nothing to himself. He looked down at the gleaming quartz crystal in his hand and wondered if it had anything to do with why he was still alive.

On the phone, Ken said to me, "Drunvalo, why am I still alive? How could I not have hit that lady? This is all impossible."

I couldn't answer him, so I told him that I would call him back. I hung up the receiver and went into my meditation room to talk with the angels.

They explained that Ken and Juan Concha had made an agreement a long time ago that on that day they would trade places, meaning Ken's spirit would move into where Juan's spirit existed, and Juan's spirit would move into Ken's body, but only for awhile, and then they would trade back. The agreement was to last two years.

This is another subject that the general public is not usually aware of, but it is known in many parts of the world. Advanced spirits can "walk into" other bodies under certain conditions. Normally the person in the body dies and leaves this world, which is when he or she would die anyway, and the new spirit will then walk into the body and bring it back to life. It's not quite this simple, but everything takes place in a single breath. Whatever killed the body is instantly repaired by a deep knowledge of how creation works. (Believe me, life on planet Earth is not what it seems. It is not even close.)

There are only a couple of reasons why a spirit would use the walk-in process. First and the most obvious is to save time. The advanced spirit doesn't have to go through the beginning stages of life, but sometimes the walk-in process happens even at an early age. The other is to select a person who has special skills, knowledge, or a position within the Earth's hierarchy that will be needed when the walk-in spirit takes over his or her body to fulfill their reason for coming to Earth. This process is used all over the universe.

To give you a little of my personal experience, I walked into this body on April 10, 1972. For almost nine years before I actually made the switch, I had been telepathically speaking with the person who was in that body to prepare him for what was to happen. Then when he breathed his last breath, I breathed into his body for the first time and immediately remembered all of my own memories. But within twelve hours, I completely forgot who I really was and was taken over by the body memories for almost three years. I really thought I was the person who was born into this body.

One day the angels told me, "It is time for you to remember your memories." They asked me to lie down on my bed and prepare. I didn't know what they were talking about, but almost immediately I began to remember everything. Coming from another world, entering this galaxy through the Crab Nebula (behind the middle star of the Belt of Orion), being met by my great-great-great-great-great-grandfather, Machiventa Melchizedek, moving to the Pleiades, then to Sirius, then to Venus, and finally to Earth in 1840. (Ten years later I entered my first human body, and it was accomplished through a normal birth.) So I understood the difficulties that Ken was going through.

In Ken and Juan's agreement, Juan would walk into Ken's body for two years, and then Ken would retake his body to continue his life. This particular agreement is very, very unusual. Juan had died a few years earlier, so Ken had to enter into another world in order to accomplish this feat—not easy.

At any rate, the angels asked me to tell Ken this. I remember sitting there, holding the phone in my hands, unable to dial his number because I didn't know how to tell him. I knew from the three days with him that he knew nothing about higher consciousness. Finally, I decided to just lay it out, realizing that he probably would not understand.

"Ken, is that you?"

"Yes, did you find out what happened?"

"Yes, but you're probably not going to really know about what I am about to tell you."

"It's okay." Ken said, "After what you told me about crystals, I would believe anything."

Okay. "Ken, according to my inner guidance, this is what happened." I explained about Juan Concha and how actually at this moment he was not really Ken, but was Juan. I explained everything down to how Juan would leave in two years and Ken would return.

There was complete silence on Ken's end.

"Ken, are you still there?"

Ken sighed and spoke in a slow drawl, "Man, you are really crazy," and hung up on me. I figured I may never hear from him again, but I had followed what my inner guidance felt was the healthiest pathway: just speaking the truth. I left the results up to Great Spirit.

Juan Is Alive

Some time went by, and I heard nothing from Ken. I decided to keep going on my way, believing that he would remember at the right moment. I was preparing to go to the Yucatan in Mexico to place specially programmed crystals in jungle temples, and I had never been there before in my life.

I figured that from then on out, I was probably going to do this without any help except from within my heart. And this first journey into the original world was to be secret. No one was to know, except my family and a few friends. I was alone.

The phone rang one morning shortly before the trip, while I was packing. It was Ronda, Ken's wife, who I also hadn't seen for ten years. Obviously angry, by the sound of her voice, she started, "Drunvalo, I know we haven't talked for years, but there is something I must ask you right now. I am really worried."

I said, "Hi, Ronda. Are you okay? What is it you need to ask?"

She said, "I know that you have been working with Ken, and I want to know what you did to him. Did you give him drugs or something?"

All my alarms went off. Instantly, I replied, "No, what do you mean?"

Her voice sped up, "Drunvalo, right now Ken is upstairs in the bedroom completely naked with an eagle feather in his hair, dancing and drumming in a circle. He is out of his mind, and I believe you had something to do with this."

What could I say? No way could I explain to her what I told Ken. So I just told her the truth, "Ken didn't seem to be himself the last I talked with him." I told her I hoped Ken would be all right, and she hung up. I sat there trying to understand where this was leading.

Less than a week later, a few days before I was to leave, Ken (Juan) called me up. "Drunvalo, I know that you are about to take a trip into the Yucatan, and you know that I am supposed to be with you on this trip."

I hadn't seen this coming. I didn't know what to tell him. I told Ken I'd have to check, which I did. I was told that he was definitely supposed to be on this Mexican/Guatemalan journey. Thoth told me both of us would have things to teach each other.

The Journey Begins

Ken said that he decided to drive out from California to Albuquerque, where we would meet to catch our plane. On the way through Arizona, along the hot, dry desert, there are "rock shops," where old miners sell the stones and crystals they find out in the sagebrush and in the nearby rivers and mountains. These places are nothing like the beautiful, refined shops where most of us purchase our crystals. These old rock shops are downright sullied. But sometimes a great crystal is discovered.

Ken had stopped at one of these shops and was gazing into a glass case where the better objects were protected, when he noticed a pendulum made of black onyx. It was sitting on the bottom shelf, far back in the case. His curiosity aroused, Ken asked to see it.

The old man hesitated. "Do you really want to see that pendulum?"

Ken was surprised and thought, why not? "Yes, please."

"I custom made that pendulum for a man in the 1920s, and he never picked it up," the old man said. "You are the first person to ever ask about it in all that time."

Ken took this as a sign and said, "You made it just for me. It just took a while for me to get here." He bought it, believing that, indeed, the old man really had made it just for him.

When he showed it to me, I could hardly believe this pendulum. Most people use pendulums that are small and light and easy to carry. This one was six or seven inches long and at least two inches at the widest part moving into a cone with a point. It had a carved hole at the top from which to attach a string. It was actually big enough to hang by a heavy cord. And being made of onyx, it was jet black, polished shiny, and rather weighty. It was also the same stone as the first crystal that Katrina had chosen to be placed, at the temple in Uxmal.

Ken was so proud of his pendulum. I didn't know what to say. I didn't have the heart to tell him no one uses psychic tools that big. Or do they?

The Eight Temples

We landed in Merida and rested only one night. We thought about going out and exploring the city, having a little fun before we started, but Ken and I were so excited to begin our work that we just started right in. We rented a little red Toyota with air conditioning, which they said would cost a lot more, but boy, were we glad to be able to escape the heat sometimes.

I explained to Ken exactly what we were doing there. I showed him the Mexican map and the list of the eight temples, and I let him feel the eight beautiful crystals that would never come home with us. They had each been programmed by Thoth specifically for each temple. I explained to Ken that the eight temples we were going to visit had not been placed in their locations at random. They had been placed in an ever-widening spiral. The exact center of the spiral was found in Uxmal, and it was said to be smaller than a single atom.

Each one of these astounding pyramids was also built in a specific geographic location in order to represent and channel the energy of the land. The energy of each of these specific temples represented a chakra energy of the human body.

1. Uxmal (Mexico): the base chakra of a new cycle

2. Labna: the sexual chakra, union of opposites

3. Kaba: the third chakra, willpower

4. Chichen Itza: the heart chakra, unconditional love

5. Tulum: the throat chakra, sound currents and manifestation

6. Kohunlich: the third-eye chakra, the pituitary gland—psychic abilities

7. Palenque: the pineal chakra, preparing for the next world

8. Tikal (Guatemala): the base chakra of a new cycle

The Maya knew this long, long ago. They also knew a lot more, as the world is about to find out. What this female part of the Unity Consciousness Grid is connected to is many more spirals of female energy. Tikal is connected to the beginning of another octave of temples that are directed south. It also is connected to a different octave of temples headed north, which eventually reconnects and forms an enormous circle coming from the south.

To understand this better, just imagine how the eight primary chakras in the human body are arranged. Then look at the temple complexes, and you'll realize their energies are connected together in exactly the same manner. Each temple holds the energy of a specific chakra. For example, just as the fourth chakra in the human body is the heart chakra, so would the fourth temple hold the same heart energy.

There is more esoteric information concerning purpose, which has to do with the Unity Consciousness Grid around the Earth. It is these temples, and other sacred sites, that actually create the impetus to form the Unity Consciousness Grid around the Earth. Without them, we would be unable to move into the higher levels of consciousness.

So these spirals of temple energy keep reversing direction each time an octave-of-eight temples is reached. They move south from Guatemala into Nicaragua, Costa Rica, Panama, Columbia, and then Peru. In Peru, at Lake Titicaca between the Island of the Sun and the Island of the Moon, there is a ninety-degree turn of the energy, which then heads out toward the Pacific Ocean by passing through Chile. In the Pacific Ocean this female energy continues along the ocean floor until it reaches Easter Island, where it continues until it reaches an incredible island called Moorea. The center of the axis of the Unity Consciousness Grid is in the middle of the island of Moorea. If you continue through the Earth with this axis, you come out of the surface of the Earth in Egypt, about one and a half miles from the Great Pyramid. This spot in ancient Egypt was clearly marked.

Moorea holds a vast significance for humanity. She focuses the entire energy of the Unity Consciousness Grid through the center of her heart-shaped island landmass. I feel that Moorea is the most female location in the world.

From Tikal in Guatemala the energy also heads north, moving through more Mayan temples and then into Aztec temples, continuing through Mexico until it reaches the U.S. border. Just over the border in New Mexico (according to the Apache, who told me this was true), this female energy continues to move through three physical pyramids that were built by Native Americans long ago. These pyramids were needed to bridge this energy further north, as no natural energy field existed there.

As it reaches the Taos Pueblo and Taos Mountain, it continues to Blue Lake, the most sacred lake of the Taos Pueblo, where there is a 90-degree turn, just like at Lake Titicaca only in the opposite direction. Blue Lake, though it is much smaller in size than Lake Titicaca, channels this female energy in exactly the same manner and with the same power.

From Blue Lake, the energy moves to Ute Mountain, the same sacred mountain we spoke about earlier. It continues west at this point, moving from sacred site, to mountain top, to sacred site, until it reaches Lake Tahoe, Donner Lake, and Pyramid Lake in California and Nevada. It then moves rapidly into the Pacific Ocean, continuing along underwater mountains and energy points until it reaches the island of Maui and the Haleakala Crater. From there it begins to head south, following the chain of islands that long ago used to be ancient Lemuria. Its final destination is again the island of Moorea, competing the circle.

This female energy of the Unity Consciousness Grid more or less makes an enormous circle in two parts, both meeting in Moorea. Moorea is an interesting and awesomely beautiful island. It is formed in the perfect shape of a heart and has a coral reef surrounding it that is also in the shape of a heart. Each house on the island has a heart shape somewhere on it facing the street. Your body can feel the love.

For now, I told Ken, the Ascended Masters were only interested in correcting the grid within Mexico and Guatemala. That was a ceremony that would come later.

Ken sat in disbelief. "As I understand you, this Unity Consciousness Grid was started over 13,000 years ago, and is just now being completed. The complexity of this energy field is beyond anything I could imagine."

"Ken, you have no idea. What we have just spoken of is but a small portion of the entire web of pyramids, temples, churches, monasteries, synagogues, ashrams, kankas, sacred buildings, mosques, stone circles, et cetera, along with natural phenomena such as mountains, valleys, springs, rivers, lakes, bodies of water, and most importantly, vortexes, et cetera, that have been consciously altered through geomancy and function as a single unit that truly creates the Unity Consciousness Grid that surrounds the planet. If you really knew the interconnected relationships between all of these sacred sites that are represented by over 83,000 worldwide sacred sites alone, not to mention all the rest that are natural, you would be in awe. Especially when you realize that it was a single consciousness that conceived, organized, and created this astounding Web of Life that the world calls the 'grids.'

"Ken, what has been explained to me is that this Unity Consciousness Grid is the only thing between human extinction and human ascension. For sure, at this point in the cycles, it will be one or the other.

"So you can see the importance of our journey. The female aspect of the Unity Consciousness Grid needs to be balanced to make the geometrical changes in the grid that allow the possibility for the new sacred female consciousness to become a living reality. So that women everywhere will remember their intimate connection with God and thereby know exactly what to do to bring balance in this world, and further."

I just had to say it. "Ken, the time in the Precession of Equinox is upon us. There is only about twenty-eight years left and 2012–2013 will be here, the time the Mayan calendar says will be the end of this long cycle. After that the changes become rapid. Since the female is about to be given the power to decide the direction in which the Earth moves, she needs to be prepared. And we can help."

Uxmal

Ken started the engine of our Toyota and pulled out of the hotel. We had made sure that we had all the maps we would need for the whole journey. We tried to think of everything we would need, like bottled water, car food, and sunscreen. We knew that we were going to be in this car for a long time.

Actually, when we first left, we thought that this whole journey would take two weeks or less, but in the end it took over a month.

Moving through Mexico and Guatemala is not easy, as the roads are minimal in many places. An American looks at the road maps and says, "Okay, that's an hour." But in reality, it's three or four hours. We just had not slowed down to the Mexican way yet, but that was inevitable.

We had planned to go to the first three temples in the first day, since they were all at the beginning of the spiral and were not very far apart. And then we would go back to Merida that night and finish the last five temples over the next twelve days or so.

Uxmal was about seventy miles inland from Merida, so I sat back for the ride, as Ken wanted to drive. This was my first time in the Yucatan, and I hadn't expected it to be so flat. Somehow I had the idea that there were mountains and jungle here. There are mountains and jungles in Mexico, but not really in the Yucatan. The overgrowth is incredible and nearly impossible to pass through without a machete, but it isn't really jungle until one heads more inland.

We arrived at Uxmal with ease and no problems. This was the time before the Mexican government began to put walls around the temples to control the people. In these days, there were almost no people who cared about the temples, and so there was no need for walls. We were able to walk right into the sacred sites, at least most of them, without any control and to stay as long as we wished. But we were on a mission and felt that these first three temples had to be finished that first day.

As we entered into the temple grounds of Uxmal and approached the Temple of the Magician, I felt the vibration move down to my bones. There was an energy there, distinctly different than any I had felt in Mexico so far. I had felt something similar in Egypt in the Great Pyramid. It just does something to you that's hard to describe.

Standing at the base of the temple, I had to lean back to see the top of the pyramid. It was magnificent. I was holding the onyx stone in my hands, and Ken said, "Drunvalo, come here." Ken was leaning up against the pyramid looking very close at the stone. "Just look," he said and gestured to the mortar between the stones. Here was the reason for the onyx stone. The gray-black mortar was made with ground onyx and covered the entire pyramid.

This, of course, supercharged us both. We knew for certain at that moment that we were doing exactly what we were supposed to be doing—whatever that was. We started laughing.

As we moved to another location, for the first time we were able to see a larger overview of the temple site, and we became more serious. We knew that the pyramid that we were supposed to place the onyx crystal near was the one called the "Great Pyramid," and it hit us at that moment how colossal this sacred site was. It stretched for miles. We didn't know where to start.

It wasn't long before we found someone who knew exactly where the Great Pyramid was. We made a beeline toward it. It took a bit of walking, but there it was, sitting royally before us—a huge, impressive pyramid. All I knew from Thoth was that the crystal was to be placed somewhere directly in front of the north face. We had brought a compass to be certain which side faced north.

The front of the north face had a totally flat lawn that framed the pyramid. It was a rectangle, perhaps a hundred feet long and forty feet wide, I'm guessing, with no distinguishing features. Ken pulled out his now-famous pendulum, which he had tied a cord to. The cord was about three feet long.

Again, I was speechless. So I hid my smile, sat down on the steps of the pyramid, and watched. Ken was in full action—only Ken had never used a pendulum before. He had only heard me talk about them in Taos and how you could find anything with one. He didn't know that pendulum stones are usually only one to two inches long, and the chain or cord on them is perhaps seven inches. And that small circles are used for finding out locations or the answers to questions.

None of this mattered. Ken was in his heart, and he was working for God. His seven-inch pendulum with its three-foot cord began to swing in large circles that almost hit his legs as he walked. He was a man who appeared to know exactly what he was doing, and I let him. Who was I to say what he was doing was wrong?

Ken did this for about twenty minutes, walking back and forth across the grass several times. Then he stopped swinging the pendulum just as he was about to walk past me and said, "Drunvalo, how do I know when I have reached the special spot to place the crystal?"

With a straight face, I said, "Ken, follow your heart and somehow you will know." I really did believe in him, but he was challenging my own narrow pathway of spiritual understanding.

Ken seemed to understand fully and started to use the pendulum again with still more energy and even wider swings. This went on for another twenty minutes when it happened.

As Ken went over this one spot, the pendulum spiraled instantly into a single position and began to pull toward the ground. Ken pulled back. He was actually up on his tippy toes with his arms up in the air, pulling up as hard as he could, when the cord broke, and the onyx crystal buried itself in the ground about three inches with great force.

Ken turned his head to me and gave me a look that said, "It wasn't my fault." His actual words were, "What do I do now?"

"Ken, you just found the spot, of this I am certain." I pulled out the pendulum, and it left a perfect cone-shaped hole. There was no doubt. This was the spot to bury the crystal.

I stood back for a moment and looked at the spot relative to the whole complex, and it was instantly clear. The spot was exactly in the center of the pyramid, and if you drew an imaginary line along the end wall of the building on the immediate left of the pyramid, it perfectly crossed the spot. This would make it very easy to find in the future, if that were necessary.

We performed our first mini ceremony and buried the onyx crystal in the little hole and covered it over. The spot disappeared like it never had been there.

It is interesting to note that ten years later I was asked by the Mayan shaman and priest Hunbatz Men to perform a ceremony with him and his tribe at Uxmal. I returned to the spot to see how it would feel, and to my surprise, a small tree had grown over the precise spot where the crystal had been buried. It was the only tree on the lawn. I feel that Mother wanted to make sure no one moved or touched the crystal. What a natural way!

Kaba

We hurried to finish the other two temples. Labna was to be next, but as we were driving there Thoth appeared to me, saying that he wanted us to change the order and go to Kaba next.

As we approached Kaba, the center for willpower, the sky darkened, and it began to softly rain. The temple had a chain-link fence surrounding the grounds and felt strange, almost prisonlike. I didn't want to enter, but I knew that I had to. But if I could, I would have passed on this place.

We were met at the entryway by two old men—I should say, two old grumpy men. They tried to tell us to go away and come back another day, but as you understand, we really needed to complete this action, as each temple had to be in sequence or as we'd been instructed.

Finally, disgusted, they let us through into the temple ground. This place was much smaller than Uxmal, and I don't think it took more than about fifteen minutes to find the spot where the crystal was to be buried. I used my "normal" pendulum, and we had it in minutes. We buried the crystal behind an ancient wall and got out of there as soon as possible.

Labna

We sped away from Kaba like we just robbed a gas station and headed for Labna, only a few minutes away. As we approached, the sky cleared, and this beautiful rosy light emitted like a fog everywhere. Labna was the sexual center of the Yucatan, and its energy was easy to feel.

We were met at the edge of the temple grounds by a young, beautiful couple who seemed to be in love with life. They were so gracious in the way they asked us to "enter their home." They told us to go anywhere we wanted to go and to stay as long as we wished.

The stone for this temple was carnelian, a reddish stone, and the dirt and roads in the temple were the same color. I remember placing the stone we were to plant there on the ground, and it seemed to disappear. The stone and the ground were both exactly the same color. I thought of Katrina.

Again, it only took about fifteen to twenty minutes to find the spot, and we buried it in its home. "Wow, this is so easy," we said to each other. "We should be able to finish this journey in maybe another seven or eight days." Little did we know.

We made it back to Merida just in time for a short meal, and we went straight to bed. We both fell asleep in minutes. The energy of the day was greater than we had realized, and before we knew it, we were in dreamland.

Chichen Itza

The next day we were on the road again, Ken driving our little red home away from home. We expected to finish Chichen Itza and continue on to Tulum, by the Caribbean Sea, where we would spend our third night. But the day didn't manifest as we had planned. Delays became commonplace, leading us into a far more complex journey than we ever considered.

The beautiful blue sky and green jungle were mesmerizing as the hours passed. The smell of the jungle made me feel so alive. I even started daydreaming about my childhood in California. When I was growing up, the thing I remember most were the smells of the countryside where I lived. And the aroma of all these tropical flowers triggered memories inside of me. Sure, these memories were from a period of my life before I walked into this body (in April, 1972), but they were dormant in the cells and felt like my own.

Suddenly I was jarred back to reality by Thoth attempting to reach me. Appearing in my inner vision, he began to inform me that he had made a change with the placement of the crystal at Chichen Itza. He was communicating telepathically, and this manner of communication revealed so much more than just the words that are said.

What he was completely saying was that the placement of the crystal at Chichen Itza was so critical for everything to work properly that he didn't want anyone to know where it would be. So he had previously given me a false location in case someone happened to read my list. Thoth looked me squarely in the eyes and said, "Drunvalo, I ask you to open your eyes, and I will show you where I want it to be placed."

I did as he said, and immediately a bright spot of light appeared in front of me, very much like the one that had appeared with Bupi Naopendara many years before. The sphere of light expanded into an oval, and a window opened into another location on Earth. When completed, it looked like a very bright, shimmering gold ring of light about three feet across and two feet high. Outside of the shimmering ring was the reality of where we were driving. Inside the ring was somewhere else.

I saw a small lake or pond of emerald green water that was impossible to see into. Around the outer edge was an off-white rock ledge maybe forty feet high. Plants and flowers hung over the edge, and jungle enclosed the water. It was beautiful. I kept looking at this deeply romantic hole of water, when Thoth interrupted me and said, "Do you see what is inside the gold ring?"

I described the pond and its high white walls, and Thoth seemed satisfied. He said, "Instead of placing the crystal on the north face of the Castle Pyramid, as I first asked you to do, throw it into the water when you find it. Do you understand?"

I asked him where the water was, and he said, "You will be brought there. You don't have to do anything," and he disappeared.

I came out of the meditation, turned to Ken, who was driving, and told him everything that had just happened. It didn't seem to phase him. He just looked at me and said, "Okay, no problem." I guess after the pendulum buried itself in the ground at Uxmal, old Ken was ready for anything.

As we approached a sign that said, "Parking for Chichen Itza," Ken turned into the lot and began looking for a place to park. He turned to me, "Drunvalo, the last three times we were in temple grounds we were always lost. I read that this place is very big, and I think this time we should have a guide with us. Is that okay?"

I answered, "Why not?" as he pulled into a place and turned off the motor. We started to gather our things when an old Indian man in his eighties or older knocked on Ken's window. Ken was startled and literally moved closer to me as he sized up this old man. The old man was asking him to open his window.

Ken rolled down the window about two inches and asked him what he wanted. The old man, with a kind smile, said, "Do you want a guide?" In retrospect, this was not just any old man. He had been sent by the Universe and knew exactly what he was doing.

Ken got all excited and turned to me as if he had just created this miracle. And who knows, maybe he did. We got out of the car to meet the man. This old Mayan man had an energy that I had felt many times before with certain teachers of mine. I knew immediately he was there for much more than just showing us the temple grounds. I bowed and showed him the respect that he deserved.

He was very friendly and did actually "show us" the temple grounds. He spent about four hours taking us from temple to temple, telling us the secret history behind each of these building. Toward the very end, he led us to the Castle Pyramid, the focus point of the temple grounds, where Thoth had originally asked us to place the crystal. He said that this pyramid was the entryway into the human heart, and the key to Mayan understanding.

But he then said something that surprised me. He turned to us and seriously gazed into our eyes, "This pyramid," he said, pointing to the Castle Pyramid, "and all of this huge complex is here for only one reason. And that reason has nothing to do with the buildings we Maya created. There is something here far more powerful and important in this jungle. If you will follow me, I will show you."

Turning, he began to walk away from the temple grounds, and in minutes we were deep into the Mexican jungle. He kept moving through dense plant growth for about a quarter mile, and then we suddenly emerged from the jungle into an opening—an opening I already knew intimately.

In front of us was the image that Thoth had shown me on our way to Chichen Itza. In real life, there was the emerald green pond of water and the white stone wall behind it. It was exactly as Thoth had shown me. Exactly.

The old man began to speak, as Ken and I were both speechless. He became a little excited, and his voice seemed to have more power. He said, "This pool of water is called a *cenote* in Spanish, and to the Maya, it is a sacred pool of water that opens directly into the heart of the Mother. In ancient times as well as today, we Maya believe this pool of water is holy, and is the very reason why the Maya built Chichen Itza in this location. Not for any other reason, only to honor this sacred pool of water."

He continued, "In 1950 *National Geographic* magazine came here to this pool and dredged the bottom and found the bones of over 300 Maya who had sacrificed themselves to this water. It was done in a ceremony, and the person who was chosen to be sacrificed received a great honor to return to the Mother in this honorable way."

He then said, "But while they were dredging this cenote, *National Geographic* also found thousands and thousands of crystals mixed in with these bones. These crystals held the prayers of our ancient forefathers, and they removed them. As if that was not enough to demoralize us, they came back a few years later and dredged again to find every single last crystal in the cenote, and then they left.

"The sadness of my people was great, but we know why you are here. In great respect and honor, I leave you with our holy cenote. May the Great Sun bless what you do!"

With these words, he turned and disappeared into the all-encompassing jungle.

Ken looked at me. We knew what we had to do. We removed the crystal from the cloth to bring it to the light. We knew that Thoth had programmed into this crystal words that were designed to heal the Unity Grid, but we both felt that more were appropriate.

I don't know what Ken spoke into the crystal, but for my part, I had seen into this old man's inner being, and my heart connected with him. I could feel and know the beauty of the Mayan soul through him, and all I wanted to do was to help them. And so I prayed into this crystal that the Maya who were now alive would awaken and remember their ancient past, remember their sacred knowledge and wisdom, and that they would be allowed to bring this power back to life. It was not a prayer that I decided to speak—it was a prayer that came out of my heart.

With these words still echoing in my heart, Ken threw the crystal into the very middle of the cenote. As it sank to the bottom and the water began to be charged with these prayers, I knew somehow, that my relationship with the Maya was just beginning. I cried with joy, knowing that this crystal was going to bring life back to the Mayan people. As the tears rolled down my face, I could feel the power returning into the land. I felt so humbled and so excited for what was going to come in the future.

Khan Kha

The ceremony felt complete to us, and we entered back into the jungle to return to our hotel. But as we came out of the jungle, the first thing we saw was the Castle Pyramid, and the sight of it made us want to go up to the top one more time.

We were just tourists now, but so what? It was fun. There were four doors into the pyramid at the top. Three of the doors were connected to each other by an interior hallway forming a U shape. And at the opening of the U, there was one more doorway, facing north, that led inside the U to the very center of the pyramid. Why the Maya arranged the doors this way, I don't know.

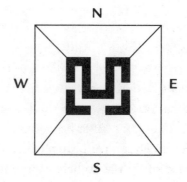

Figure 4: Drawing of the four doorways

We entered the three connected doorways from the east, and once we were inside, it began to lightly rain. Thinking that we had better hurry in case it really began to rain, we quickly entered the fourth doorway just to feel this place one more time.

For me, the energy in this pyramid was one of the strongest in the world. Just as the Great Pyramid in Egypt channels the energy of the mind (male) aspect of the Unity Consciousness Grid, Chichen Itza channels the energy of the heart (female) aspect. And as the new, pristine female movement of the Earth's Kundalini begins to move through the physical bodies of us humans, and then into the grids, we will all change.

I just had to feel it one more time.

We stayed about fifteen minutes, feeling this energy, and then the sound of pounding rain brought us back to reality. Realizing we should go, we looked at each other and hurried to the opening, but it was too late. A torrential rain was pouring out of the sky, so much so that we could see only about a hundred feet. Everyone else had left, and we were all alone at the top of this incredible pyramid, except one small dog that had somehow ended up in the same situation. There was no way down!

Sheets of rain came off the steps of the pyramid like small waterfalls. To understand what this meant, truly you would have to have been there. The Mayan steps of this pyramid were polished like glass from the thousands of people who climb them every year, and unlike the steps of the Great Pyramid in Egypt, which were huge, these steps were only about ten inches wide. They were so slippery that it was impossible to get down. Even the dog wouldn't try it. There was nothing to do, but to wait until the rain stopped.

After an hour or so, Ken became restless, but there was nothing we could do. I looked down at the enormous lawn that surrounded most of the pyramid and saw that it had disappeared under water. It looked just like we were sitting on top of a pyramid in the middle of an enormous lake. The rain blocked the view of the jungle, leaving only water from the sky to the ground to the edge of the pyramid. I don't think I will ever forget this image.

As Ken leaned nonchalantly up against the wall of the doorway watching this rain, I decided to go into the center of the pyramid and meditate. I carried this picture of a pyramid in the middle of a lake with me into the pyramid and sat down on what I felt was the exact center, facing the open doorway where Ken stood waiting for his freedom. I closed my eyes.

I began to feel the flow of energy from within my human light body, the ancient Mer-Ka-Ba field of the Egyptians and the Jews. I rested for a few minutes, just feeling the flow from above and below. I began to enter deeper states of consciousness, but not with a purpose or intention. At one point I could feel the entire energy field of the pyramid, and I felt like I connected with the Maya.

What happened next was most unusual for me. I forgot where I was, and like a little child, I decided I would go down into the pyramid to see if I could find a chamber. I didn't ask permission, nor did I have a purpose.

I clearly remember the Earth slipping past me as my spirit and body of consciousness moved deeper and deeper into the interior space of the pyramid. I could see the change in rock and ground structure as I descended. And then it happened.

Actually two things happened simultaneously. A large black bat came out of the torrential rain, flew past Ken and the dog, and came right up to my face. He stopped inches before he flew into me, screamed, and lightly clawed my face.

At that exact moment, from within the pyramid, a man's voice screamed into my left ear inches away, "NO."

These two events occurring at the same time, blasted me back into my body with great force. Maybe "slammed back into my body" would describe it best, but for sure, I was back. The bat was touching my face.

Instinctively, I raised my arm, and it flew up onto a stone ledge, kind of flopped down off center, and watched me.

I watched him for a while, until I could see that he was not going to attack me again. And then I closed my eyes once more, attempting to bring myself back into balance after such a shock.

It took a few minutes to get my breath to slow down, but when it did, I was back in spirit. I felt ashamed, because I knew that I should never have tried to enter into this sacred space without permission. How could I have done such a thing?

The male voice that shouted "no" began to speak again. He said, "We can see your heart, so don't feel bad. We know you didn't mean any harm, but still you cannot come into this sacred area."

He was talking to me in a very loving and respectful voice, and my heart opened to him. This guy was pure. Seldom in life do I find someone living in this level of awareness. I asked him his name, and he said, "Khan Kha." He asked me mine, and I told him my name.

He began to talk with me like an old friend. He told me that he was the architect of this pyramid and one of its protectors. I told him he was doing a great job. He laughed like a child. He said that he was also the architect of a pyramid in Palenque that we call the "Temple of Inscriptions." But he said, "These are the only two temples that I have ever given birth to."

I heard Ken make some sounds, and I knew that I should go. I told Khan Kha goodbye and honored his light. I opened my eyes, and Ken, from the opening, was asking me to get up and leave. I felt Khan Kha's energy and thought to myself that I liked this person. Too bad that I probably would never see him again.

We had no trouble getting down now, as the rain had stopped sometime before, and Ken waited until the steps were more or less dry. In minutes we were back at the hotel, where I told Ken everything about what happened in the center of the pyramid with Khan Kha.

After a few days, I completely forgot about Mr. Kha.

A Note on History

Ken and I both decided to stay one more day at Chichen Itza, as we were told that a secret Mayan phenomenon was going to take place the next evening at sunset. The next day would be March 21, 1985, the spring equinox.

Why was this important? At the base of the north face of the Castle Pyramid is a huge stone carving of a snakehead. It is facing to the north. But if you sit facing the west face of the pyramid at sunset on this particular day, something happens that you have to see to believe. The pyramid steps on this specific day create a shadow that, for a short time just at sunset, connects to the stone snakehead and gives the appearance of a full snake body moving down the edge of the pyramid. It is awesome! This snake told the Maya when the spring equinox had arrived, when to plant their seeds, and other spiritual matters.

But there is something even more important for the reader of this book to realize. Spiritual people are growing in numbers everywhere, but in Mexico you can see how fast they were awaking. Contemplate the following:

Ken and I were there in 1985, and the government put up a set of metal bleachers for the tourists to watch this event. There was seating for maybe 100 people, and the bleachers were not full.

Ten years later, in 1995, I was asked by the Mayan priest Hunbatz Men to participate in ceremony with him at Chichen Itza, and it happened to be on the same day, March 21. The expanding awareness of spiritual matters was obvious, as there were 42,000 people present.

In 2005, I was again asked to perform ceremony with the Maya at Chichen Itza (as well as other temples), and there were over 80,000 people in attendance. (See chapter thirteen.) It was a sea of people. The visual of so many people awaking to consciousness made my heart sing and my mind realize that humanity was finally beginning to slowly unfold like a lotus in the early dawn light.

Life may seem to be business as usual, but it is not. We are evolving exponentially even in the face of ordinary, everyday life that seemingly knows not where it is going, but still proceeds with uncanny accuracy. The cosmic DNA turns, and life responds.

CHAPTER SEVEN

The Balancing of the Female Grid Around the Earth
The Yucatan and the Eight Temples, Part Two

The Last Four Temples

Time slowed down—slower and slower until I had no idea what day it was. It wasn't even about thinking anymore. It was about second to second and the eternal now. All my sensors were wide open, as each temple dissolved more and more of my city ways of being, and as my spirit slowly became aware of the third-dimensional world in a new light.

Here we were down on solid everyday Earth, deep in between the nanoseconds. Life was one opening always into another opening.

I felt great. I could hardly wait to get to Tulum. This was the throat chakra, connected to the world of the sound currents, one of the primal energies of creation. As we traveled to each temple, we were moving higher and higher up in consciousness levels of the female part of the Unity Consciousness Grid. I could feel it, even if I was having trouble tuning to it.

Tulum is on the Caribbean Sea, facing out over the water. Chichen Itza had been easy to connect to because it felt so familiar, but Tulum vibrated on what felt to be a much higher level. And it was beautiful—grass, living stones, blue sky, and deep blue water everywhere. I could see with my eyes why the Maya chose this place, but knew that soon I was going to have to see with my third eye, my "single eye," energetically why they came here.

Thoth told us before we left the U.S. that he would tell us where the first four crystals should go, but for the last four temples, Ken and I would be on our own to find the precise location that would bring each temple back to life or to another level of vibration.

At Tulum, I was confident when I began the search for the spot, but as time went on, I began to think that this job was beyond my understanding or capability. I had been using a pendulum to sense the ancient energies just as Ken had, but at Tulum, each place felt so incredibly strong, it seemed an insurmountable task to pick one spot over another. I told Ken that it was like trying to pick out the song of only one violin in an orchestra of a hundred voices. It all felt the same—powerful!

We searched for five hours without even one possibility. We stopped at one point to eat. Ken was saying that he was completely bewildered and that if I couldn't find the special place, we might as well go home. Nothing like putting pressure on me, when I was feeling the same way.

I said, "Okay, let's meditate and see if there is something within us that can feel in a new way. Obviously, what we are now doing is not working."

We both found our place to sit a few feet from each other, and we went within. About a half hour later, I came to a "knowing." I couldn't tell you how I arrived at this conclusion, but I felt like I could find the location for the crystal by allowing my intuition to take control of my mind through making a humming sound and "following" the sound. After all, we were in the throat chakra.

Ken just said, "I'll follow you. Go big guy!" (Having Ken there was like having a straight man in a comedy routine follow me all over Mexico.)

Well, it worked. I began to move without thinking, but by listening to the sound in my throat. This method led us within minutes to a tiny temple up high, near the edge of a cliff overlooking the ocean— a place we had not noticed before. If I went away from the spot where the crystal was to be buried, the sound would lower and change tone, but when I went toward the spot, it increased in strength.

When we entered this small building, no more than twelve feet square, the sound in my throat stopped completely. I knew I was there. I knew I was there for absolute certain when I pulled out the crystal, and we could see that the ancient paint that covered the inside of the dome was the very same color. We buried the crystal under this dome, and our work was done.

Kohunlich

We were pretty quiet as we drove down the coastline toward our next temple. After Tulum, we knew that we were in for far more than we suspected back in New Mexico. Were we going to have to change psychically for each temple? Were these kind of abilities within us? Were they in everyone? What were these experiences going to do to us as humans? Was there a purpose in our being here beyond what Thoth had told us? The questions in my mind would not stop.

The ocean stayed on our left as we moved from the east coast of Mexico toward a little town called Chetuval, near the country of Belize. At first we were not sure if the Kohunlich temple was in Belize or Mexico. It had only recently been found and put on the map, and it appeared to be exactly on the border.

But once in Chetuval, people told us that no, Kohunlich was in Mexico. This was a great relief for us as we quickly found out that the Mexican government would not let us take our rented vehicle into Belize. "Are you crazy?" they said. "If you bring that car into Belize, it will be stripped into a million parts and sold before the end of your first day."

So we slowed down even more and rested for the night in an out-of-the-way hacienda. We decided to drink a little tequila for the first time to relax our two tired bodies. Man, it really worked. I'm only used to drinking in very small amounts. The next morning we woke up very late, but with happy smiles on our faces. We were ready for anything. So we thought.

We threw everything into Old Red and took off excitedly, like we were on the Yellow Brick Road. We were sure that something magical would happen today. Tulum had been so incredible that Kohunlich was certain to be more so. It was even higher up in the energy spectrum.

We'd bought a map of the surrounding area that showed in much greater detail the small roads and towns. Kohunlich was clearly marked on the map, and the route to it appeared quite simple. Our day seemed to be laid out before us.

But when we arrived at the location where the map said Kohunlich was, it was not there. There was nothing there at all. The local people there looked at us like we were nuts. Confused, we headed back to Chetuval. We didn't know what to do.

Back in town, we decided to ask someone who should know where Kohunlich was really located. There was a military man standing by an old run-down Mexican restaurant, and Ken began talking with him, since the man knew English. Ken asked him if he knew about Kohunlich, and the man's eyes lit up. "*Si*, I have taken my family and children to Kohunlich only last month, and I know right where it is."

He perused our map and began to laugh. He said whoever made this map had no idea where Kohunlich was. It wasn't even on the same side of the map, according to him. He marked on our map where it really was and told us the details of how to get there. We thanked him and set off for Kohunlich, feeling that finally we would be able to begin this part of our journey.

About forty-five minutes later, we arrived into the area where he said Kohunlich was, but it was not there. No one there knew what we were talking about. Kohunlich was becoming a problem.

We drove back to town one more time, thinking about whom we should ask for directions, and decided that a taxi-cab driver should know best. We found a whole line of taxis in front of a nice hotel and walked over to talk with them. We picked one and asked him about Kohunlich. He took our map and pulled about five other taxi drivers into a huddle. They began to talk very fast in Spanish. They came out of the huddle, and he said, "*Bueno*, we can show you exactly where it is on this map. We have all been there many times, but I was trying to find the best route for you from here. I have marked with my pen the route you should take. It is a beautiful place. You will like it."

We thanked him, and Ken gave him a tip for helping us. His smile became almost bigger than his face.

We followed the route he suggested, and it took us directly to the spot he intended us to go to, but, as usual, no Kohunlich. After three trips, the day was slowly being lost. We pulled over to the side of the road, dumbfounded. We said nothing, but stared out into the countryside. It all seemed so impossible.

Suddenly, Ken sat up straight very fast and yelled, "I got it. I know what we are supposed to do." It made me jump, as I was kind of drifting off into my thoughts.

"What, Ken?"

"Isn't Kohunlich the sixth chakra, the third eye? Remember in Tulum we had to change? Maybe we are supposed to use our third eye to find this temple. Drunvalo, I am sure this is right. I'll tell you what, you use your psychic abilities to find Kohunlich, and I'll drive."

All I could say was, "Thanks, Ken."

I realized he was probably right. Thoth said that for the last four temples we'd have to find the special spot on our own and that we both would learn from this journey. Perhaps it was time now to learn.

The idea excited me, and my spirit woke up. "Okay, you drive," I turned to Ken, "and I'll tell you when to turn. Keep going the way you are headed." Ken pulled off of the roadside onto the road, headed to wherever.

I closed my eyes and kept repeating the sound of the temple name, "Kohunlich," over and over to myself. After three or four minutes, I let go of thinking and began to sense and feel. Every time we came to an intersection or Y in the road, I would let my body sense and respond. Whatever my body suggested, I accepted.

"Ken, turn up here to the left at this next intersection." Without asking any questions, Ken would turn. We continued to do this for almost seventy-five miles, making turns whenever my body said to.

We were totally lost. Everything was unfamiliar, and we were a long way from our hotel.

I remember the last turn onto a seldom-used dirt road. It was narrow and filled with potholes. Worse, we were moving into very deep jungle. I think Ken was becoming a little nervous by the way he sat up straight in his seat, and for the first time, he expressed doubt.

"Drunvalo, are you certain about this road?"

"Ken, I'm not certain about anything. I'm just attempting to use my possibilities."

And the road guided us deeper and deeper into jungle. No more civilization, just jungle.

Maybe five more minutes down this road, we noticed the brown governmental sign: *Kohunlich*, with a gold arrow pointing the way.

Ken and I almost went crazy with excitement. Wow! It worked! Nothing in my life had ever stirred up my emotions and gotten my adrenaline moving like seeing that simple little sign. That sign also taught me something about myself and human possibilities that has continued to this day. Thoth was right. We would learn from each other.

The Third Eye

We pulled into the compound deep inside this jungle where the sky was completely hidden from view. There were ponds with lotus flowers floating on the surface of water and tropical flowers everywhere. It was unbelievably gorgeous—and so surrealistic. Nothing seemed real. I felt like I was on the set of a Hollywood movie.

There was a lone man there, an archeologist about to go home for the day, and he told us that his team had just found Kohunlich about a year and a half before. They were only working on the first pyramid, but the site extended for miles in all directions. Go ahead and take a look, he said, but please don't touch the superstructure around the pyramid. And then he left us all alone.

We walked up to the only pyramid exposed, and for the first time we saw something that brought home the concept of each of these

Kohunlich faces showing the third eye

temples having a chakra connection. Covering each surface of this four-sided pyramid were human faces in relief. Each face was about ten feet high and stuck out from the pyramid perhaps eighteen to twenty inches. And on every single human face, in the area between the eyebrows, rose a round dot emphasizing the third eye. I had never seen anything like this in all of Mexico.

Kohunlich was connected to the sixth chakra, which is located exactly at the third eye. Here, on the forehead of each of these kingly faces, was proof that the ancient Maya also knew the energy function of this sacred site. It was pretty impressive.

But we had work to do, and so after maybe fifteen minutes of being tourists, we began to psychically search for the secret spot where our crystal was to be placed.

Kohunlich was the most powerful place, in terms of pure energy, that we had been to so far. But, as if we were brain dead, completely forgetting the lesson of Tulum, we once again started using our pendulums to search. About an hour later we gave up. It was not working. The reality reminded us of our initial dilemma.

We sat down on the steps of a little temple near the large pyramid and began to reason as we had in Tulum.

"Drunvalo, this is not going to work," Ken said. "We should have learned something from Tulum. Since this is the third eye, and we found this temple with psychic abilities, I think we need to use only that method to locate the spot. You found this place, but now I want to do what you did and somehow find the place in my meditation. Do you think I can?"

"Ken, I believe in you. Go within and let me know what you find."

He closed his eyes and was gone for maybe twenty minutes. Then he opened his eyes and became very excited. "I know what we are looking for. Let me show you."

Ken took out a piece of paper and pen and made a drawing of what he had discovered in his meditation. He said there was a hole in the ground that looked like the drawing and that directly in front of this hole there was a small tree. In between the tree and the large hole there was a small hole about three inches in diameter. It was in this small hole that we were to place the crystal.

This large hole was so unusual that if we were to find it, there would be no doubt what it was, but it seemed unlikely that such a hole really existed. Instead of expressing my doubts about this, I stood up and said, "Okay, let's go. If it's out there, we'll find it."

Ken was quick to say, "Drunvalo, I found what the hole looks like. It's your turn to actually find it." He has such a great way with words.

I took the challenge. I held the image of this hole in my mind and sensed out into the reality for it. My body was pulled in a direction away from the main pyramid and out into pure jungle. Within

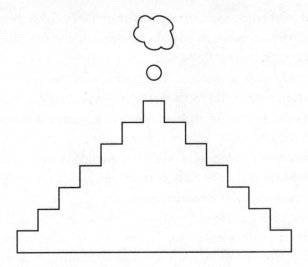

Fig. 5: Drawing of the hole and tree

seconds, all remnants of civilization had vanished, and we were in nothing but nature. But the pull on my body continued.

We had difficulty moving through this dense jungle, and we didn't have a machete, which most Mexicans would use for this purpose. We didn't let this stop us. We just tore through the undergrowth and kept on moving. I was scraping my arms, so I unrolled my sleeves and buttoned up to protect myself.

We must have moved through the jungle maybe a mile or more when the pull on my body changed. We were passing two very large hills off to the right, when the pull literally turned my body to face them. In between the hills was an open space, and I knew we had to enter this area. "Ken, come with me. I'm not sure, but I think it is this way."

This open area between the two hills was about sixty feet across and for some reason was clear of undergrowth. Able to walk easily for the first time, we traveled halfway into this opening, when both of us were stopped in our tracks. We were witnessing something that could not be there, but it was.

On the hillside to our right was a staircase leading up to the peak of this hill. Here we were in the middle of a dense Mexican jungle, and there was a staircase that looked like it had come from Greece. It was made of swirling tan and off-white marble, polished like glass. It looked like it had been made yesterday, and a marble railing led up what must have been 150 to 200 steps. On each side of the staircase were rugged jungle and the snarling roots of ancient trees. It really did appear as if someone had built this staircase right over the top of the jungle and was probably hiding somewhere now, watching us. It was so creepy.

We had completely forgotten our mission. This was too fascinating. Finally Ken said, "Do think that anyone knows about this?"

I didn't know what to answer. Instead, I said, "Let's go up to the top and see where it leads."

In complete silence, as if we might wake up some mythological creature, we climbed those stairs that seemed to stretch to the sky. At the top the staircase turned to the right and opened out into a sitting area about forty feet square with marble flooring and benches. The whole top of the hill was jungle except for this sitting area. We sat down on one of the benches in utter confusion.

"What do you think, Ken? You think the Greeks somehow made it to the Yucatan and claimed this hill as their own?"

He just silently shook his head.

For some reason I took out my pendulum and tried it. It worked. I could feel through it that Ken's strange hole was here on this hill. I got excited. "Ken, it's working. I think it's here."

"Where? You mean on this hill?"

Without answering him, I asked him to follow me, and I moved in the direction that the pendulum was suggesting. It led directly over the top of this hill. We were back in dense jungle again, moving slowly.

And then there it was. It felt like we had just hit the lottery and didn't know what to do with all the money. As I looked down on this very strange hole in the ground, a feeling went through my body that I will never forget. The feeling said to me, "Remember this, for Life is going to present stranger things to you in your lifetime, and they all have meaning and purpose."

This hole was probably about ten feet deep and twelve to fourteen feet wide. The walls and the floor going into the earth were hand made and lined with stones cut perfectly into rectangles. There was something obvious that Ken didn't see in this meditation: there were two red-clay tubes sticking out of the floor. Each tube was roughly a foot in diameter and stuck out of the floor about a foot. I contemplated what these tubes could be, but nothing came to mind.

I looked up and saw the little tree that Ken had seen in his meditation. I jumped up, guided myself through the brush to it, and looked to see if there was a little hole in front of it. There it was, just as Ken had seen in his inner vision.

I shined my flashlight down inside the hole to see what was there, but nothing came back. It was pitch black. But as far as where we were supposed to place the crystal, there was no doubt.

Ken came over and he peered inside too, but could see nothing. It was like looking into the stars, only there were no stars. All we could see was mystery! Mystery, but trust.

We took the crystal out of the cloth. We both held it for a moment in prayer for the Maya, and then I was elected to place this crystal into the Earth. I remember that during our ceremony, at the right moment, I dropped the crystal into this darkness, and I could feel it falling. It was not hitting anything. Psychically, it felt like I had released it into deep space, and the crystal was floating away from the planet.

We were quiet for a long time. Without saying anything, we both moved to sit on the edge of the large Mayan hole and look at the little tree. Our eyes closed. To me the Maya were all around us, and now they were my brothers and sisters. We were of the same spirit. Our purpose was the same: to bring heaven to Earth.

I was meditating a long time, and then instantly I was back in my body, sitting in front of the sacred Mayan hole, staring into the Earth. Ken was still meditating. Silently, I stood up and followed my heart through the jungle to the edge of the hill, and what I was suspecting to be true revealed itself. The hill was a Mayan pyramid! It was the red-clay tubes that had caused me to suspect this. I think they are breathing tubes for interior spaces.

Everything fell into place. I understood so much at that moment. I felt incredibly honored to be one of the people who were helping to bring back the ancient memories—something that happens to consciousness on Earth whenever the mankind of the moment begins to remember who it really is.

Palenque

We drove all afternoon to get to Palenque by sunset, but we didn't make it. It was much farther than we thought. Palenque was gated up and would not open again until 8 a.m. the next morning, so we turned around to find the closest hotel.

Ken pulled in and paid for the room, and I unloaded the car. We'd found a small, unpretentious room with two well-worn twin beds that nearly filled it. The door hit my bed before it was even half open, which I thought was kind of classy in a Mexican sort of way. (Don't get me wrong—I love Mexico and Mexican people. Therefore, if you know what I mean, then you know what I mean.)

We leaped out of bed at sunrise and were at the temple grounds as soon as they opened. We were the first and only people to enter at that hour, and all that space was perfect for us. Soon, hundreds of people would be swarming over this land like ants. So we wasted no time in beginning to search for the sacred spot.

Realizing that the temple we were connecting to was the seventh chakra, the pineal chakra, we found ourselves in the same situation as at Tulum and Kohunlich. We knew we had to change ourselves somehow in order to be sensitive enough to find the special spot.

When someone arrives at the level of consciousness associated with the pineal chakra in the human body, they are preparing to leave their body and to ascend into the next level of awareness beyond human. In the previous 200,000 years of human consciousness, only three Ascended Masters were able to reach this level. Now, of course, all that has changed. All of the 8,000 Ascended Masters have moved past this level in the last ten years, bringing human consciousness to the frontier of new and truly awesome possibilities. In time we will all know of what I speak, for not one of us will escape the changes that are upon us.

The pineal gland, very near the pineal chakra, in the center of the head, is the key to the third eye. And the third eye has far-reaching possibilities beyond what most teachings allow to be known in the outer world. It is the link between the Mer-Ka-Ba field and the Sacred Space of the Heart, and when these are linked, a human being becomes more than human. He or she extends into Divinity. (The next book I write will explain this in great detail.)

Jesus could not have walked on water until his third eye was opened and the eight beams of light coming from the pineal chakra extended past the surface of his head. It's simply a cosmic fact.

After several hours of searching, Ken and I simply gave up as we had done before, and we sat on the steps of a small but very elegant temple on the edge of the jungle. We had tried the pendulum, the psychic approach, and everything else we knew. Nothing worked. I think we were just really tired; a feeling of being lost moved through our spirits. We both just stared into the jungle and inside asked for help.

Suddenly, a young Mayan man ran past us wearing nothing but a loincloth and disappeared into the jungle. The image was like stepping back a few hundreds years in time. He was so Mayan and so real.

A jolt went through us. We turned to look at each other, and we knew exactly what we were to do but not why. Without a word, we ran after him into the wall of growth.

A well-defined trail led away from Palenque, and within minutes we were moving through the densest jungle we had seen in Mexico. Palenque was not in the Yucatan, but in an area called Chiapas, farther into the interior of the country, where the hills actually approached what some would call mountains. Palenque is beautiful for that reason; all the temples are on mountainsides at different levels, which gives Palenque an air of mystery.

Our young Mayan friend was nowhere in sight. Either he was a lot faster than us or he took another trail, but it didn't matter. We knew that this was the way to find the special spot, but we didn't know why or how.

We must have run for at least seven or eight miles in the jungle. At this distance from civilization, the jungle came alive. Snakes were dripping from trees, and rare colorful birds flew past us to see who would be crazy enough to enter this eerie world. Everything was wet and slimy, causing us to slip and fall every once in a while, which gradually made us look like dirty beggars running from the law. But nothing was going to stop us.

The terrain suddenly changed, and we began to run uphill. It seemed to never end. At the top, we were practically climbing, using our hands to pull us up to what appeared to be a ridgeline. And then, when we reached the top of this mountain, we broke free into the other side of the mountain to discover another world. The entire south side of this mountain was a cornfield. It felt so weird to go from wild, wet, cool jungle, which we thought would never end, to a manmade field of corn that was hot and dry. It actually shocked my body.

We stood there in disbelief. But when our eyes refocused after the darkness of the undergrowth, we could see that down in the valley before us was an authentic Mayan village, perhaps a half mile away. We stood very still and then sat down to observe the Maya.

My heart was so happy to see that the Maya were still living in the way they had hundreds of years before. I began to cry. I couldn't help it. They were still alive. Somehow, I had been led to believe that the Maya no longer lived in the old ways and had been assimilated into civilization.

There were at least fifteen round grass huts with dogs and other animals running around them. A fire was burning in a pit toward the middle of the grouping. A few people were moving back and forth from hut to hut. It was like we had run into a distant past time before modern man arrived.

A peace descended over me, and my breathing slowed down to where my body was barely functioning. Someone was communicating with me. Then an image appeared to me of a temple and the space beside it. I didn't recognize the temple. The image zoomed in to a small area, no bigger than a square yard, next to one of the walls of this temple. The special spot for the crystal was vibrating with energy. I knew now where it was supposed to be planted.

We had been sitting there for about a half hour, and without any warning to Ken, I stood up and said to him, "Ken, let's go. I think I know what to do." Ken didn't say a word. I could tell that this experience had been powerful for him too.

When we got back at Palenque, my body was pulled directly through the temple compound from behind the Temple of Inscriptions, past the palace and the astronomical observatory, to a small temple off to the side, about 300 meters away.

When I arrived at this temple, my body moved toward a particular wall. When I arrived at the area, I looked down at the ground, and within a few minutes, I found the exact spot. I recognized every stone in this single-meter-square area next to this wall. I had been there before.

Right as the sun was setting, we buried the crystal with prayers that the dreams of the Maya and others connected to this land would synchronize and create a new reality, a new beginning.

The seventh note in the octave was complete. The eighth note is actually on another dimension, another octave, but on another cycle. In other words, the return of energy to the temples of Palenque was completing the first spiral. The next spiral was not in Mexico, but in Guatemala, and represented the beginning of a new cycle of consciousness.

The eighth chakra is a ball of energy, actually a tiny Mer-Ka-Ba field, floating in space one hand length above your head. It is the first note of the next octave of higher consciousness.

Khan Kha: One Eye

I turned from the wall and the spot where we had just buried the living crystal, the sacred point of light, and, facing the gate, I took a step. Pain shot through my head, especially across my eyes, pulling me toward the ground. I caught myself and took stock of my condition. I rarely get headaches, one about every ten years or so, and they seldom last longer than a few hours. But right now, I had one of the worst headaches I'd ever had in my life. It seemed to come out of nowhere.

When I traced it back to the source, I found that my own child-like psychic abilities were simply being overused. It was like using your leg muscles for the first time in years and then making a fifteen-mile trek up mountains. The muscles give out and so did my psychic abilities. I needed rest as soon as possible.

They locked the temple gate behind us. We'd been the first in and the last out. The hotel was only a few hundred meters down the road, so in minutes we were parking our car. Ken parked at the curb, in between two other parked cars.

I got out, and the first thing I saw was the license plate of the car in front of us, which read 444-XY-00. Long ago, the angels taught me that when you see a triple number in the Reality, it has significance relative to what you are thinking or the environment around you. It has to do with music and the fact that all notes in an octave separate themselves by eleven cycles per second. Therefore, the separations of each note to each other are 11, 22, 33, 44, 55, 66, 77, 88, and 99 cycles per second, or multiples of these numbers, which presents a perfectly harmonic tuning or moment in time, since the entire Reality was created through the harmonics of music.

Therefore, when triple numbers or more appear, in any manner, it physically represents a mathematical moment in time that contains the harmonics of the value of that number. In human words, 444 would best be described as the Mystery School, which is where one learn about the Reality. Alice Bailey was the first to write about this number having that meaning. Quickly, these are the meanings of the triple numbers.

111 = Energy Flow: Any energy flow, such as electricity, money, water, sexual energy, etc.

222 = New Cycle: The beginning of a new cycle, the nature of which depends on the next triple number you see.

333 = Decision: You have a decision to make. The decision will lead to either 666, which means you must repeat the

lesson again in some other way, or it will lead to 999, which is completion and you have learned the lesson.

444 = The Mystery School: What is occurring in life is a lesson around the learning about the Reality. This school is learning, such as reading books or studying a subject, but not actual doing.

555 = Unity Consciousness: This is the number when someone has attained Unity Consciousness. They have mastered all levels of the Mystery School. It is the highest number. It is the number of Christ.

666 = Earth Consciousness: This is the number of the Beast in the Bible, so it can represent pure evil, but it is also the number of mankind and life. Carbon is the basis of life, and carbon has six protons, six neutrons, and six electrons. Generally when you see this number, it means to watch out for physical events that are presenting themselves at that moment, and you must be careful.

777 = The Mystery School: This is the part of the school where you are not just reading books about life, but are also practicing it.

888 = Completion of a particular lesson within the Mystery School.

999 = Completion of a particular cycle of events.

000 = Has no value.

Standing outside the car and looking at the 444, I wondered what it was that was going to present itself. I turned around and noticed that the license plate of the car behind me was 666. This told me that the lesson would have something to do with the physical plane. I then turned toward the hotel, and for the first time I saw its name. It was the Khan Kha Hotel. I stood speechless for five full minutes contemplating what this meant.

Halfway into the hotel, Ken saw me standing there and came back out to get me. "Drunvalo, what's the matter?"

"Ken, look at the name of this hotel."

"Isn't that the name of the Mayan who talked with you in Chichen Itza?

"Yes, it is." Then I showed him the two license plate numbers.

"Wow! What do you think this all means?"

"Ken, I really don't know, but I feel it is important. Remember, Khan Kha said he was the architect of the Temple of Inscriptions here at Palenque. Maybe he really is."

We walked to our room, still talking about this lesson that Life was presenting to us. We opened our door, stepped in, and immediately found a note folded in half on my bed. I picked it up, and Ken stood beside me as I read the message. It said, "Thank you for all that you have done. You are in the hearts of the Mayan people forever." And it was signed "Khan Kha."

Before I could even react to this note, Ken grabbed it out of my hands, looked at it for a second, looked me in the eyes, and said, "You did this. I know you did. Khan Kha never wrote this note." I tried to tell him that I had nothing to do with this, but he didn't believe me. He grumbled for almost a half hour saying things like, "Sure, sure. A spirit wrote this note and placed it on your bed. Do you think I'm stupid?" He wouldn't quit. On and on, until we finally went to sleep.

Just so you know, I kept this note for years. It is an inspiration to me even now.

I had a hard time getting to sleep, as my headache would not quit. But eventually, I dropped off. And then suddenly, in the middle of the night, I woke up instantly. Something pulled me out of a deep sleep. I rolled over and looked up into the space in our room. There was an enormous human eye staring at me. At first I thought I was still dreaming, but it did not go away, and the room was real.

The eye was about six feet across and maybe four feet high. It was mostly a golden color, but the eye itself was green and black. Every once in awhile, it would blink.

I have seen so much psychic phenomena that this did not disturb me, but I knew that I had to understand what was occurring. As I was trying to understand what this was, a male voice began to speak. Immediately I recognized who it was. It was Khan Kha.

He began to talk to me about Palenque and what had happened in this day. Then he stopped for a second, and said, "Drunvalo, you have a terrible headache. We need to fix this. I'm going to send you knowledge in a moment, and this will heal your headache. But, Drunvalo, it has meaning and purpose far beyond your headache."

In the next instant, in the blink of an eye, I received ancient knowledge having to do with the pineal gland in the center of the head and the beams of light that come out of the pineal chakra when the conditions are correct. I did what this knowledge said, and instantly my headache was gone. It was dramatic, going from pain to no pain in a few seconds.

Khan Kha said, "Ah, that's better." And he began to talk about Palenque again.

At that moment, Ken moved in his bed. I guess my moving around was waking him up. Ken turned to look at me, then up into the room, and he saw the huge eye of Khan Kha.

He bounced into a sitting position, pulled the sheet up around his chest and screamed as loud as a grown man could possibly scream. I'm sure he woke up every person in that hotel. Quickly, I tried to calm him down, "Ken, don't worry. It's only Khan Kha." But that did almost nothing. Ken was staring at the psychic phenomenon and appeared to be in shock.

After a few minutes, I finally got his attention, and he listened to me when I told him that it was okay. I think this was Ken's first experience of a real psychic phenomenon appearing in the Reality itself and not just inside his head.

It was quite awhile before we were able to get back to sleep, but eventually we did. Ken's initiation into Palenque, the pineal chakra was complete.

Ken's reaction to Khan Kha ended the conversation, but the information that Khan Kha gave to me was most interesting. And over the years I have discovered how incredibly important it really is to human expanding consciousness. It is too complex for a book of stories, but someday, in another book, I will outline it clearly for you to understand and to apply, if you choose.

Guatemala

I felt complete. To go to the next temple in Guatemala felt like work that almost didn't need to be finished, but we knew that it did. Tikal was where we were to finish our journey. This is the place where the oldest and most knowledgeable Maya live. It was the Jaguar Temple, which held the sacred spot of light that needed to receive the final crystal.

However, something happened in Guatemala that the Maya will not let me speak about. I am sorry. Our story will have to end here. Perhaps in the future, when the time is right, the story of what happened can be told, but to honor the Mayan wish for this information to be reserved for now, I must obey.

In Lak'esh. That is the Mayan greeting and goodbye, meaning "You are another me."

CHAPTER EIGHT

"WE NEED YOU AGAIN"

After returning from the last trip into Mexico and Guatemala, I thought that I would have time to play for awhile. Boy, was I wrong.

I think Mother Earth uses every minute of her time to continue expanding consciousness and, in every way that she can conceive of, to keep trying new ideas.

Thoth returned during one of my meditations and said, "Drunvalo, we need you again. There is another correction to the grid that must now be made. Are you ready for service?"

The last journey would have pretty much wiped out my finances, except that Ken had money and paid for most of the trip. So it was possible that I could afford to continue.

Thoth was clear from the beginning that Ken was not to be part of this journey. But he was very unclear as to what was to be accomplished. He wanted me to commit before he told me the situation.

I assumed that he was testing me again. It seemed that he always was. So I answered him by saying, "Thoth, you know that the only reason I came to Earth was to help humanity, so tell me what it is that you need."

He began with a long explanation that actually lasted almost two hours. In a nutshell, he said that the sexual energy of the female (all females on Earth) was out of balance relative to that of the male, and even though the imbalance was small now, it would become huge when the planetary ascension began in a few years. This sexual energy had to be brought back into near perfect balance now or the consequences would later be enormous.

Not really understanding him, I could only try to absorb what he was saying.

"Okay, how do I begin?"

Thoth started speaking as though he had rehearsed it. "You need to buy a green calcite crystal that is about one square foot in size and very high quality. Then you should break this crystal into precisely forty-two pieces of approximately the same size, except for the last two pieces, which should be a little larger."

I knew exactly where such a crystal existed as I had seen it a few months before, assuming it was still there.

"No problem," I replied, "I know where one is."

Thoth looked at me for a full minute without speaking, then said, "After you have the forty-two pieces in your possession, you must dream that forty-two women are going to come to you to help you with this project. These forty-two women know who they are, but you must create the dream. Do you understand?"

I almost laughed out loud. Thoth knew what I was thinking, slightly lowered his eyes, and gave me a sideways glance. I mean, how do you get forty-two women to cooperate together with anything? (Only kidding.)

"This is not about your concepts of human energy," he said. "It is your *dream*."

"Okay, after I have the forty-two crystals and the forty-two women appear by magic, then what?" I asked.

He straightened up, going back to his usual calculated self. "What you are about to do must be timed perfectly. There will only be a few minutes in which the alteration of the Unity Consciousness Grid is possible. There will be no room for even a minute mistake.

Therefore, in your dream, you must see it occurring as if a computer was controlling the events. Do you understand?"

I didn't say anything. He continued. "There are forty-two sacred sights on Earth that must be changed simultaneously. These forty-two places are related to the forty-two primary chromosomes in the human DNA. Forty-one of them are in the female circle of the grid, and the last one is in Egypt, about a mile and a half from the Great Pyramid, out in the open desert.

"The forty-first and forty-second sites are intimately connected. The forty-first site is located in the center of the island of Moorea in the South Pacific."

Moorea and Egypt (the forty-second site) were the axis points of the Unity Consciousness Grid, so this made sense.

Thoth took a deep breath, and began again. "When this adjustment takes place, you must have a man and a woman at both of the axis points, in Egypt and Moorea, and the forty other women must also be in location at the forty specific sacred sights that I will name for you. You must believe in your dream. Prepare this far, and I will give you the final details as you approach the time."

Thoth left the meditation, and I came back out into the room thinking that I had just been given an almost impossible mission. How was I going to find forty-two women (and one man and me, so altogether there were forty-two females and two males) that would do this exactly on the same day in forty-two different locations in the world? I honestly didn't believe that I even knew forty-two women.

But, as he implied, it would not be about what is normally considered possible, but completely about the dreaming process. I sighed and left this entire possibility up to God. I felt that there was no way that Drunvalo could accomplish this.

I went back to the crystal shop where I had seen the green calcite crystal a couple of months before, and it was still there. Somehow I knew it would be. I bought the crystal and while driving back I tried to visualize how I was going to break this crystal into exactly forty-two pieces. I really didn't know.

I decided to start by breaking it in half, and that turned out to be easier than I had imagined. Then I broke each of those pieces into half. I continued doing this until I had sixteen pieces, but then I had to be far more careful, using a lot of thought on how each piece would be cut to end up with the forty-two pieces I was hoping for. It turned out to be quite simple, except for the thinking process. When I broke the last two pieces, making forty-two crystals, I was so proud of myself. It just seemed to happen effortlessly.

Now came what I thought would be the hard part—the forty-two women. I wasn't too concerned about the one man. I was pretty sure that I had one male friend that would do this journey for me.

But finding the women wasn't the hard part that I had imagined. I just sat there without doing anything at all. One woman, some-times two, would come to the Nakkal Mystery School and tell me they were leaving for a sacred site in the Pacific Ocean, or perhaps in Peru, or maybe in California—all places exactly where Thoth wanted them to go. They would always end up asking me, "Do you want me to do anything for you while I'm there?"

Each time I would explain the mission and ask them if they wanted to take part. And each woman would reply, "Of course, I would love to do that for you. I have my plane ticket and I'm ready to go." It was one of the most amazing situations I have ever witnessed.

The part I didn't explain to most of them was the final instruc-tions. But it wasn't necessary; all they had to do was to be there at the precise moment in time with their crystal and to hold the space. We actually synchronized our watches based on my timepiece to be as accurate as possible.

About a month before I was to leave on this journey, Thoth appeared in my meditation once again.

"Drunvalo," he told me, "the male at the north pole in Egypt will be undergoing a sexual change within the female part of himself, and the female at the south pole of the grid in Moorea will simul-taneously be undergoing a sexual adjustment within her female aspect. The female that is with the male in Egypt will be controlling the entire adjustment, while the male, which will be you, will be the secondary controller at the south pole controlling the female undergoing change.

"At a very precise moment in time, space and dimension, the female in Egypt will drop one of the green calcite crystals into the hole in the ground that is near the source of this Unity Grid coming out of the Earth. As this crystal is falling and for a few minutes afterwards, the adjustment can take place.

"In order for this to work, the forty women must be in location around the world, holding their piece of the original one crystal and meditating on this Unity Consciousness Grid balance change."

Thoth wanted me to be the male in Moorea and said that I should select who the female would be. Well, that was fixed in stone. I had a girlfriend, and if I had chosen anyone else I probably would not be alive now to write this story.

With everything seemingly in place, my girlfriend and I headed for Moorea, as all the rest of the women and the one other man began their journeys to their specific locations around the world. All I could do was trust in Great Spirit, as only Great Spirit could possibly coordinate such an elaborate event.

I was in contact with only one other person—the woman in Egypt—to make sure everything was going properly.

CHAPTER NINE

THE ISLAND OF MOOREA, THE FORTY-TWO WOMEN, AND THE FORTY-TWO CRYSTALS

Moorea was a surprise to me. It was the most succulent female place I had ever visited. It wasn't just that the island was in the shape of a heart, it was also the beautiful sexual energy throbbing out of the Earth and the ocean.

Everywhere we looked there were gorgeous tan men and women moving about, all wearing nothing more than a small piece of cloth on their bottoms and nothing on their tops. The sight of such beautiful people in near-naked form only emphasized this mission and its purpose—to change the sexual balance of females worldwide.

Thoth wanted us to arrive on the island at least a week before the adjustment so we could get used to the energy of this island. He suggested that we contact the natives to really understand. As it turned out, we were there for ten days and completed our purpose on the ninth day.

My girlfriend and I were both novices at scuba diving, but dragged all the equipment with us, as we had heard that Moorea was one of the best places in the world to dive. We were not disappointed, to say the least. The coral reef around Moorea is like liquid glass. When you're swimming through this almost-body-temperature water, you can see the millions of multicolored fish and animals surrounding you for a hundred feet in all directions. I remember thinking that it was like swimming in an aquarium. We couldn't leave the ocean. When we got out of the water, it felt like the energy dropped by half, and we kept finding ourselves walking back into the ocean like zombies. It was like a magnet pulling us back. And we were swimming in this water from six to eight hours a day, both of us completely addicted.

After a couple of days of this bliss, a carefree young native Polynesian couple approached us and asked us if we would like to visit their home. We both found them so unassuming and natural that we didn't think twice. We went home with them as if we had known them all of our lives.

Their "home" was a beach hidden from the tourists. It had grass huts for storing stuff, but not really for sleeping in. There must have been about twenty-five people in their home—a few more women than men. Everyone slept on the sand by the ocean, except when it rained.

Higher up on an ocean ledge their ancestors had built a special stone building for one purpose only. The women and the men would take turns using this space. It was a place where the women would massage each other, and then the men would massage each other. They would alternate each afternoon. In their culture, it was important that each sex took care of each other physically, and so each person was massaged and loved by other members of the tribe almost every day.

Why not? They had mastered life beyond what most of us know. They didn't use money, as they found that money only enslaved them. When they were hungry they would go to a mango or papaya tree. There were hundreds of plants and herbs growing everywhere, and they knew exactly where they were. The ocean was part of their home, and they would simply walk into the water with a pointed stick and in minutes come back with the fish of their desires. They seldom became sick, but if they did, their ancestors had told them how to heal, so doctors were people they never knew.

If paradise exists on Earth, they live it.

Playing and loving were their primary purposes in life. At night they would bring out their musical instruments, which they made out of materials from the jungle or ocean. They would dance and sing for hours until the moon was high in the sky. Work was something that was necessary only once in awhile, such as when a boat that had been destroyed by a storm needed to be rebuilt, and when it was necessary, all of the tribe would come together as one to help. Even then they turned work into something fun, even exciting. Music would flow through the air, tribe members taking turns between playing the music and working on the project. What a life!

It became clear, after even a couple of days, that their way of life was not based on ego, but on something more holistic.

They loved each other in every way, taking care of each other. No one ever combed their own hair or made themselves ready for the day; it was always done by someone of the same sex. They turned the simplest acts into a way of showing love.

They shared each other as if they were all in one large marriage. The women had their choice of all the men, and the men shared the women. I don't think that the word "jealousy" was even in their vocabulary.

After only about three days of being with them, I had forgotten why I had come there in the first place. Never had I felt such release and relaxation. My old life in the States had disappeared completely. My body had become part of the tribe, and the island owned my soul. How could this happen in such a short period of time?

Neither my girlfriend nor I had ever mentioned to any of them our secret intention for being on their island, but somewhere towards the seventh or eighth day, the young man who brought us to the tribe asked us to come sit with him. He looked into our eyes with complete love and began to speak.

"You are my white brother and sister, and we know what is in your hearts. We know why you are here, and we want to help you. You must reach a sacred place near the center of this island to complete your purpose, but it is forbidden that you go there. It is too holy for us to let anyone into that area. But your purpose is beyond our rules.

"Tomorrow one of our elders will be here to guide you. I can't tell you his real name, but you can call him Thomas. You are in our hearts, and we will do whatever we can for you to complete why you have come here."

The next morning, as the sun was rising and exploding with color over the blue, blue ocean, painting the billowing clouds shades of purple and orange, a man in his middle fifties walked straight up to us and said his name was Thomas. He was six feet tall and dark brown. His almost-black hair hung down to the middle of his back, and he wore nothing but a white cloth around his waist and leather thongs. He seemed to know exactly what we were thinking.

Without asking any questions, he proceeded to tell us that the place where we needed to be to do our "ceremony" was deep inside the interior of the island, that it was a little dangerous to get there, but he would show us the way.

I asked if there was anything we needed to bring, and he looked at us like we were children. "No," he said simply and turned and began to walk away. We looked at each other and followed him.

While living on the beach, I had noticed that the middle of the island seemed mountainous and covered with jungle, but hadn't thought about it except to feel its beauty. Now we were about to feel its power.

Leaving sea level, which had been our only experience of Moorea, was a shock. The terrain really was jungle. Without this guide, I quickly realized that there would be no way my girlfriend and I could have ever made our way. You had to know the pathways in the dense jungle and how they connected to other, smaller, almost unnotice-able pathways that branched off, eventually leading to our goal.

Several times we passed ancient stone ruins that were situated just off this trail. I asked Thomas about the first one, and he said, "There were ancient ones that lived here long before we came to these islands. We don't know who they were, but these ruins have been pro-tected always. There are certain ones that we do ceremony at every year to honor those that came before us. But where we are going is the most sacred place of all."

After several hours of climbing always upward, we came to a mountain ridgeline that I had thought from a distance was our destination. But when we stepped onto the highest point, we could see into the center of the island for the first time. I couldn't believe my eyes. Honest to God, it looked like something out of an Indiana Jones movie.

The mountainous ridgeline that we were standing on formed an enormous circle of mountains, and in the exact middle was a mountain that was the most phallic physical mountain I had ever seen. It was like a giant penis pointing at the sky, forcefully penetrating the female circle of mountains below.

All I could say was, "Wow," and was forced to be silent by the sheer power of what I was witnessing. I couldn't help but remember that Moorea was shaped like of a heart. And this was at its very center? The three of us stood speechless. The only sound was wind blowing through my hair, and the silence allowed me to notice that the three of us were breathing in perfect synchronicity, as one. I felt connected to all life everywhere.

Perhaps five minutes later, Thomas pointed to an area to the left of the phallic mountain and said, "There. That is where you need to be. You must go on by yourselves now. You will know when you are at the right place. My heart and those of all of my people will be with you." And he turned and walked away, leaving us alone.

For a long time we stood there holding hands, not wanting to break this magical moment.

Finally, a bright green parrot flew uncomfortably close to our heads and screamed, startling us out of our trance.

We laughed at how we had jumped, but the seriousness of why we were there together began to take control. We knew we were running out of time. We had to be in position at this sacred location within an hour and a half or all would be lost.

"Come on, let's get going."

It wasn't easy without Thomas, who knew every inch of the island, but it was up to us to decide how to get from here to there. We decided to drop almost straight down the side of the mountain into the bowl to save time, which was probably a mistake. We lost the trail within five minutes.

But finally, we reached the sacred site, which was a fairy-tale picture: a flat stone altar where ceremonies had been performed for countless generations before us. We had only fifteen minutes before the all-important moment would expire.

Really, life is amazing. After months of planning something so critical for the human experience on Earth, we barely made it on time. But we were there, and as fate would have it, so were all the other forty women and our two counterparts in Egypt. This massive ceremony was about to become reality.

Very quickly, we set up the four directions to center and protect this internal space where the ceremony would be performed. From my training with the Taos Pueblo on creating sacred space, I knew certain intentions had to be projected and brought into reality. One has to connect with Mother Earth and Father Sky within one's heart and ask the spirits of the six directions to contain the space and protect the humans doing the ceremony. One had to consciously bring in the presence of Great Spirit. Of course, Great Spirit is always everywhere, but it is about the human awareness of the presence of God. Without these intentions, this ceremony would be nothing but a fantasy and powerless.

All around us, this amphitheater was reflecting back to us the energy of thousands of years of sacred ceremony. Thomas had given us local herbs and articles to be placed at the center of the circle, as was the islanders' tradition, and, knowing how important it was to follow the local beliefs, we did that. And so, with a mere three minutes left, all was prepared.

I looked into the eyes of my girlfriend. I could see her anticipation of not knowing what was going to happen. She was practically holding her breath, frozen with the reality of knowing that she was about to be used by Mother Earth as a tool of immense energetic change that would affect every woman on Earth.

I took a moment to assure her, held her hand, and the words came out of my mouth, "You are, at this moment, the most important and beautifully sexual woman alive. Close your eyes, and let your spirit enter your body and be here fully in this moment. For the next few minutes, you are the Earth creating a new way to express femininity."

I checked my watch. We had fifty-five seconds before the stone would be dropped into the sacred hole in Egypt. I turned to my female friend, and she was gone. Time and space meant nothing to her now. She had entered a place in her body that only she, in the whole world, would understand.

A silent countdown began to happen in my head. I couldn't help it. I could not imagine what was about to take place.

Five, four, three, two, one—now.

She, of course, could not have possibly known exactly when that split second spent itself, but at that precise second, everything changed.

She had been on her knees, resting back on her haunches, but the moment the ceremony energy arrived, an expression of shock swept over her face. Her whole body responded by dropping down closer to the Earth.

And then another wave of energy moved through her. And another. She was obviously having an experience of intensity, and for me, as a male watching her, it was also a sexual experience.

I knew what this ceremony was about, but it was not until I was actually seeing her and feeling what she was feeling that I realized the power of sexual change on this level.

She stretched out on the Earth, opened her legs as wide as she could and let out a moan from deep within her secret hidden chamber. It almost sounded like pain, but it was something far more primal. She had entered a region of sexuality where she was totally male and, for the first time in her life, knew the urge of wanting to merge with a beautiful woman. Her normal sexuality had disappeared, replaced by a reality that she later said she'd only fantasized about, but this was real. This was body-energetic real.

Then, as fast as this experience swept over her, a new wave of energy entered her body, and she involuntarily swayed herself into another position. She clutched the Earth and moaned even louder to Father Sun directly above her. Her sexuality had now swung to the opposite pole. She was entirely, totally female now, wanting to be penetrated as deeply as humanly possible.

All she could say was, "Oh my God. I love you." The words went to someone only she could see.

Then another wave of energy surged through her, and now she was male again. But this time there was a little female mixed with all that masculine desire. Each time the energy from the Mother entered her body, she would enter the opposite sexual polarity, but closer to balance. Like a pendulum swinging from side to side, her sexuality kept changing from energy surge to energy surge, until finally it returned to somewhere near the center.

As the energy stabilized over the next half hour or so, we both knew that she had been forever changed by this experience, and so had the Earth.

The females in the future of this dear planet were now to be altered ever so slightly, to be centered more within their own feminine sexuality, as the last 13,000 years of male domination had pulled them a little too far into the world of male experience. Now females would be ready for changes that were to come in the future, changes they could never experience or be able to absorb while plagued by the sexual imbalance of modern times. It was only the beginning, for what actually changed was the Unity Consciousness Grid high above the Earth. This grid was the future of humanity, and the future of humanity was about to become almost completely dependent upon the women of all the countries, cultures, and religions that humankind has created from its mind.

The Precession of the Equinox was about to enter a new 13,000 years cycle, this time led by the female wisdom that all women have held within a small secret chamber within their beautiful female hearts. Without this unconditional love, humanity would be lost to the mental constraints that men have built to protect us over the last 13,000 years. This protection was needed in the past, but now it is our greatest hindrance to survival, to the expansion of our consciousness, and to the ascension of the human race into a new world of light.

Thank God for the female heart. It has always been this way. The men protect us as we enter the dark part of the cycle, and the women lead us back into the light as the Grand Cycle returns toward the center of the galaxy.

My girlfriend lay limp on the ground, every muscle in her body spent. She had just had the most amazing and unusual orgasm of her life, and by doing so, had saved humanity.

Suddenly, lightning bolted out of the sky, and thunder exploded all around us. It shocked us both. She jumped into my arms, and we looked around into an atmosphere entirely different than the blue sky and white billowing clouds that were there when the ceremony began. I'd been so wrapped up in the energy of the ceremony I hadn't noticed the enormous storm that had quickly engulfed the entire island. Lightning began to build, striking everywhere around us. It was rapidly becoming a serious situation.

We grabbed our things and began to look for shelter, but it was too late. Fifteen minutes after the ceremony the fury of hurricane-like rains were everywhere. Never in my life had I seen anything like this. We couldn't see more than a few feet in front of us. A wall of water was pouring from the sky.

We found a place under a rock formation to get out of the torrential downpour and held each other as the storm raged on. What we didn't know at the time was that this rain was not going to stop for three days and three nights. Eventually, we made our way back to our "family" near the beach, but our lives had changed in ways I can't really explain on these pages.

A storm of this magnitude was not unusual in Moorea, but for the same thing to simultaneously happen in Egypt definitely was. Fifteen minutes after the ceremony in Egypt, torrential rains began in Giza and continued for three days and three nights in this normally dry desert region of the Great Pyramid. Newspapers reported three feet of water in the streets of Giza. Three people died from drowning.

The reporter said that Egypt had never experienced anything like this in its known history.

In retrospect, I saw this as an emotional release from our Mother to find a balance one more time in her inner needs. Though this new female sexual balance would not manifest in the world for a few more years, to our Mother it was real, here and now, and the beginning of a new cycle of life for her dear body, the planet Earth.

CHAPTER TEN

The Island of Kauai and the Fourth-Dimensional Ceremony of the Transfer of Power From the Male to the Female

Finally, my girlfriend and I were free to move without any pressure from the Ascended Masters. We had no choice, however, about leaving Moorea, as we already had our plane tickets, and we didn't feel we had the money to change them.

It was terribly difficult for us to leave the island. Our hearts were forever there on that tiny piece of sand and trees. But the idea of going to Australia was also exciting. It was the place we had decided to go after this spiritual journey, and the more we talked about it, the more pumped up we became. The Great Barrier Reef, here we come!

We took a slow boat to Tahiti, and from there flew to Sidney. Sidney was remarkable—such a beautiful city, with its harbor of white sails floating side to side across its dark blue waters. We didn't stay there long, though, for the reef was pulling us. By now, we had become almost experts at scuba diving, and we had heard that the reef here was at least as good as Moorea. So we hitchhiked up the eastern coastline, talking with the locals and beginning to understand the amazing nature of the Aussies. They were so open and fun loving. I don't think I've ever laughed so much in my life.

Eventually, we ended up in a place called Byron Bay. There the northern ocean and the southern ocean meet, creating one of the greatest places to surf because of the huge waves that come rolling in like clockwork.

I'm convinced that all the hippies of the 1960s somehow found their way to this little town and established a beachhead, never to allow the man to enter again and take away their peace, love, and good vibes. Being one of the first and original hippies, I thought I had died and gone to heaven. It was deja vu to the tenth power. For sure, I spoke these people's language. My girlfriend and I were both having a pretty hard time leaving this place, so we decided that we were not really in a hurry to get to the reef and would just lay back for awhile.

Two weeks into being a beach bum again, I was meditating high up on a ridge overlooking the Pacific Ocean, when Thoth appeared. At first I thought he was just checking in, but no, he had other plans.

This was the first time I had ever seen Thoth look timid. I asked him what was the matter, and he replied, "Drunvalo, I'm very sorry, but I have to ask you to do something for us again."

All the hairs on the back of my neck stood up. Oh no. I could feel it. "What do you want?" I squeaked out barely able to speak.

"I really am sorry," he said. "But you must leave immediately for Hawaii, the island of Kauai, as soon as it is possible."

"Thoth, I thought that we had time to rest for awhile. Can't this wait at least a couple of more weeks?"

"No," he said simply. "This is even more important than what you did in Moorea. Please try to understand."

I was silent for sometime. I didn't know what to say. I knew that this spiritual work was one of the primary reasons that I traveled across the universe to be here on Earth. It took precedent over all other parts of my life.

I also realized at that moment that my girlfriend would not take to this idea very well. She was through running around and really wanted a vacation. At last, I looked up at my mentor and said, "Okay, if you say it is important, it must be. What do you want me to do?"

"Not now," he said. "Wait until you are on Kauai, and I'll explain everything. Thank you, Drunvalo. If there were anyone else that could do this work, I would not have asked you." And he disappeared.

I sat there for a long time trying to figure out how to tell my girlfriend, but nothing seemed to be appropriate. I knew I was in for it.

She sat by our tent fixing some piece of clothing that had torn. She glanced up as I approached her, then back to her work. "What's wrong, Drunvalo?"

I told her everything trying to make it sound like a great idea to leave Australia and head for Kauai. She looked at me, very disappointed, and said, "Honey, I can't leave here without seeing the Great Barrier Reef. If you must leave, I understand, but I'm not going. Do you understand?"

"Yes, I do understand. I don't really want to go, but I must. It's what I do in life."

"Then I'll meet up with you somewhere, I don't know where, and I don't know when. This place feels so good I may never leave."

We hugged, and I packed and left early the next morning alone. I felt a little funny leaving her there in a foreign country, but she was a world traveler and a very savvy girl. And Australia was a beautiful and safe county. We didn't see each other again for almost six months. Life can be strange sometimes as well as amazing.

I landed in Maui and took a small island-hopper, carrying mostly locals between the islands, to reach the shores of Kauai. Kauai is the oldest island in the chain and a remnant left over from Lemuria. The energy there is ancient by anyone's standards.

As I was drifting out of the sky to land, I began to wonder what it was I was supposed to do here. I had no idea. How could I not wonder?

There were dense rain clouds hanging over the center of the island. It is almost always raining in the center of this island. It is the wettest place on Earth. If a location gets four or five feet of rain a year, that is considered a very wet place. But Kauai gets forty-two feet of rain a year—hence, the awesome waterfalls that grace the side of almost every mountain on the island.

Soon I was standing in the airport with that out-of-place feeling airports seem to cause in people. I decided to rent a car to not only get me around, but also to give me a sense of having a home again. I think I was missing my girlfriend.

The decision to rent a car was paramount, as Thoth eventually had me running all over this island. The land here is so rugged in the northwestern area that they have never been able to build a road that completely circles the island; the primary road is in the shape of a horseshoe about thirty-three miles in length. Wherever I needed to go next always seemed to be at the opposite end of the horseshoe. Every time I would get to one location Thoth had asked me to go to, he would turn me around and head me back to the other side of the island. I will never forget when I returned this car to the rental establishment. Most people bring a rental back with maybe sixty or eighty miles on it, but I had over 800 miles on mine. The guy could not believe it, but I sure could.

The first night I was there I slept in my tent by the ocean, on a grassy knoll. For the first time in awhile I felt peace, and the sound of the ocean lulled me into a deep sleep.

When I woke the next morning, I remembered that Thoth had still not told me why I was there, but I knew it wouldn't be long before this slumbering attitude would turn to work. Right I was. In fact, Thoth must have heard my thoughts, for it was only about a half hour later that he appeared to me.

"What you have to do is too complex for me to explain everything all at once," he said. "So let's start piece by piece. In it's simplest form, you must be part of a ceremony here on this island that will change the course of history, but that can't happen until certain things fall into place.

"As I said, I have brought you here to be part of an Earth ceremony, but before this primary ceremony can be performed, you must be part of a smaller ceremony that takes place every year here, which has to do with the heart chakra of this island. The location is under a mango tree. Ask and you will find it."

Then Thoth abruptly disappeared.

I began to talk with the Hawaiian people, but whenever I would speak about the ceremony with the heart chakra under the mango tree, they would walk away. Obviously this was something foreigners were not allowed to know about.

But eventually I found a young Hawaiian man who knew exactly what I was talking about. He said, "If it is true that you are supposed to be part of that ceremony, then head up this river." He pointed to a wide, dark green river that appeared to come from the center of the island. He hesitated for a moment and added, "And if by chance you do find your way, after you leave the ceremony do not look back, for if you do your life could be in danger."

I asked him to explain to me what he meant, but he just shrugged his shoulders and walked away.

"How do I find the heart chakra ceremony?" I called after him.

Without turning around, he said, "Use your heart. What else?"

As he disappeared into an old grocery store, I thought, "Does life always have to be so mysterious?"

The river wound through gorgeous foliage and expensive homes. I knew that what I had to do and where I had to go was somewhere up this river, but as usual, past that, I had no clue. I put the little rented Toyota into gear and pulled away, pointing upriver, trying to feel my heart, but it seemed senseless to keep driving without knowing where I was going. Besides, I was tired and really wanted to just pull over and go to sleep. So I did just that, pulled over to the side of the road and closed my eyes. I became sensitive to the heart vibration and waited.

Thirty or forty minutes later, I was about to leave when out of the trees appeared two young couples dressed in ceremonial clothing, holding flowers. One of them was holding a clay pot. They got into a car and in minutes drove away.

On pure instinct, I got out of my car and followed the path they had emerged from. The trail carried me deep into the trees and eventually to the edge of this same dark green river. As I was following this path, more native Hawaiians were leaving. None of them looked into my eyes or said hello. I pushed forward.

After another quarter mile along this river, I found this huge mango tree, half over land and half over the water, and at the base were offerings that appeared to be ceremonial in nature.

Sitting in quiet meditation was a young girl about eighteen years old who looked pure Hawaiian. I didn't notice her at first, as she was mostly hidden by a few small trees. When I did see her, it was obvious she had seen me first but she lowered her eyes as if she didn't know I was there.

I knew I had entered into a sacred place and began to treat this tree and this place with respect and honor. I had a small crystal with me, and I had picked some native flowers along the way to emulate the two couples I had seen. Laying the crystal and the flowers at the base of the tree, I sat down a little ways away and tried to make myself invisible. I went into meditation, feeling my heart. A beautiful sense of joy filled me, and I knew for certain that this was the place Thoth wanted me to find.

The moment I felt this certainty, Thoth appeared in my inner vision and said to me, "The crystal holds your vibration, and it must be thrown into the river. Before it hits the water turn and walk away, and *do not look back*. Leave and return to your car."

I did exactly as he said. I threw the crystal up into the air where the mango tree branched out over the river, and before it hit the water I turned and left. I kept moving, never looking back. I don't know if the young girl was still there or if anything unusual happened. I simply obeyed the rules.

More Hawaiians approached me as they were heading for the mango tree, but I lowered my eyes and continued walking until I reached the pavement and figured I was now out of the energy field. I drove away back toward the ocean.

Next morning as I woke, Thoth came into my awareness and began to speak about something new. He said to me, "You must now get permission to perform the major ceremony from the island Kahuna." He gave me her name and showed me what she looked like. She was an old grandmother, heavy set, and strong-willed, from what Thoth projected to me.

"So how do I find her?"

"Finding her is part of the process," he said. "You must do that alone. But you will find her when you find this crystal."

At that moment in my inner vision I saw an enormous quartz crystal, maybe five feet high and almost three feet across. I had never seen a crystal this big before except in photographs. Thoth asked me if I could see the crystal he was showing me. I told him I could. He said he could not tell me where it was, as finding it was also part of my spiritual process. He left me with the statement, "Find the crystal and you will find the Kahuna."

"And one more thing," he added, "The crystal is near the heart chakra of the island." And he disappeared.

So I drove all over the area where I had been the day before, asking people if they had ever seen a crystal that big before, but to no avail. After two days of searching, I decided that to find this crystal I had to use my inner abilities, those I had learned in the Yucatan.

The next day I drove to the area where the heart chakra was again, but the road was long with many roads branching off. It could take forever to find what I was looking for.

So, as I had done in finding the Kohunlich Temple in the Yucatan, I let my third eye do the driving. Holding the image of the enormous crystal in my mind, I kept moving up this road until I felt I had to turn in a certain direction. I continued doing this for several miles, making turns when I felt I needed to. Eventually I was on top of a mountain ridge, moving in a residential area with luxurious homes on both sides of the road. Abruptly, as I made a turn onto another road, I found myself approaching a Hindu temple. My car decided to turn into the parking lot and stop the motor. That's the only way I can describe how I got there: my car did it.

I got out and walked up to an enormous statue of Ganesh, the Indian elephant god. It was probably fifteen feet high and quite well done, I thought. But it wasn't the statue that attracted me there. It was this feeling that the crystal was somewhere nearby.

It was Sunday, and the temple was giving service. The parking lot was full of cars. I decided to enter the building to see where this would lead.

People were in the middle of singing a Hindu chant, and incense smoke instantly penetrated my entire body. The service was familiar, as I had spent many nights in Ram Dass's Hanuman Foundation in Taos, New Mexico, singing and chanting during darshan. I closed my eyes and joined in with the chanting, forgetting for a short time my real purpose.

It seemed like only a few minutes had gone by, but my mind knew nearly an hour had passed. Within another ten minutes, most of the people had left, and this transplanted ancient temple quickly returned to its normal silence.

For the first time, now that all the people were gone, I could see the altar, and there it was—the giant quartz crystal. It was an incredible sight, sitting high in the middle of the altar space, resonating its influence into every inch of the temple. I don't know how I didn't feel it when I walked in.

I started to move toward the crystal to see what it had to say, when the priest who had led the service blocked my approach.

"Can I help you?" he said with an authoritative tone. I looked at him and could tell that to go up to the crystal was simply out of the question. What I said was, "I'm looking for a Kahuna grandmother. Her name is . . . ,"—and I spoke her name. "Do you know how I can find her?"

He smiled and said, "You don't have to look far. Just turn around." I turned my head and directly behind me was the very image Thoth had showed me two days before. Her smile and genuine warmth melted any concern that I might be imposing myself on her.

"Grandmother," I said, "I have been looking for you. Can we talk?"

"What is it that you want from me?"

I let out a sigh of relief, and told her everything. I told her about Thoth, the ceremony that needed to be performed on her island, and how I needed her permission before I could proceed.

"Grandmother, can I have your permission to do this ceremony?"

She took my hand with great love and said, "Drunvalo, you have my permission, but that is not enough for something this important. You must now seek the permission from the spirit of this island."

She told me the spirit's name and explained, "You will now have to find him on your own and ask him yourself. May Spirit bless you and what you do."

She gave me a big hug and bowed to me in a Hindu manner, telling me "Namaste." I bowed back to her and left.

Sitting in my car I felt both contented to have finally found her and to have received her permission and let down since it seemed that I was no closer to my goal. Now I still had to get yet another permission.

I closed my eyes and went into meditation to receive assistance. Thoth immediately appeared and smiled. "You're closer than you know, Drunvalo. Don't you realize that life has already happened? The idea of failure or more work is only the part of your dream that still believes in separation."

"Okay, okay, okay. What's next?"

Thoth, in his deliberate way, said, "Take the road to Hanalei and continue on past the town until the road ends. Park the car, and wait for my instructions."

As I was making my way up the coastline, I began to contemplate everything that had happened to me in the last few months. Time seemed to be moving so fast, almost out of control. On the other hand, so much was being accomplished.

And this man Thoth had become so pivotal in the work I was doing. The angels were the primary guiding light within me, the true source of my spiritual decisions, but they made it clear that it was proper for me to be listening to Thoth at this time. I didn't know it then, but it would not be long before my work with Thoth would come to an end.

At that moment I was passing through Hanalei, which is situated at the northern end of the horseshoe road. Traffic could not pass much beyond it. It was like a home on a cul-de-sac, and I realized again how much I love that village. The area is astoundingly beautiful, the lifestyle there is so open and free, and the people reflect the environment they lived in. My heart always beats a little easier when I am there.

I arrived at the end of the highway and pulled over into a spot where I knew my car would not be in anyone's way. I had no idea how long I would be on this journey. I closed my eyes and waited for Thoth to appear.

He was so reliable. "Drunvalo," he said to me, "Here are your instructions. Take off all of your clothes including your shoes, and wrap the white shawl that you have in your trunk around your hips. Take only the medicine bag that you use with you."

This medicine bag was something that I had carried for years. It contained power objects that I used in ceremony, such as crystals, stones, powered corn, sage and cedar for purification, and pieces of feathers.

"As you enter the trail into the mountains, you are beginning the ceremony," Thoth said. "Do not be concerned about the permission from the spirit of the island as he is part of this ceremony, and has already given us his permission. Remember to breathe and stay in your heart.

"You are to look for a waterfall that splits into two equal parts about halfway down its fall. When you find this place, stand exactly in front of the waterfall, and then turn around 180 degrees. Look in front of you, and there will be a large flat rock. It is there that the island's spirit will meet you, and it is there that the ceremony will commence. We love you and thank you in advance for the work you do for this planet."

With this statement, Thoth disappeared. I opened my trunk and found the white shawl. My medicine bag I had around my neck. I stripped off my clothes, wrapped the white shawl around my waist, and held on to my medicine bag for just a moment. I closed my eyes, and the angels were there. They just smiled.

"We love you," they said.

I crossed the street to the trailhead to where the ceremony would begin, according to Thoth. There, at the beginning of the trailhead, was a large warning sign. At the top of the sign was the skull-and-crossbones image, and the sign said, "Do not walk into this area without knee-high rubber boots as there is a bacteria in the water that can kill you if it touches your skin. Do not touch the water."

Well, there I was, beginning my journey and the ceremony, almost naked with no shoes, and this sign immediately tried to put fear into my body and mind. Thoth didn't wait until I closed my eyes. He simply appeared outwardly to me and said, "Drunvalo, this is a test. You must trust who you are and your connection to the universe and the Creator. Center in your heart, and proceed. Do not worry, you will not be harmed."

I took a deep breath and did exactly as he said. All my concern left my body, and I knew that I was absolutely protected. Without any fear and with a sense of excitement, I began this sacred journey into these beautiful, rugged mountains.

At first the trail was pretty simple, as I was at sea level and near the road. But as time went on, I climbed higher and higher, farther off the ocean level and deeper into jungle mountains that looked like something from millions of years ago. If I'd seen a dinosaur, I would not have been surprised. Water was everywhere, falling off the rocks, gushing past the trail, flowing in creeks. I kept getting soaked. Even the jungle trees were dripping. Every few hundred feet or so, I would pass a spectacular waterfall. They took my breath away. Of course, I kept waiting for the one that would split into two.

At one point I stopped in one of the rare clearings where I could look out of the jungle and see the ocean below. I was shocked to see how high I had climbed. It was like looking out of a small plane—the water was far, far below me. The sense of beauty, the sounds of eternal waterfalls, rare birds everywhere, the unbelievably gorgeous flowers and plant life made me feel like I could not possibly be on Earth. It had to be a planet where life was just beginning and totally undisturbed.

Thoth told me something else that I haven't mentioned, something I should probably tell you now. Kauai was the geographical location on Earth where the memory of the planet was stored for the last 13,000 years. Yes, there is an Akashic Record stored in the atmosphere as well in the human body, but the Earth's memory is also intentionally and literally stored in a single crystal that was placed off the shoreline of the exact place where I was standing. I am not certain why this is done; Thoth never explained this to me.

There were thirteen crystals all together, but one of them was the actual memory bank. The crystals were set in the pattern of Metatron's Cube: one in the center of the island, six around that one and positioned on the island, and six more around those inner six and situated in the water off shore. This particular system had been used by other people in the distant past. We know that the Lemurians and the Atlanteans used this same set of crystals on this island for the same purpose, without changing the crystals. But from Thoth's memory, this system is much, much older than either one of these cultures. Who created it even Thoth doesn't know.

The one out in the water below where I was standing is called a skeletal crystal, and it looks like it came from space. In fact, this one did. It was about two feet long, a foot in diameter, and double terminated, meaning both ends come to a point.

Skeletal crystals are very rare, and if you've never seen one, they are hard to describe. They are quartz, but nothing like normal quartz. What is so unusual about skeletal crystals is that they have quartz "tubes" covering their surfaces. It looks like someone has glued round tubes about a quarter inch in diameter all over the surface in a random pattern. There is nothing like them in the world that I know of, and they will hold an infinite amount of data within and in the space around them.

It is for this characteristic that this crystal was selected to hold the memory of the planet and everything that lives and occurs upon it. In other words, it is the Akashic Records of the Earth downloaded into the tiny space of a crystal. It would be another story to explain why this is important, and like I said, I don't really understand it.

I turned and continued up the tail, watching for the special waterfall, and in no more than five more minutes, it appeared. I stood at its base for at least ten minutes. It was stunning. The water was falling for at least 200 feet and then hit this huge rock that protruded from the mountainside, splitting the falling water into two streams. It was truly spectacular. And partly, I was resting from the climb. I knew that I would have to go to work soon.

When the time felt right, I turned around 180 degrees and faced out over the ocean. As Thoth had said, directly in front of me there was this large flat rock, slightly lifted up off the surface of the mountainside and with a fantastic view of the deep blue ocean stretching to the horizon, creating a perfect place for a ceremony. I knew for certain that I was in the right location.

Not knowing what to expect, I proceeded as I was trained on the Taos Pueblo in New Mexico. I opened my medicine bag and placed four quartz crystals in the four directions, making a square about two feet in diameter. In the very center I placed a special crystal of mine called a Herkimer diamond—a double-terminated crystal of exceptional clarity that affects your dream world in a positive way, which is its main use.

I prayed to each of the four directions to make this ceremony sacred and for protection to not be disturbed in any manner. I used corn and tobacco as my tradition required, placing these substances on each crystal in each direction. I also prayed to the directions below the center crystal and above it, as well as the center itself—all seven directions. In a circle connecting the four direction crystals, I placed many smaller crystals and stones of different kinds as I felt needed, making a wheel. Inside the wheel, I made a cross of local stones connecting the center crystal to the edge.

When the ceremony was set, I closed my eyes and began to go into a deep meditation, waiting to meet the spirit of the island. I knew that had to happen first, but I had no idea how that would happen. All I could do was to do as Thoth asked, remain in my heart and be open.

I continued to meditate for twenty-five or thirty minutes and nothing happened. A small concern was beginning to creep into me as to why this was taking so long, but I knew I had to have patience and to continue even if it took all day.

Another fifteen minutes passed with nothing going on within me. Then I heard a noise. I opened one eye, and there on the rock was a tiny white mouse, walking around, smelling the corn, and checking everything out. He was so cute, and I didn't see any reason to disturb him. So I let him have his way.

I was about to close my eye again when this little mouse moved over to the very center crystal, the Herkimer. He put his tiny front feet up on the crystal, turned, and looked directly into my one open eye. He stared at me. I opened both of my eyes. He didn't move for about a minute. We just looked at each other. Time stopped and then expanded. And then it happened.

I don't even remember closing my eyes, but I must have. Suddenly the little mouse expanded into a giant of a man about fourteen feet high. He looked Polynesian, with dark brown skin, black hair, and brown eyes. He seemed to have a warrior vibe and a powerful muscular body.

His gaze penetrated me, and in a deep voice he said, "I am the spirit of this island, and you are invited into this ceremony."

He backed up, and as he did the space expanded into an open circle about thirty feet across. There, standing in the outer rim of the circle next to this enormous spirit was Thoth, three other men I didn't know (though my inner knowing told me they were part of the Ascended Masters, and they all appeared Polynesian), and a woman who I believe was associated with Atlantis.

In the center of the circle was a man whose name I cannot say because I am not allowed to. He was the person the Earth selected to be the male to protect humanity during the last 13,000 year cycle. When I saw him, I knew exactly what the purpose of this ceremony was.

This was the fourth-dimensional ceremony that took place every 12,920 years to turn over the power and responsibility from one energy to the other—in this case the male to the female. Everything on Earth happens on the fourth dimension first and then filters down to this third dimension, which we are all familiar with.

What this instantly meant to me was that after this ceremony, there would be a third-dimensional ceremony someday to crystallize these energies on our everyday world. When this second ceremony took place, the female energy would then lead humanity into the light for the next 12,920 years.

I was humbled. I now understood how important this ceremony was and why Thoth had asked me to drop everything to make this journey.

The man in the center of the circle was kneeling, facing toward my right. In his arms he held the skeletal crystal that holds the memory of the last half of the Grand Cycle (actually, everything back to the beginning of time for Earth).

He began to speak. He talked about his experience over the last half of the cycle and how he was so grateful that we, humanity, had made it to this point in time/space/dimension without too many disturbances. I could feel that he was on the edge of his emotions and was holding back tears from the relief of what was about to happen.

In the next instant, a beautiful young woman walked into the circle from the right, the direction the man was facing, and moved into the center, where she knelt down in front of him, bowing with great reverence. She held her bow for at least thirty seconds and then straightened up to face him, eyes closed.

Then she opened her eyes and looked into his eyes, but said nothing. He began to speak, "I have been given the responsibility to protect and guide humanity for the last half of the Grand Cycle. Now you have been chosen to protect and guide us into the next half of this cycle. This crystal is the tool that you need to link the two parts of the cycle together and to accomplish your work. As I hand this crystal to you, my work is finished and completed, and your work will begin. Will you accept this sacred responsibility?"

She lowered her eyes from his and began to speak in a soft and flowing voice. "Thank you for all you have done. You are a great man. Yes, I will accept this responsibility with my life. I will do the best I can." With those simple words, she became silent.

He paused a few seconds, then lifted the massive crystal, set it in front of her on the ground, and returned to his place. "You now have full power to follow your heart and make the decisions that will guide the course of human history," he said.

Those of us present were witnessing the most important changing of the guard in thousands of years. There was nothing to say. It was perfect.

The young woman stood up, bowed to all of us, and turned to leave. The crystal lifted off the ground and floated behind her, following her like a little puppy. The two of them disappeared into another realm of existence.

What happened after she left was visible to me. I could see her entering her ship along with the crystal and flying back to her home in Peru. She immediately flew to a place between the Island of the Sun and the Island of the Moon on Lake Titicaca, where she flew to the bottom of the lake. There she planted the crystal deep inside the Earth. Then she flew back out into the atmosphere above the lake and waited.

A short time later, a brilliant violet ray of light shot out of the lake into the heavens, and the ancient memories were connected and engaged to the present. It was the beginning of a new era of light and brotherhood for the human race—or, perhaps we now should say, sisterhood.

A side note: For those of you who have read my first two books and know the story of the woman who raised the ancient spaceship from under the Sphinx in Egypt, this is the same woman. She was twenty-three years old at the time and lived in Peru, and she still does. She is now the most important person in the world. But her name cannot be given, as her work must be secret by its very nature. You will hear about her more in this book when I speak about the journey to Peru.

As the ancient memories flooded into human subconsciousness by the completion of this ceremony, a new human dream was initiated—a dream that, higher human consciousness believes, will in the future lead the Earth into a time of peace, beauty, and super-evolution.

But no one knew what had just occurred in this ceremony, except for a few advanced souls, for the dream was a seed deep in darkness, planted literally on a higher dimension of Earth's consciousness, and would not emerge into the light of this world until after the turn of the century. There was nothing to do but to wait.

CHAPTER ELEVEN

THE ANASAZI AND THE MEDICINE WHEEL OF A NEW DREAM

The Serpent of Light and the Cycles of Time
Create a New Dream

After 12,920 years, the cycle is complete as the turning of the Precession of the Equinox approaches the constellation of Aquarius and a new movement begins. Tibet and India have served their purpose of enlightening the world with great integrity, and the Serpent of Light has nestled down into its new home high up in the Andes Mountains of northern Chile, surrounded by Peru, Bolivia, Argentina, and the Pacific Ocean. The Serpent of Light is growing with strength each day through its connection to the center of the Earth, and the world is in for a huge surprise. A new cycle of light is in the process of revealing itself to the world, just as the darkness appears to be overcoming the human soul. "Amazing grace" is an understatement.

As the events in this chapter unfold, it's 2003, and the moment that so many books have been written about, the date of December 21, 2012, is rapidly approaching. Those in the know are wondering in their heart of hearts, what will happen? How will we humans and the Earth change? Will we make it to that time before the environment or the politics of this crazy world dictate our demise? So many questions have flooded our consciousness, creating so much stress in our lives.

Just so you know, the Serpent of Light was put on this world by the highest levels of consciousness to answer your questions of survival, regeneration, and ascension. We will be fine. In fact, more than fine. Please don't worry, but trust in Life, as it is perfect. There is a cosmic DNA, and it is unfolding the world's events just as it was all originally dreamed by the One Consciousness. This reality becomes clear as your eyes become single as you move from duality to Unity Consciousness, and you enter into the heart of the Serpent of Light.

The Serpent Coils into Its New Home, and We Respond

It was a Monday morning in 2003, and the light from the rising sun entered my bedroom window almost imperceptibly, lighting up the landscape of my inner dreaming. In moments, it would reach my physical eyes, and I would respond, but now I was so deeply involved in my meditation that I barely noticed it bringing the room into view as if on a dimmer switch. The angels had been instructing me for almost an hour, and I had forgotten I was still on Earth in a human body. They were telling me that I was being asked to be of service to the Mother and that I was going to have to move around the world and perform ceremonies with and for indigenous tribes that were necessary for the coming energies. They said that there was more to do to assist with the shifting of power from the male to the female. They knew that I didn't fully understand the extent of what they were talking about, but they also knew that I trusted them. I always have. The two angels had been appearing to me since 1971, and I knew that whenever they appeared, there was a reason. They were usually very specific.

But this time seemed different. Everything they were talking about appeared to be shrouded in a veil. They talked about certain indigenous people and how important to human survival they were. These people held memories, knowledge, and wisdom, and without this experience and knowingness, modern mankind would never be able to make the transition across the great abyss, which was approaching very rapidly.

I asked them which tribes they were talking about, and they said the Anasazi, the Maya, the Inca, and the Zulu were the most important for now, but others would come in time, just as they had in the past.

"So how do I begin to be of service?" I asked.

They looked at me as if I were kidding them and simply said, "Be in your Heart, Drunvalo, and you will know what to do. On the journeys you are about to take, Mother Earth will be your guide. Listen to her. She will guide you in each step of your way."

The rising sun reached my eyes and suddenly woke me from my meditation. Inwardly, it appeared as an explosion of red and gold throbbing light. Before I knew what was happening, I was back in my body, and it was morning. I sat, wondering what the angels were trying to tell me, but then figured I might as well start my day. Surely it would become clear in time.

My assistant, Diane Cooper, who has been helping me for years with the business side of my life, phoned me later the next day. She suggested that we make a journey to the Four Corners area of the United States where Arizona, Utah, Colorado, and New Mexico meet, and that we bring a group from around the world there. She asked if I was interested.

Taking people on journeys around the world is not something that I usually do, as most of my time is involved in teaching and writing books on meditation and higher consciousness.

"This is the area of the ancient Anasazi, is it not?" I asked.

"Drunvalo," she said, "You know it was where they lived."

I said this to her, I guess, to hear the response. Sure, I knew the Anasazi used to live there, but it surprised me to hear the name of the Anasazi so soon after the angels telling me they were the first ones that I had ceremony to perform for. I told her I had to think about it, and I would get back with her.

Many years had passed since my trips to the Yucatan and Guatemala, the island of Moorea, and to Kauai, and I thought my work on these levels having to do with the shifting of power from the male to the female were over. Now, at the age of sixty-two, I considered stopping everything having to do with this kind of work—not because I was tired, but because I felt my purpose on Earth was complete. Inside I was content. But Life had more plans to use me, and who am I to argue with Life?

The Unity Consciousness Grid had been completed in about 1989–1990, and I truly thought that there was nothing left to do but wait until the planetary ascension process began to accelerate. But, as I now understood from the angels, there were unusual blocks in the grid that were slowing down the natural flow of energy within it and that had to be removed or balanced in order for the females to effectively use the power they had been given. These blocks had been created by decisions and actions made by certain human cultures that had lived long ago.

As it turned out, Diane and I set up a trip to the Southwest called "The Journey to the Ancient Anasazi," inviting anyone in the world who wished to participate. My books were translated into languages all over the world and read in at least a hundred countries, so I knew that this could be a truly international group. We would limit the number to the capacity of a single tour bus and one pickup truck that would follow with supplies. In the end, we booked solid with fifty-six people (not including our support group of five people plus myself) from twenty-two countries.

This trip was so different from the intimate sacred journeys I had taken before either by myself or with a close friend. This was sixty-one people coming from cultures all over the globe. Some of them I didn't know, but of course, I was about to. Some couldn't speak English, but it had to be this way. This was spiritual work on a level that had to be done with many souls cooperating together, really working as one.

Further, I feel that we had actually made the decision to be together to do this work long, long ago. We think time is linear, but in truth, it is spherical. The future has already happened. Probably no amount of explanation at this time would help you to understand that. Only direct experience will make a real difference, and that experience will change you forever when you discover the reality of time.

Everyone arrived in Sedona, Arizona, one of the most beautiful red-rock-mountain, high-spiritual-energy places in the world. A small town (only about 10,000 people actually lived there), Sedona swells to over 20,000 because of the 5 million tourists that come each year to feel the remarkable energy that comes out of the Earth and makes direct contact with your soul. You can feel it even if you're a materialistic nonbeliever and think that politics and the stock market are the secret keys to Life. Just park your shiny black Mercedes by the side of the road, and step out into the vortexes of the infinite past. You'll see.

The reasons for creating this journey were interwoven and complex. First was the purpose of helping the Anasazi, which the angels had spoken to me about. The Anasazi had to be brought back into this world in order for the second reason to be fulfilled, which was unblocking the grid associated with this ancient culture.

There was another reason, which had to do with the weather. This may sound unimportant, but the weather is part of the problem associated with why the Anasazi had to leave this world in the first place. And the weather was the key to unlocking the energy field that kept the Anasazi hidden inside the Earth's inner worlds. Let me explain.

The Native Americans believe that we are now in the Fourth World and that soon we are all going to leave here and go into the Fifth World. They believe they have been in the other three worlds prior to coming to this world that we all now live in together. They believe that the other three worlds are literally inside the Earth, and that when they came from the Third World, they actually came out of the interior of the Earth to the surface, which is what they call the Fourth World.

The ancestors in the Four Corners area of the United States were a group of people that disappeared long ago, a people we now call the Anasazi. *Anasazi* means "the Ancient Ones," but to some it means the ancient enemy. The Anasazi seemed to have disappeared in a single day. Food and clay containers were left sitting on their tables. Everything looked as if they had simply decided to take a walk and return. It looked as if they had stood up and altogether, en masse, disappeared into thin air.

Why would they do this? Where did they go?

In the last few years, it's been learned that in the final stages of the Anasazi culture, the Atlantic Ocean current slowed way down, just as it is doing today in our world, and that change caused the Four Corners area to enter an extreme drought, just as it has today and for the same reason. But for the Anasazi, the rain stopped completely for forty-six years, and this dried up every lake, river, and underground water supply they had. The Anasazi had no choice: They had to leave or die.

In addition, the Anasazi were being threatened by the Spanish conquistadors, who were trying to eliminate them. It was all too stressful for the Anasazi; they took desperate measures.

Many of them decided to return back to the Third World inside the Earth, thinking this would save them, but they had no understanding of how this would affect their future evolution or the evolution of the world.

So the Ancient Ones went into their underground prayer rooms, their kivas, where there was always a symbolic *sipapu*. A sipapu was the opening left on the surface when the Ancient Ones came out of the Earth from the Third World. The Anasazi (though not all of them), using special knowledge, went back into the Earth and back to the Third World, where they thought they would be safe.

But, as we were to learn on this journey, it was not so simple. Now that their spirits were connected to the outer surface of the Fourth World, they found that their life in the Third World rapidly became hell. Only slowly did they realize they had made a mistake to try to go backwards in evolution. They also realized that there was nothing they could do about it—not until their prophecy (their collective dream) could be fulfilled. And our group was that prophecy they had been waiting for, for hundreds of years.

This choice made by the Anasazi over 700 years ago had to be corrected before the female could take power. And as the angels said, it was not just the Anasazi that were creating distortions in the Unity Consciousness Grid; there were other ancient indigenous cultures also.

Simultaneously, our group was charged with the triple task of creating a means by which the Anasazi could return to this world, the Fourth World; changing the weather patterns in the Four Corners area; and, through the first two, performing certain ceremonies to unlock specific blocks in the Unity Consciousness Grid to prepare the female to use her new power. And all of this would be accomplished through ceremonial "magic," or call it science, if that is what you understand and prefer.

In 2002, my world, Arizona, had seen the worst drought in over 100 years, caused by global warming and the slowing down of the Atlantic Ocean current. Forest fires were burning everywhere. *Time* magazine suggested, based on evidence it had acquired, that this drought would not end for 150 years. Our group had to change this prediction, ending the drought now or at least altering it. We believed that this weather pattern was, in truth, connected to human consciousness and to the ancient people called the Anasazi.

In order to guide this group through this difficult multicultural terrain, I did as the angels requested. I began to meditate with Mother Earth everyday, asking her to guide us. I love her so much, and I can feel her love for me. She began to instruct me as to how each action should be handled.

The Ascended Masters, through Thoth, had assisted me through the first levels of my remembering, but this present journey demanded that my guidance come from cosmic levels beyond the Great White Brotherhood. The actual living spirit of the Earth, Mother Earth, and, of course, the dear angels were going to lead me now.

Thoth had been one of my primary guides for about ten years, but in the mid-nineties he and almost all of the Ascended Masters left the Earth to make the journey into the future that we will all make someday.

When he returned after the turn of the millennium, he appeared to me to let me know that he was back, but that our relationship with each other was complete. It was time now for a new form of guidance, one that is within each one of us: guidance from our own Divine Mother.

The First Medicine Wheel

I was living in Payson, Arizona, at the time, and the forest fires surrounded my town. The biggest fire in Arizona history was burning out of control only fifteen miles from my house. Mother Earth told me and my family to make a medicine wheel on our land and to pray for rain.

We did this in a sacred way, speaking to each stone, seeing it as alive, and at the end Mother Earth spoke through me to my whole family and said that it would rain in two days.

The next day, the sky was filled with moisture. The local newspaper headlines called it the "Miracle Day," because the moisture went straight into the fires. The rain turned the smoke from black to white and allowed the firefighters to get a 5 percent hold on this completely out-of-control megafire. It was the beginning of the end for this fire.

The following day, it began to rain lightly, but only in this area around Payson. Slowly, each day, it began to rain more and more until the Payson area was wet with water and the fires were extinguished. The medicine wheel was working, but unfortunately only near my home. The fires continued elsewhere in the Four Corners, and so the problem was not solved. But this medicine wheel was superimportant, as it began the healing that would be completed by our international group and the special talents they were to bring to this Native area from all over the world.

Mother Earth wanted me to go into all four states of the Four Corners—Arizona, New Mexico, Colorado, and Utah—and perform ceremony to heal this relationship between the Ancient Ones and the Modern Ones, all humans alive today. In so doing, the outer and inner worlds could come into balance, and simultaneously a block on a portion of the Unity Consciousness Grid would disappear.

The Anasazi

The Anasazi existed from the time of Christ to about A.D. 1300, when the Atlantic Current began to slow down (historically, the Little Ice Age began in 1300 and continued until 1850), and their area of influence mostly centered in the Four Corners. They created buildings, and incredible science is embedded in the location and placement of their sacred sites, as well as their use of sacred geometric patterns. Their recently discovered story has been told in a documentary film, narrated by Robert Redford, called *The Mystery of Chaco Canyon*, which describes how the Anasazi were functioning scientifically on a level similar to the ancient Egyptians.

The Anasazi were not barbaric human beings, they were civilized people who understood a reality that would look like science fiction to us. The other worlds, the other dimensions, were reality for them, and they knew how to move within them (at least to a limited degree).

To be clear, the Third World is an overtone of the third dimension of the Earth, in which they were trapped. The Anasazi tried going into the fourth dimension, but they were not ready and couldn't make it. So they found an overtone world not of this world and felt safer there.

Perhaps it is time to explain, at least in a simple manner, the ways the different dimensions and overtones are related. (There is an expanded explanation in my first two books, *The Ancient Secret of the Flower of Life: Volume I* and *Volume II*, if you wish more clarity.) This description of dimensions corresponds to the ancient view, but not to the modern view, which sees the first three dimensions as the x-y-z axis of space and the fourth dimension as time. Then the modern view continues up the dimensions mathematically as defined by modern science. It is not that the scientific way is wrong, it's just based on different concepts.

What I am explaining is entirely different. In this explanation the universe is seen as purely sound or vibration. The relationship between the dimensions is also purely vibrational and corresponds perfectly to the laws of music and harmonics. The dimensions are separated from each other in exactly the same proportions that notes on the chromatic scale of music are separated from each other. Instead of cycles per second as in music, for dimensions they are separated by wavelength, but the proportions are the same.

There are 12 major and 12 minor overtone dimensions, for a total of 144 dimensions in each octave of dimensions. There appears to be almost infinite octaves of dimensions that keep repeating themselves over and over, except that the experience of them changes as one moves up the dimensions. All dimensions interpenetrate each other, so in the space where you are at this moment, all dimensions are passing through your body.

The universe that we see with the stars and planets is defined as the third (major) dimension within the twelve major dimensions. So the Earth is within the third dimension, but within and around the Earth and the entire universe are twelve overtones of the third dimension. Although you cannot see these third-dimension overtones, they are worlds that have been known and experienced by shamans, medicine men and women, and the Ascended Masters for thousands of years.

If a person were to enter into an overtone of the Earth's third dimension, or any other dimension, he or she would disappear from view here on Earth and reappear in another world. This is not easy to do without great knowledge.

The ancient Anasazi, out of desperation, did move from the third dimension of the Earth into an overtone of the Earth. The problem was that because they were moving backwards in consciousness in making this movement, it was akin to suicide, and they became trapped, unable to move out of this lower overtone world.

Let me tell you something of their nature; maybe you will feel the compassion I have for them. Their life span from birth to death was usually only about eighteen or nineteen years. If an Anasazi lived to be twenty-five, he or she was a very old person. A female would usually have her first child at least by twelve or thirteen, only to die within five or six years. This meant that children had to be on their own and able to survive very early in life.

So, even though they had an astounding understanding of the Reality, they lacked the wisdom that age brings. This is what I feel after having experienced the Anasazi on these other levels in my meditations many years ago.

The Sacred Journey Begins

I'm writing this in late 2006, and as I remember this 2003 journey, my heart is alive with energy. What happened on this journey changed my life.

On the morning of the day I left for Sedona to meet the group, I sat in front of our "family" medicine wheel, praying to Mother Earth that she guide and protect us as we entered the Anasazi worlds. The angels said these prayers were my way and my guidance until they changed the path. Thoth had been a brother and a great advisor, but now a new type of challenge faced our group. In my heart I said to her, "Dear Spirit of the Earth, I will listen to you, and do my best to follow your advice."

I left the wheel and headed north to Sedona for the first meeting with the international group. After this initial connection together, we began to follow the Native American path that we would follow during the rest of the journey. On that path, it is agreed that before a ceremony or a sacred journey, the group purifies themselves with a traditional sweat lodge.

The sweat lodge is a small structure that will hold between ten to thirty people. It is usually built of red willow branches woven in a specific pattern and tied together to build a frame. Then different types of materials, such as animal hides in olden times and blankets in modern times, were tossed over the frame until the inside is completely dark. In most cases, the tiny door with a flap is placed toward the east.

An enormous fire is built in front of the doorway, and special "lava" rocks are placed in the fire to heat up until they are orange-red. The rocks are carried into the kiva with a shovel or pitch fork, one at a time, until usually seven are placed in the ground in the middle of the sweat lodge. When these rocks cool, another group of hot rocks are carried in to begin another round of prayer. Sometimes the sweating can be almost more than people can handle, but it serves its purpose; it allows the unclean part of us to leave. It prepares us for the integrity that must be honored at all times in order to fulfill prophecy.

Our group went into the sweat lodge with the understanding that they were entering into Mother Earth's womb, and there they would sing and pray to Mother Earth, Father Sky, and Great Spirit, asking to be purified and prepared for the sacred journey ahead of us.

After the sweat, we walked to a friend's house, where we simply got to know each other with a beautiful meal and fine local musicians vibrating songs from the heart and the didgeridoo. We quickly began to merge our energies. The following morning, we slipped into our ultramodern land ship called a tourist bus and headed for ancient land to seek an invisible people.

The Navajo

Navajo was a name given to them by the white man. To each other, they are the *Diné*, pronounced "dee-nay." In their language, *Diné* means the Children of God, but the name *Navajo* is Spanish and means "stealer." Obviously, they don't like the name Navajo. We visited them first to get their permission to perform ceremony in their land, for they were the guardians, along with the Hopi, of the doorways into where the Anasazi existed. It all began here.

My mentor from the Hopi, Grandfather David, once lit up my heart with his great power of vision. Grandfather David was the elder who held the Hopi Prophesies for the tribe before he left this world. I had his permission, but I needed the Navajo to open their hearts to us and also give us permission to perform ceremony on their land, which extended from Arizona into Utah, Colorado, and New Mexico—everywhere we needed to go.

I had never seen the Navajo be open to the white man, as he had shown them only deceit and lies from the beginning of their relationship. The Navajo saw the white man as having a "forked tongue" like a snake, always saying one thing, but doing another, and their disgust had been passed down through the ages. In my lifetime I had never seen the Navajo be trusting or even friendly with the white man, but knowing that life is a dream helps the impossible become reality. I have seen this distrust in the eyes of the Navajo many times, but what I found when we arrived in Canyon de Chelly was just the opposite. The Navajo people there took us close to their hearts and led us to parts of their sacred land that normally are not shown to the outside world.

Our Navajo guides took us down into the canyons of their homeland and pointed out the pictographs made by the Anasazi, the Ancient Ones, who were there before the Navajo. But in our case, and with great caring, they also showed us sites and told us stories about their sacred land that others of their white visitors had never heard.

Most of our group didn't know the history. They thought it was normal for the Navajo to be so friendly, but many of us understood that this simply was not the case. Our guide said that he had brought many groups to the canyon, but that ours was different. He kept revealing to us knowledge about his tribe and the Anasazi that normally was saved for family discussions.

On the second day at Canyon de Chelly, on a rocky cliff overlooking the secret heart of the Canyon, our Navajo guides joined us for our ceremony. Together, we went into the "space of the heart" and prayed for the healing of the land. It was a truly moving and extraordinary experience.

But it had been the night before, the night of our first day at Canyon de Chelly, when many of our group experienced the first opening of the Diné heart. I left in the middle of this experience because I needed to meditate and prepare for what was to come. So I will give you the story from the memory of someone who was there.

One of our group, John Dumas, decided to sit in with a Navajo flute player who, with two helpers on drums, was entertaining guests at the Navajo restaurant where we ate dinner. John plays flute and didgeridoo, and the music he so skillfully and feelingly created became a true blending of our group with the Navajos—an incredible jam session that went on until late in the night.

Although those of us who were there were very tired from hiking all day, we could not bring ourselves to leave. It was a beautiful experience. The music itself was extraordinary. And the heart communication, not just between the musicians, but [also] between the Navajos and the people in our group, was one of the most amazing experiences of what friendship and caring means that any of us had ever had. For the first time, at least in that small room, the Navajo and the white man were One. John played with shining eyes, and the joy that streamed from him was something to behold, mirrored in the faces of our Navajo friends.

At the end, just as we were preparing to leave, a very, very old man walked out to the microphone. He was, he said, a Navajo code talker from World War II, and he had been among the group that planted the flag on Iwo Jima. There had been three other Navajos with him at Iwo. They were all dead now, all but him. Softly, matter-of-factly, he gave us their names, and told us how they had died.

He said that he had written a sacred song for that day, for Iwo Jima, and the battle they had fought there. And then, in the hushed room, without accompaniment, he honored us in the ancient way by singing us his song.

When he left the room, he stopped to hug each one of us.

This story only makes inner sense when you realize how unusual it is for the Navajo to befriend what they call the white man. But they knew that our purpose was their purpose, to heal the inner Earth and the Anasazi.

The Second Medicine Wheel

From Canyon de Chelly, we traveled on to Chaco Canyon—the master center of the Anasazi—in New Mexico. We were hoping to do a medicine wheel at Chaco, but once we got there we found that the government had sealed off all possibility for such a ceremony to be performed in that place. We talked to local officials, but they made it clear that we couldn't even bring drums into the area.

Instead, we all went to the major ancient ruin there and were drawn to one of the abandoned kivas where the energy felt powerful. It was open to the air, since the departing Chacoans had torn down much of their civilization, and the roofs of the kivas no longer existed. There was no way to go inside. Instead, we circled the kiva and began ceremony with only our bodies and our spirits.

Here we asked for permission to make contact, but what ensued was silence.

Afterwards, we decided to move around this enormous site and connect as individuals to the land and to the Ancient Ones. It was the only pathway left to us.

At first I climbed with a few of the group members up the side of a cliff until I reached the top where I could see out over the entire canyon. I played my flute for a while, tuning my heart to the land, and then my inner voice told me to continue by myself up to a ledge that was hidden from the group (and from the government officials).

Chaco Canyon was in a drought—dry, with no rain at all or even any moisture. Life was hanging on by its fingertips. Mother Earth asked me to create a small medicine wheel in this hidden spot and to connect the wheel energetically with the one on my land in Arizona, hundreds of miles away.

I found some little rocks made of iron, and on a large flat rock I used these iron stones to make the wheel. I prayed to Mother Earth in the same way as if this were a normal-sized medicine wheel and asked her to connect it to the wheel near my home, as I had been told to do.

After about an hour and a half, it felt complete. I returned to the group and became a tourist again.

Now, you need to understand at this point that back home in Arizona it had been raining for almost two weeks, and everything was turning green and beautiful. The fires were history. But when the Chaco medicine wheel connected to the one in Arizona, the energy created by the Arizona wheel was sucked out of Arizona and into Chaco Canyon. By the following day, my family reported that the Arizona weather near my home had returned to the same dry condition that had existed before we made our small family wheel.

Actually, I felt this shift the moment it happened as I completed the small medicine wheel in Chaco Canyon. It was as though life force had been taken away from me. It felt personal.

I explained these events to the others and said that we needed to keep moving to find the right place to create our group medicine wheel. I knew it had to happen very soon to bring balance to the region.

The Kiva Ceremony

During the next day of our journey, seeking a location for the medicine wheel ceremony, we visited two of the ancient Anasazi ruins from the Chacoan culture. They are enclosed and managed very tenderly by official caretakers.

In the Salmon Ruins, we were able to walk through the insides of the sacred structures and houses actually inhabited by the Ancient Ones. We knew that the Anasazi were of small stature compared to us, but the size of their doorways really brought this home.

At the Aztec Ruins, which are actually Anasazi, for the first and only time on our journey, we found ourselves inside a roofed-over underground kiva. We could feel the energy and the mystery of it. Our group sat around the edge of the circular, cavelike chamber on benches that had been provided for visitors, and I talked a bit about the creation story of the Anasazi—how they had emerged from the Third World, and how the kiva stood for that world, with the symbolic "sipapu" at the top, where the Ancient Ones had climbed through onto the surface of the Earth. Then we all entered the sacred place of the heart, as we did so many times together on this journey, and performed a ceremony of healing there.

I don't remember what I said, but I remember the energy. I remember that a family of visitors came upon us and stood reverently, joining us in our ceremony. And I could feel the Ancient Ones all around us, connecting with us. The way was being prepared as we meditated together in that dark chamber inside the Earth.

A side note: While we were praying in this kiva, we asked the Anasazi to be present with our group. After the ceremony was complete, many people in our group took pictures. These pictures revealed the Anasazi spirits that were present. There were, in total, more than twenty cameras that the same spheres of light appeared on the photographs, but now we only have the photos from three of them. These spheres of light were not the result of the way light refracted in the camera lens; they appeared on the photographs from each camera. The Anasazi were really with us, as became evident as our journey continued.

Ceremony in Anasazi Kiva. John Dumas playing the didgeridoo during ceremony. Photo by: Nicole Andraud

Sphere's Anasazi 1

Sphere's Anasazi 2

Lionfire and Destiny

The next day, we slipped into our home on wheels and headed north for Colorado, the third state of the Four Corners and the northernmost region of the Anasazi's empire.

As we approached the wide-open spaces of Hovenweep National Monument, we all could feel the awesome power of this remote area. We stopped at the primary Anasazi Hovenweep ruins and were met by a ranger with the U.S. National Park service for the entire Hovenweep ruins. His name was Lionfire.

When Lionfire saw who we were spiritually and discovered what it was we were attempting to do, which was make a medicine wheel for the healing of the Anasazi, he knew that the government would not allow us to do this on national park land. His heart opened and he offered to take us to his own land, which was within the Hovenweep National Monument area and was also covered with Anasazi ruins. He called his land simply Hovenweep.

From his property, which was a very special vantage point, sacred mountain peaks and land formations of the Anasazi and the modern Native Americans could be clearly seen in all directions. Hundreds of thousands of Anasazi had once lived in the area surrounding his land, and hundreds directly on his land, evident by all the ancient ruins that could not be avoided in all directions. The presence of the Anasazi was so strong in this place, and we all felt it and commented on how it was affecting us by pulling on our heart strings.

The smell of sage filled the air. Secret side canyons were the home of the eagle spirits. Ancient pieces of pottery lay on the ground, as if thrown there to lead us to our destiny.

Lionfire not only was a U.S. National Park Service employee who guarded the northernmost Anasazi ruins, but he was a shaman who had studied the Ancient Ones for most of his life and knew much about how they lived their lives.

Hovenweep itself is on the same longitude as Chaco Canyon, directly on the "sacred line"—the Great North Road that leads due north from Chaco. Today, nobody knows where this road was intended to go or why it was so important. But Hovenweep lay on its route and was once a place of great power.

Arriving there, I knew that we were in the right spot. Everyone in our group felt this. We were "at home" in Hovenweep and sensed immediately that this, finally, was where we would build our medicine wheel to heal the Anasazi.

We began our visit by going through a complex of ancient dwellings. We were able in some cases to go inside and to notice once more how small in stature the Ancient Ones must have been.

We received permission to build our medicine wheel, not only from Lionfire and his wife Mary but also from Mother Earth. She told us to "let go" and treat this land as if it were our own. The wheel, once built, would be protected by Lionfire and Mary, faithful keepers of the land. And as Lionfire and Mary told us, they had received a prophecy many years before telling them that we would come and perform this ceremony.

Before we arrived, not even knowing why we were coming to Hovenweep (remember that we had originally intended to build the medicine wheel at Chaco Canyon), Mary had written a poem in honor of our journey. She says that it came to her all in one piece, and she simply wrote it down. As we gathered together in a giant kiva—unroofed, but so deep that we had to climb down into it by ladder—she read us this poem.

The Weaving
We stand here, surrounded by the sacred mountains, at
    the sipapu, where our world began. We come from the
    four corners of this earth, walking in love, bringing our
    knowledge of many cultures, many languages. Seeking
    understanding, growth and change, for ourselves, our
    nations, our world.
This is our intention! Here at this time we create a new world,
    we weave a new reality!
We pray for assistance and request witness, from the sacred
    energies of our world!

* AIR - Winds of the 4 directions, winds that move the stars
* WATER - Rain, rivers, springs
* FIRE - Our sun, lightning that dances on the sky
* EARTH - Our mother, her sand, her cliffs, her mountains
* OUR BROTHERS - The four legs, the winged ones, water
    children and those that creep and crawl
* OUR SISTERS - The standing people, from mighty tree to
    smallest flower
* OUR OWN HUMAN RACE - From our ancestors who
    first walked this land, to our children's children, seven
    generations distant, most of all we call upon
* OUR SELVES, here and now, to witness and strive.
We are here to create a weaving of a new reality.
In any weaving, beauty is created by the warp, weft, and the
    pattern.
We bring: For the foundation, the warp thread,
Human energy, the experiences of diverse cultures.
Strength and pride from our societies, our families,
History, our struggle to manifest our own path.
These we braid together and string on our loom to form the
    warp, the shape of our weaving.
Onto this we weave the weft of our daily journey, the thread
    of beauty, spun, one moment at a time, with each step of
    integrity, as our actions spin time into history.
And the Pattern?
The pattern that will call the rest of the human race into under-
    standing, changing?
This pattern is formed by our teachers and by our intention.
We set our intention to manifest a world where every spirit,
    human, animal, plant and mineral, walks in harmony and
    balance, health and joy.
We ask our teachers to guide us to actions that flow into this
    intention.
We seek to manifest that divinity within our selves that will cre-
    ate this new reality.

This is our time.

We are called.

Together we will weave a new world!

Mary's poem astonished us. It spoke of what we had all been thinking and talking of, and yet we had only met her the day before. More amazing was its mention of "the four corners of the earth," and "many cultures, many languages." Mary had had no way of knowing that fewer than half of the people with us were Americans. Our group members came from many, many nations. Two did not even speak English, but listened to us with their hearts.

After our kiva ceremony at Hovenweep, it was time to find the exact spot to place our medicine wheel.

The Third Medicine Wheel

Hovenweep is vast. I moved back and forth over the land, searching and "feeling" for the right place for this most important ceremony to be located. Finally, as I walked over a certain area, all the mountains and the ancient nearby Anasazi canyon seemed to come into alignment. Just off to the south, only a few feet away, was an Anasazi ruin that commanded primal importance long ago because it was on the highest point.

I knew in my heart that this was the right place.

As I looked around, a large rock "spoke to me" to be the central stone, and I placed it on the ground in what would become the very center of the medicine wheel. Four more living stones were found to mark the four directions. With this basic setup, the wheel ended up being about thirty-five feet in diameter, and it was ready for the group to complete it.

All the people were still in the air-conditioned bus, out of the heat, waiting for me to finish my job. By now I was almost a half mile away, so a runner was sent to bring in the group.

They all piled out of the bus, eager to begin something we all knew would help to heal not only the Ancient Ones and the Modern Ones, but also each person's family tree going back thousands of years. For the spiritual health of all of our ancestors, and to heal the land of the Four Corners, we began as children of the Earth and as one family of man.

First, each person went out in a different direction to "speak" with the spirits of the stones that were spread over the land, asking permission to use them for our wheel. One by one, people came back, holding the living stones close to their hearts, collecting them in readiness for the moment when we would begin creating the wheel. For some, it took several trips.

Two males and two females were chosen to represent each of the four directions. They took up their places behind each of the directional stones.

I began the prayers by once more asking permission, then setting the purpose and intention of the medicine wheel. After that, the chosen guardians of the four directions gave their own prayers, to protect their direction and the space within the wheel, that it would be holy and sacred.

Now, to the accompaniment of drumming and chanting, people carried their stones one by one into the sacred space, entering through the "doorway" in the east, dedicating each stone to the guardians of the four directions and then placing it in the wheel. First was created a circle of stones, each stone touching the one beside it. Then a cross of stones in the center marked the four directions. (Remember that cross.)

Since this wheel was about thirty-five feet in diameter, it took over two hours to make. The energy kept building until we could "see" the Anasazi dancing with us, leading us on to completion. Each member of our group would place one stone, then join the others who were dancing, praying, chanting, or drumming outside the circle, and waiting to place another stone.

And so, in a heart rhythm, the Medicine Wheel of the New Dream was constructed.

We all sat down, and after a moment of silence, the individual prayers began. Each person, holding the "talking stick," spoke

Medicine wheel

beautiful and sacred prayers into the wheel–prayers for the healing of this land and its life-forms; for the rain to reappear and the rivers to flow; for health, love, and beauty to flourish; for the relationships of mankind to blossom forth in harmony; for the rift between the white man and the Indian to heal.

The hearts of the people were open, and the energy and power of the space kept building until at last each person had spoken. A sense of immense energy and purity surrounded our ceremony.

At the final moment, I led a special ritual based on the Taos Pueblo ceremonies. This ritual breathed even more life into the circle by establishing a pyramid over many miles of the land, high into the sky and deep into the Earth, connecting the Earth and the heavens with the medicine wheel at the center. The pyramid's purpose was to bring rain and spiritual balance to all beings existing in the Four Corners.

At the end of the medicine wheel ceremony, Mother Earth told me that it would rain in five days, and I announced this to the group, which was my training from the Taos Pueblo. Since we were in the middle of an historic drought, this message presented a spark of hope to those who lived close to this land.

It was our intent that this rain would begin the restoration of the Southwest, bringing water to the land and love and healing to the relations between the white man and the Native Americans.

We could all feel the love and peace. We could feel the Anasazi all around us. It was very good.

Meeting With the Stars

As it became dark and the stars began to peek out of the heavens, we all gathered at the main Anasazi ruins, at the highest point on the land. There, Daniel Giamario, a shamanic astrologer who was traveling with us and teaching his wisdom, invited us once more, as he had on other occasions, to look up with him into the night sky.

Daniel's knowledge and perception of the ancient ways is truly outstanding. Throughout the journey, Daniel was a star who gave of himself to help others. On this momentous night, he led us into an understanding of the heavens in a way that few of us had ever known. Together, we gazed into Galactic Center, as he had taught us, and spoke our own individual prayers into the cosmos. Father Sky heard our prayers.

Then, slowly, we all found our way in the dark back to the bus, guided only by the light of the stars, just as the Anasazi had walked this land so many hundreds of years before. Hugging each other, we tried to immortalize the feeling that we had in our hearts.

I could feel the three medicine wheels—the one in Payson, the small one at Chaco Canyon, and this one we had created today—linking. I knew that the rains would come.

And, even more important, the Anasazi would now have a vortex to allow them to reenter this world, so that they could come with us as the Earth enters the higher levels of consciousness, what many have called ascension. In so doing, the Unity Grid above the Earth comes closer into perfect balance.

Ancient Cliff Dwellings

The next day, we wanted to visit the Anasazi cliff dwellings in Mesa Verde, near Hovenweep. Mesa Verde was one of the Anasazi's most beautiful living places, a high plateau surrounded by rugged mountains. But, because of the incredible drought, a forest fire was burning out of control, and Mesa Verde National Park was closed to visitors. So the Ute Indians, guardians of Mesa Verde, allowed us to privately visit a portion of the reservation that belongs only to them and not to the National Forest Service. It was a site that very few white people have ever seen or even heard about.

To get there, our huge bus, with its airplane-type seats and air conditioning, had to negotiate a lot of tiny little dirt roads that wound through cedar forests. Our bus driver was quietly freaking out, fearing that we would never make it out of this primitive place. But all was well.

The Ute treated us with great honor, for they knew also the purpose we were living. While we ate lunch, our guide told us stories of Ute tribal history. Then he led us to the edge of a deep canyon. It appeared impossible for a human being to climb down into it without ropes, but he showed us three handmade wooden ladders that dropped down over the plunging cliffs.

More than one person in our group was forced to deal with a lifelong fear of heights in order to make that trek down the precipitous ladders to the ledges below, where the cliff dwellings were. One woman could descend only with the help of protectors above, below, and on each side of her, but she made it down and back up again. The fears were faced. People took care of each other. Our group had truly become One Heart.

Once we were inside this magical place, it felt so alive, so filled with the Anasazi spirits. I felt so honored to be allowed to be there that I could hardly speak. The voices of the past were all around me, telling me about their lives and the greatness of who they were. I could actually enter their homes, touch the stones that they touched, feel with my fingers the pottery they had made so many hundreds of years ago.

That night, after Mesa Verde, I had a dream.

The Lost Children

This dream was one of a clarity that always alerts me to a dream being special. I usually remember these dreams, as they are important to my spiritual growth.

In this dream, I was living with my family in an area near Mesa Verde, in a home I had never seen before. I was going into my garage to get my car—in this dream, the garage was a huge place—when I saw that some Indians were living there. I went up to them to ask if everything was okay, but they ran away. Nothing like this had ever happened before. I remember thinking, "How odd that they would want to live in my garage."

Then, as I headed for my car, I saw three young Indian children running into the back of my garage to hide from me. I went over to see where they were hiding and to speak with them, and I saw that they had gone into a round hole three feet in diameter. I knew I had never seen this hole before.

I looked in the hole and saw that it went down deep into the Earth, so I dropped inside to find out what was there.

The underground space opened into a very large tunnel about twelve feet high and wide that slowly sloped into the depths. I could see no one, so I simply went forward to explore this place.

I'm sure I hadn't gone more than a quarter of a mile when I realized that people—lots of them—were blocking my way a few feet ahead. Mostly, I could see only their eyes.

At first I couldn't tell who they were, but as my eyes adjusted, I saw that they were all children, from about ten years old to about eighteen or nineteen. No one said a word. They just looked at me. And they would not let me through.

Then three men who appeared to be in their late thirties gently pushed their way to the front, walked up to me, and looked into my eyes. These men were covered with scrapes, bruises, and infested sores. They were dirty and appeared to really need help.

The oldest one, he might even have been forty or so, began to speak. He said he was the chief of the Anasazi, as we called them, and he wanted to know why I was there. I told him I wished only to help.

He turned to the children and motioned for me to look at them. I could see that they were in the same shape as the men. It was heart-rending to see so many children covered in sores and in such pain. All I could think of was how to help them.

The leader saw my reaction. "Thank you for being here," he said. "But you must go now." So I turned and went back out the opening into my garage. There were more children around my home now, but I let them be there. I didn't know what to do. The dream ended there.

During the medicine wheel ceremony, I had deeply felt the Anasazi presence the whole time, and so had many of our group. But at the time, I didn't put two and two together— I didn't connect this dream with the Anasazi's felt presence on our journey.

A Miraculous Ritual

The next morning there were the usual clear skies as we approached the Navajo national monument known as Monument Valley.

We were moving along a smooth, flat road, about to enter this sacred Navaho valley with the red rock mountains stretching to the sky, when a vision began within me. Ahead of us, I could see a throng of Anasazi facing us on both sides of the road. There could have been hundreds of thousands of them.

One man appeared to move closer to our approaching bus until he was centered in my vision, only a few feet away. It was the Anasazi leader from my dream, only now he was regal and stately, dressed up in feathers and beautiful clothing of many colors. He began to speak.

He said the medicine wheel ceremony we had performed was prophesied by his elders and would offer them a connection to this outer world. He said that through this wheel and our loving intent, his people could be saved from the terrible trouble and pain they were in. He thanked us dearly, many times, for our effort.

But, he told me, as a group we were not aligned properly in our energies. He "showed" me to myself wearing a t-shirt with the image of an X in the middle of a circle. What was needed, he said, was to revolve the X of our energy so that it would appear as a cross. He said that to do this, we all needed to come very close together.

He said he and the others were caught "between the worlds," and that we had come there to release them. For each one of us on that bus, it was a mission that had been given to us for this lifetime. And all of the work and hardship we had endured, both in our own lives and now, trekking through the hot sun of a southwestern August, had been needed just for this task we were there to perform.

Using the microphone at the front of the bus, I told our group about my dream and my vision. One other member of the group had received a vision that matched mine. In describing these events to our group, I could barely speak, because I kept feeling such grief at the suffering I'd witnessed in those Anasazi children—their bruised and emaciated bodies covered with weeping sores.

At this emotional moment, as I sat down again, everyone on the bus spontaneously joined hands and went into a profound heart connection. And, again spontaneously, with tears flowing, we all began singing with one voice the hymn, "Amazing Grace." We could "see" the children all around us and feel them rejoicing.

"I once was lost, but now am found."

At the very moment we began to sing, the driver changed roads, from Route 666 to Highway 160, headed for the meeting place of Utah, Colorado, New Mexico, and Arizona, the point at which the Four Corners come together.

The visionary Anasazi leader reappeared to me and said, "Look." The image of the circle and the X he'd shown me before turned into the image of our medicine wheel, with the four center stones in the shape of a cross.

"You must do ceremony now," he said. "You must be standing on Mother Earth."

We needed to find the very next possible place were we could pull over and do ceremony out on the land, and that "next possible place" just happened to be the junction of the Four Corners. Diane Cooper, our "lady of all needs," directed our bus to this monument, which is managed by the Navajo.

From past experiences, we had concerns about being allowed to perform our ceremony in public places. I looked into the eyes of the Native American lady who was selling the tickets and asked her for permission. Without hesitation, she said, "You can pray here, you can do your ceremony here. We will let you." She pointed to a particular area. "Pick somewhere out there."

As a group of One, we went into the area the woman had pointed to and found out that we were now in Utah—the only state we had not yet visited. This was perfect, because Mother Earth had said that we must do ceremony in each state of the Four Corners.

We gathered in a tight circle and built a tiny medicine wheel in its center, using many little stones, the fourth wheel. We tried to use a compass to site the stones, but none of our compasses would work there! Each time we put one onto the earth, it showed north in a different direction. So we found our direction from nearby tourist information signs.

We burned sage and cedar and offered tobacco. We poured water and breathed life into the circle.

All of our hearts opened at once, and the beauty and power was overwhelming. You could feel the love and purity in the air. I began to cry, for I knew that our Mother was loving and caring for us. It was really good.

Once more, the song "Amazing Grace" lifted around us. One of our group knew all the words, and her clear, sweet voice carried us through to the end: "God, who called me here below, shall be forever mine."

And so it was that the Anasazi children were released from their imprisonment of hundreds of years.

CHAPTER TWELVE

THE LIGHTNING CEREMONY

Antelope Canyon

Yet we were not finished, and I wasn't certain why. It had seemed complete. I asked Mother Earth what was left to do, and she simply said, "Drunvalo, what is left is a gift for you. A gift in understanding." But I didn't understand.

So we were on the road again. Ahead of us lay the long, mesmerizing ride to Page, Arizona, to the upper reaches of the Grand Canyon. Here we would create our final ceremony. But first, we would spend the afternoon and early evening at a unique natural cathedral known as Antelope Canyon, where we would meet with Dalvin, a Navajo shaman whose fierce protectiveness of his people would provide us with our last test of faith and love.

Antelope Canyon is so sacred to the Navajo that visitors are allowed in only when accompanied by Native guides. These guides—Dalvin and his two aunts, Carol and Lisa—met our bus, and we all piled into their pickup trucks for a fifteen-mile drive into what seemed like pure desert.

Next, on foot, through an almost hidden entrance, we trooped from the heat of an Arizona August afternoon into the quiet coolness of a cavelike canyon. The light-colored, sandy floor was smooth under our feet. Multihued light from occasional openings high above filtered down into the swirling vortex of energy that could be felt surrounding us.

Antelope Canyon is a long, winding, narrow passageway—no more than twenty feet at its widest part—leading from one bit of desert to another, with red-rock walls on either side that look as though they've been molded by some divine sculptor. The space flows and swirls like the water that formed it. It is a place like no other that I have ever seen.

Dalvin led us silently through the canyon, and when we emerged on the other side, he sat down on a rocky outcropping and began to tell us stories about his culture.

He spoke very slowly, in a measured cadence, so quietly that we had to gather very close in order to hear him. He told of a near-fatal accident that he had had when he was young, and how this accident had marked the beginning of his path as a shaman. In a coma for

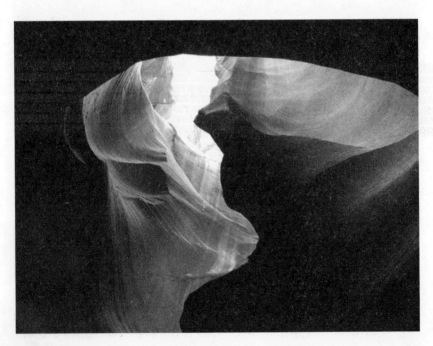

Antelope Canyon

SERPENT OF LIGHT

a long time, he had "traveled to the back of beyond," and when he returned, he was changed.

He told us about his Way with peyote, saying that this canyon was a living peyote church. And as he spoke, he looked deep into our eyes, as though searching for who we really were.

After talking to us for a while, Dalvin led us back inside the canyon. I realized that he was not sure of us, not certain how he felt about our doing ceremony in this sacred place, and not totally convinced that we had had the right to make our medicine wheel in Colorado, which one of the group told him about. Many members of our group sensed his questioning.

Coming finally to a kind of circular spot deep inside the canyon, we gathered around Dalvin again. He played his guitar and sang, then said that he wanted to sing a peyote song for us, but that he didn't have his rattle. Then Vina, a part-Indian member of our group, gave him a medicine rattle that she had brought. He shook it a few times, looking at it carefully, listening, seeming to consider. Then, using this rattle, he sang two peyote songs, the medicine songs of his path. Afterward, Vina said, he returned the rattle to her and said that it was a good rattle. "It helped me sing good," he told her.

After hearing Dalvin's songs, we returned his gift with what had become our song "Amazing Grace." He nodded.

One of Dalvin's aunts asked us if we would do ceremony. We agreed, and we went into the Space of the Heart together, praying for rain to come to the Four Corners to change the weather in this sacred Navajo land, and for the Native American and the white man to become as One.

The canyon lit up with a soft glow, and it was easy to feel the hearts of everyone melting into oneness—everyone but one man.

Susan Barber, one of our members, sat with Dalvin's two aunts and spoke with the elder of them, a beautiful woman whose name was Carol. She asked about Carol's experience of our ceremony.

"Many, many groups come here and do rituals that never seem real or true to me," Carol said. "This is the first time I have ever felt the same way in ceremony with white people as when we do our own ceremonies." Smiling then, her face radiant, "I 'saw' the rains coming," she said.

Then Dalvin spoke, and what he said gave goosebumps to those who were near enough to hear him. For he said that the medicine wheel (with his index finger he drew an imaginary circle on his t-shirt) has a cross in it (he drew the cross, north-south and east-west). And the problem was that some people were doing ceremony "almost right." But instead of having energy in the form of a cross, he said, they had it in the form of an X. He indicated the imaginary X inside the imaginary medicine wheel on his shirt and said, "The X leads to the dark side."

This was the exact same image—right down to the t-shirt—that I had been given in my vision on the bus before we sang the Anasazi children on their way to freedom! And, as I explained before, I was later shown that our misalignment had been healed. Now, here was this teaching in "real life," confirming my visions.

So Dalvin still was not convinced.

A Blind Man Can See

Back outside, as we were getting ready to be driven back to our bus, Dalvin pointed up at a snake shape on the wall of Antelope Canyon's entrance and began to tell us about it. He illustrated each detail of what he was saying by pointing up at the snake shape, moving his finger along the forty-foot formation. As he was doing this, his aunt Carol turned to me and quietly said, "Its amazing, isn't it?" I asked her what she meant. "You know, he's totally blind."

That was how I learned that Dalvin—who had driven some of us there in one of their trucks (and would drive us back in the dark!), who had led us unerringly through Antelope Canyon, looked deep into our eyes as he spoke, and was now pointing out features of the snake that guarded his peyote church—had lost the sight in both eyes as a result of that long-ago accident he'd told us about.

According to Carol, visitors to the canyon were never told about Dalvin's blindness. In fact, not even his own children knew.

Once again, we had been given a gift of secret knowledge normally withheld from the modern technological minds of most of the visitors to reservation lands. But little did I know that Dalvin was prepared to go much deeper to test our group.

Rafting on the Colorado River

That evening we arrived at Lake Powell, in Page, Arizona, a resort village at the very northern tip of the Grand Canyon formation. Here, Diane had a gift for us: a rafting trip up the Colorado River through Glen Canyon—a fifteen-mile ride through one of the most gorgeous places on Earth.

Out on the river, red-stone walls as high as 1,800 feet rose above us on both sides. We were literally in a deep crack in the Earth. We saw great blue herons skimming the water, and we listened to the stories told by our river guides of the people who had lived there before the white man came.

At one spot, we debarked from our rafts to walk on the shoreline, where we saw petroglyphs left by the Indians who had inhabited those canyons centuries ago. We speculated on what the images might mean. One seemed to be saying, "It's okay to hunt here." Or perhaps, "Go this way to find some good ducks."

The next morning, we left for our final destination, Grand Canyon National Park. I knew that here, near the rim of one of the seven wonders of the natural world, was where we would hold our final ceremony.

The Giveaway Ceremony

We chose the Giveaway Ceremony because it was used by the Ancient Ones long ago and even by Native Americans in our own time. It consists of identifying an object that we are attached to and want very much to keep—and giving it away as a sacrifice. In doing so, the Native world believes that we heal both ourselves and our relationships.

It sounds simple. But because we place so much value on our possessions, and because our emotional body is also often connected to these possessions, profound healings often occur.

Three of us—myself and two of the other men—searched for a long time in the Grand Canyon forest land, finally agreeing on a place among the trees, hidden from the rest of the park. We marked the spot with a special rock and drew a small medicine wheel in the red dirt. Then the two men left me and went to bring the others.

When they'd gone, two elk—a mother and her daughter—approached me to see what was going to happen. We looked at each other, and they both sat down to observe. In that moment, I knew that what was about to happen was perfect, whatever it was.

I arranged everything in preparation for the ceremony, and when finished, I sat down on the ground to meditate. As I did, Dalvin appeared to me very clearly in a vision. He said, "I want you to prove that you and this group are truly connected with Mother Earth and Great Spirit. If you do, I will join with you in my heart and help you in every way. But if you cannot, then you will be my enemy."

I told him that I also sought proof that we had truly accomplished our purpose on this sacred journey and offered to him what that proof would be. I knew that the only proof that Dalvin would accept would be one that came from Mother Nature, one that I would have no control over. So I said that when the Giveaway Ceremony begins, at the exact moment that the first person hands their gift to Grandmother, the leader of the ceremony, lightning will come out of the sky and strike the ground very close to the circle. In my vision, he accepted.

The members of our group began appearing through the trees, first one, then many, and arranged themselves around the little circle of stones. The elk became nervous as so many people arrived, and they quickly disappeared into the forest.

When we were settled, I asked for the oldest woman to come forward to be the Grandmother. She would receive the gifts, hear the words of those who gave them, and then, at the end, select a gift for each person in the circle to receive in return. Susan Barber, or Moonhawk (her medicine name), became our Grandmother.

As Grandmother settled in the circle on one side of the small medicine wheel, we all became aware of a change in the weather. It was almost sunset, and instead of the still, hot air we'd been accustomed to for nearly two weeks, it suddenly was growing cool. The wind gusted, whipping the tall pines that encircled us. Stormy-looking clouds scudded across the darkening sky. There was an eerie, otherworldly feeling.

I gave an opening prayer that all would be done in a loving way. Then Grandmother asked the first person to approach with his gift.

This was Osiris Montenegro. He came forward with tears in his eyes—for his giveaway in the ceremony was an object of huge significance to him—and knelt on both knees in front of Grandmother, holding his gift in both hands.

Just at the moment he was about to hand his gift to Grandmother, a bolt of lightning shot across the sky, an ear-splitting clap of thunder exploded around us, and the lightning struck the ground only about seventy-five feet from the circle. The people sitting in our circle jumped into the air, startled.

I was not startled. I was happy. I started laughing. I couldn't help it for I knew that we'd succeeded with our sacred journey. I remember looking at the group and realizing that before me were souls of great depth and compassion—a global community of masters. I couldn't say anything. I looked down at the ground, but the joy kept coming out of me.

After the ceremony, Vina—who had loaned her rattle to Dalvin for his peyote songs and knew nothing of what had happened in my meditation shortly before the ceremony—said that Dalvin had appeared to her after the ceremony and asked her to give her rattle to me. I knew that the gesture had come from him and that from now on Dalvin would be a friend to help us as we continued with our sacred ceremonies in other lands. The gift of Vina's rattle had been for us all. We were truly breathing with One Heart.

The Giveaway Ceremony lasted roughly three hours. Throughout this whole time, the wind kept blowing. The limbs of the trees above us whipped and clattered. Many thought a huge storm must be coming our way. This was day four after the medicine wheel in Colorado.

But at the moment the ceremony ended, this entire display of weather ceased as if by magic. The wind stopped, the clouds went away, the trees were still. And above our circle, a million, billion stars glittered in the night sky.

And Then the Rains Came

We headed home the next morning. As we entered Flagstaff, drops of rain began to pelt our bus. It was just as Mother Earth had told me after the medicine wheel ceremony. It had been exactly five days since Hovenweep.

When I picked up my own car later that day, the sky was dark with clouds. I drove into my hometown in the pouring rain.

The medicine wheels were now One Heart also, for they were our creations.

The people who met in the space of the One Heart for this journey also went their own ways, to their homes and their loved ones. Although we are now separated by distance, in our hearts we will always be One. We will always remember how our love guided us upon this pilgrimage, remember meeting the people we met, and joining our creative power into one force, performing ceremonies for the healing of the world.

I know the Anasazi are now our brothers and sisters, and that a time will come when their presence in our hearts may make a crucial contribution to our great ascension.

May Great Spirit bless us as we return to the ordinary world and bless all those our lives will touch.

CHAPTER THIRTEEN

JOURNEY TO MAYALAND

The angels began to speak again about the need to journey into the land of the Maya, for, like the Anasazi, this ancient culture had also made a huge mistake in the distant past. It was a mistake that, if not corrected, would thwart the world's ascension and hinder the female from performing her responsibility for the next 13,000 years. In a nutshell, another grid problem.

Almost a year had passed since the ceremonies in the land of the Anasazi, and I was in no hurry to begin running around the world again. One of my biggest problems is that I am lazy. So the dear angels actually had to prod me into action to begin a journey that I knew would be a lot of work. I'm such a silly guy. I travel from such a great distance to be here on Earth to do this work and then only want to hang out and play.

The Four Corners journey had been breathtaking. We had participated in the intimate involvement between the ancient Anasazi, Mother Earth, and our tiny group of brave souls who breathed as One Spirit. Now I was being asked to push still farther into the indigenous world and deeper into the darkness of the ancient past.

As I had become aware of Lionfire, the shaman of Hovenweep in Colorado, and his Herculean knowledge of the Anasazi, I had also become aware of his impressive knowledge of the Maya. And so before I even started this journey, I asked him if he would come along as an expert in Mayan history. Thankfully, he agreed.

The Timing and Purpose of Entering the Mayaland

The timing of our trip to the Yucatan coincided with an invitation by the Mayan shaman Hunbatz Men for us to participate in the equinox ceremonies at Chichen Itza on March 20, 2003.

Hunbatz, the Mayan Council of Elders, and about 250 indigenous elders from North, South, and Central America would perform ceremony for world peace, joining their spiritual powers together for a world healing. Our own group would support this endeavor by performing ceremony in an outer circle around the inner core of indigenous shamans and elders. We would also be joined by a European group led by Carolina Hehenkamp, who had been with us on the Anasazi journey.

After the ceremonies at Chichen Itza, our plan was to continue on a spiral journey to fulfill our own group's further purpose of going to Mayaland. And, very much as it was in the Anasazi journey, our purpose here would be to help the ancient Mayans, who were also trapped in the inner Earth, to be released.

Not known at that time—in fact, unknown until it actually unfolded before our eyes—was yet another enormous purpose that is still unfolding to this day.

Healing the Inner and Outer Mayan Worlds

Just as it was in the Four Corners, the Mayaland healing would mean restoring the balance of nature between the Inner and Outer Worlds of the Maya. By so doing, the Inner Worlds could begin to move with us, the Outer World, in harmony—or, better yet, we would move in harmony with them.

And this needed to happen soon. For—if you believe the present-day version—the Mayan calendar was to end in 2012, a little less than nine short years after our 2003 journey. In the tradition of the Mayans, the period we are now in will usher in a moment of history called the End of Time, which they understand to be the ending of a very long cycle and the beginning of a new one.

So our job would be to open the channels for the Mayans in the inner Earth to connect with those on the surface in preparation for the final ascension. In so doing, the Unity Consciousness Grid was to become more focused, and the energy of the Serpent of Light high in the Andes Mountains in Chile would grow brighter and stronger.

And again, just as it had been in the Four Corners last summer, the Yucatan and surrounding areas were in a terrible drought. Another part of our job, then, would be to perform the ceremonies that would bring rain—the physical symbol of the balance we were seeking.

Why would this ancient culture want a group of international people to do this kind of service for them? Had they forgotten how? Had they, for some reason, lost the spiritual power to do it themselves? I don't really know. It still seems strange that they would give such a personal task to someone of another culture. Yet it reminds me of the time I was asked by the Taos Pueblo in New Mexico to bury their dead. They believed that it was better for them if another culture performed this task.

Perhaps the Mayans need an outside force to open the energy channels. Or perhaps, as with many of us, they have simply become overwhelmed by circumstances and need help.

Whatever the reason, we had been invited by the Mayans, both the living ones and the ancients, to come to Mexico and perform these ceremonies with them and for them. We could not say no.

Coming Together in Merida

I felt the heartbeat begin as soon as we touched Mexican soil. I felt a strong sense of connection between this and the Anasazi journey. It was the same energy, as though it had already been dreamed. I felt inside that this new trip to the Mayan chakra temples would possibly be life-changing for me; I just didn't know how. Who but God, and perhaps the Ancient Ones, knew what was about to take place. I was clearly stepping into the unknown.

Upon arrival at the circular city of Merida, I was swished away to the Hotel Los Aluxes—which means "the Little People" and is pronounced "a-loosh-as"—where we found that Lionfire and Carolina had already arrived. For the next twenty-four hours, our vagabond group of sixty souls slowly came together from all over the world.

A Mayan Welcome

For our first meeting circle, Lionfire had arranged a special evening for us with his Mayan friends.

We met in a small room at the hotel, where a Mayan elder—a beautiful grandmother—stood before us and, in the Mayan language, gave us her permission to participate in ceremonies and visit places that in the past had been reserved only for the Mayan priests. We felt incredibly honored by her words. There were many tears.

Then a Mayan musical group called Wayak played their haunting music for us. Their throaty cries and native instruments seemed like sounds from an ancient past. It was unlike anything we'd ever heard before. The enchantment of that evening was the perfect beginning to a pilgrimage of ceremonies that would hopefully bring health and balance back to the Mayan people and their land, helping to prepare them for vastly important ceremonies in the future—ceremonies that the whole world will someday depend upon for its very survival.

As we sat in that circle, I noted that we would be moving in the same spiral of temples that Ken and I had moved through almost twenty years before, except there would be new ones. I felt like an old veteran and a kid at the same time. I could hardly wait.

Temples of Uxmal

Upon arriving at Uxmal, our international group was just beginning to remember to breathe as One Heart. They gathered around while I told them the story of Ken's giant pendulum and the amazing happenings of 1985. Then we all walked to the Great Pyramid, where I saw that the tree that sealed in the obsidian crystal was still there. The tree was much bigger now than it had when I last saw it in 1995, when I'd been at Chichen Itza with Hunbatz Men for that year's spring equinox ceremony. It was the only tree in that grassy space, and it was perfectly aligned with the center of the pyramid and the edge of the building next to it.

We made our way to the top of the Great Pyramid—a steep climb and a dizzying height for some of our group who had never done anything like this before. From the top, we could see the entire, immense area of Uxmal, its pyramids and temples spread out over miles in the jungle. It was easy to imagine how at one time this site had been a great center for the Mayan people.

Our ceremony here took on an unusual shape—the geometry of the vesica piscis. Picture us, a group of sixty people on top of a pyramid, attempting to arrange our bodies in the form of two overlapping circles. But we achieved this end result, with some people hanging on the edge, and our first ceremony of the journey unfolded. The two interlocked circles represented the inner indigenous ceremonies and those of our international group, functioning together as One.

By the end of this ceremony, I realized that we were beginning to connect with the Ancient Ones already. I felt them there watching us, feeling us, testing us. And in response, the hearts of the people in our group kept opening wider—just what was needed for us to be

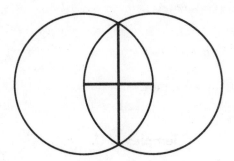

Figure 6: Drawing of vesica piscis

Ceremony in the shape of vesica pisces

accepted both by the Mayans on the surface and the Mayans in the Inner Worlds.

Our weary but elated departure from Uxmal was attended by splendor. All over the Yucatan, the Mayans were burning their fields in preparation for planting their spring crops, and the slight haze this put in the air caused the setting sun to go down in an unusually brilliant blaze of glory.

As we responded to the beauty of this place and our experiences, I knew that Great Spirit had brought the right people together for this work. It couldn't have been better if we had planned it.

Labna

After Uxmal we traveled to the temples of Labna and Kaba before we returned to Merida.

Labna is the second chakra and represents the sexual center. The land of Labna is a rusty red color, much like Sedona, Arizona, where

I live now. The entire temple complex has a soft, seductive flavor to it and an energy that somehow always gets to your heart.

We held a simple ceremony there that was designed more for purification than anything else. I walked around each person with burning sage and cedar smoke, while one of the group slowly gave a heartbeat rhythm on his drum. But while we were in this circle, something appeared that later would be an enormous problem.

One of the women from South America began to go slightly out of control as the ceremonial smoke swirled around her body. Her face began to distort, and these strange sounds emerged recklessly from her body. After a few minutes she began to flail her arms and body, sending fear into some of the people. The people on both sides of her responded immediately and tried to comfort her, but it was obvious to me that something associated with the dark side of life was beginning to express itself.

I simply made a note to myself and watched her from that moment on. It was clear to me then that this could be a disruptive influence on our work together, but I didn't understand then what this meant or where it was coming from.

Kaba

The last temple of the day was Kaba. Kaba used to have another name long ago, and this temple is extremely interesting to me since the Maya came from Atlantis where the Jews first entered into human consciousness. (See *The Ancient Secret of the Flower of Life: Volume I*.) The original name of Kaba was Kabala, a name that every Jew would recognize as a sacred book of Judaism. It only makes sense when you know the history of the Maya.

After what happened at Labna, we let the group just explore Kaba, with no ceremony this time. The energy had to crystallize for us to understand what was coming our way. We headed home to Merida, waiting to see what would come next as the Maya gently unfolded their needs to our outer consciousness.

Merida

We all went to bed early that night, because we had to arise at 4 a.m. This was in order to be present by sunrise at the ancient site of Dzibilchaltun, where the equinoctial sun rises each year in the keyhole of a temple of a civilization that dates back to 500 B.C.—a place perhaps older than anywhere else we were to visit in the Yucatan.

After that, we would return to our hotel at Merida, pack, visit the extraordinary Caves of Balancanche, and then make our way to Chichen Itza for the equinox ceremony the following day.

Meeting With Hunbatz Men

Before I tell you about Dzibilchaltun, where we went to participate in the ancient rite of the spring equinox, I need to relate a conversation I'd had with Hunbatz Men at breakfast the day before.

As Hunbatz drank his coffee and I sipped my tea, we went over our schedules in order to synchronize our movements for the coming events. Since we were going to perform ceremony together at Chichen Itza—the Heart Center—we needed to determine exactly how we would place our energies relative to the Incan, Mayan, and hundreds of indigenous elders who were coming from all over the Americas to participate. In other words, Hunbatz wanted to know precisely where we would be and how we were going to interact with this group. Also, Carolina Hehenkamp's group would be going with Hunbatz when we parted at Chichen Itza, and we wanted to know where each other would be during the coming days of these numerous ceremonies.

After that conversation, Hunbatz changed the subject. He wanted to tell me about the future and especially about the importance of the crystal skulls to future ceremonies. He talked about how these skulls were alive and how they would soon all come together in our ceremonies as we approached the End of Time.

Interestingly, the Native American Council in the United States had sent a crystal skull to my home in Arizona before I left. I was to keep it for an undetermined period of time. But the crystal skulls had not been part of my understanding of what this Yucatan journey was about. So, while I listened to Hunbatz, I considered that the information about the skulls was really meant for another time.

Little did I know. As usual, I'm the last one to understand.

The Temple of Dzibilchaltun

I had seen this equinox ceremony in 1995 with Hunbatz, and I was feeling excited to be with this wonderful group to experience it again.

We arrived at the site, which has been a major initiation center for the mystery schools of the world, about twenty minutes before sunrise. Many others, most of them Mayans, also had come to celebrate the equinox in this way.

The sunrise temple is a stone edifice with an opening where the equinoctial sun, the first light of the spring equinox, appears each year. The land that leads to the temple is a long, rocky corridor, almost like a landing strip, with low brush on either side. The temple sits way at the end of this corridor.

Lionfire had also been there before, and he helped our group to align themselves at a distance from the temple so that they would be able to see the sun appear in its opening.

About two minutes before the sun was to rise, something happened that I will never forget.

An elderly Mexican couple, people that I had met before, came near to me and said, "Drunvalo, is that you?" I turned to talk to them, knowing that I had only a few seconds before the sun would rise.

The lady, Maria, was carrying a piece of white cloth wrapped around some fairly large object. She opened the cloth to show me what was inside. There, nestled between her hands, was a fantastically beautiful, lucent white, ancient Mayan crystal skull. She looked at me and said, "Please, hold this to your heart."

I placed the crystal skull over my heart, turned to face Dzibilchaltun, just as the first sliver of sunlight began to emerge into the opening of the temple. In seconds the sun entered fully into the opening

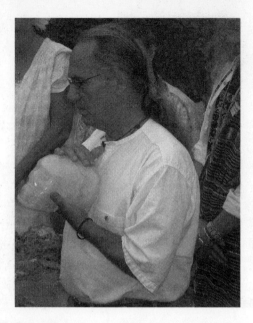

Mayan crystal Skull

of Dzibilchaltun, and the first rays of light began to explode from within me.

I had a vision. I saw two human Mayan spirits within this crystal skull I was holding to my heart. They were male and female, they were very much alive, and they were together in sexual union, facing each other in eternal love for one another.

At that moment, in a flash of understanding, I knew for certain what the Maya were doing with these crystal skulls.

Certain Maya were chosen, usually at birth, to be part of the crystal skull ceremony. Each chosen to capture the essence of Mayan culture in its entirety at one of thirteen different periods of time, from the very beginning to the very end of their culture, these people received lifelong training for this purpose. At the right moment in their lives, in solemn ceremony, they would ingest a specific natural psychedelic and, drawing on their training, would consciously die, remaining aware while they were leaving their body and forcing their spirit to enter into the crystal skull. The skull would then become their home, their body for hundreds or even thousands of years.

Dzibilchaltun

They would live within the crystal skull, holding and preserving the knowledge, memories, and wisdom of the ancient Mayan people, so that in this time—in the End of Time—it would be remembered. Their purpose was being fulfilled now, at this moment. The skulls were all slowly coming together all over Mayaland because that was their purpose from the beginning. There are thirteen skulls in all, and in the near future the Ceremony of the Thirteen Mayan Skulls will become reality and the Mayan prophecy will be complete, meaning the ancient transmission will have entered into the modern Mayan spirit.

As this realization flooded into me, I saw an old grandmother sitting quietly in the background inside the crystal skull. I knew that she was the one who had arranged this eternal marriage with the two lovers. I knew that she had planned everything that this crystal skull was to do for her people, that it was the ancient grandmothers who had devised this method of transmitting information across the millennia, and that they were still guarding the skulls.

The knowledge, memories, and wisdom that the Mayan lovers held was from the period of time when the Mayan culture was first blossoming. It was from the time when love and compassion were the rulers of all that was Mayan. And it was this extraordinary love, compassion, and knowledge that was to be reignited in the modern-day Mayan heart.

The experience of the sun rising through the temple and the crystal skull and its spiritual lovers opened my heart in a way I would never have believed if it had not happened. Dramatically, the ancient Mayans were beginning to speak to me about what was important to them.

I listened, and I prayed. I knew then that this was going to be another journey of the heart that would even more deeply change life on Earth and heal the relationships between people. I believed that it could even heal the suffocating clouds of carbon dioxide that are choking our planet. It brought such hope to my being.

But I had no idea that another experience of equal intensity lay but a few hours in our future. We were to enter a place so power-ful, so deeply heart centered, that after simply being there, no one in our group would ever be the same. We were about to speak with the Ancient Ones directly.

The Cenote at Dzibilchaltun

The cenotes are sacred pools—sometimes even good-sized lakes—fed by underground springs. Remember I saw one at Chichen Itza in 1985 when I was there with Ken. For the Mayans, all sacred sites must be near a cenote, for these springs are seen as doorways to the Inner Worlds. The waters of the cenotes are thought to have pro-found healing properties, and the cenote at Dzibilchaltun is among the most notable in Mayan understanding.

So after we watched the sun of the spring equinox rising through the stone temple at Dzibilchaltun, we went to its cenote, a beauti-ful pond at the jungle's edge. We gathered among the stone ruins beside it and held an impromptu service, meditating in behalf of the Mayans, our journey, and healing for the war in Iraq, which had begun on exactly the eve of our quest. It was interesting that the

Maya had set this date for this Ceremony of World Peace two and a half years in advance.

Following the ceremony, the keepers of the ancient crystal skull that I had held to my heart placed this sacred object upon a cloth draped on a rock ledge and allowed each of us to touch it and feel its power.

Suddenly, a strong and horrific manifestation of dark energy tried to enter our circle by taking control of the body of one of the women in the group. It was the same woman that it had manifested through at Labna. This lady the entity had entered raised the crystal skull above her head and, with everything she had, tried to smash it on the enormous rock ledge where it had been resting. Three men, led by Lionfire, tackled her and tried to grab the skull out of her hands. Their struggle lasted several minutes, but in the end, the skull survived. The woman foamed with fury as the entity moved within her.

We had been keeping careful watch to protect our group from this entity. We knew we were in its home. This was the entity that entered the Maya consciousness at the height of their culture and turned it from love and beauty to human sacrifice and fear. Knowing this, Lionfire had been closely guarding the skull. Nevertheless, it took all of his strength and that of the two other men to save this priceless sacred object from harm.

We now knew just how strong and determined this energy was. Without question, it would have to be cleared from this woman's body before we could participate in the next day's ceremony at Chichen Itza.

It was generally understood, as many of our group commented, that this dark-side energy was among us for a reason. It was very much a part of the problem we sought to help heal in the world, and we knew that we had to deal with it in a good way—with love, compassion, and even gratitude, especially toward that member of our group who had agreed, at some higher level of her being, to play such a difficult role. We had to plan.

Exhilarated, awed, yet chastened, we returned to Los Aluxes for breakfast, then set out for the next adventure of our journey at the incomparable Caves of Balancanche. (I say "caves" because this one cave has many arms that branch out in different directions.)

Our Guide, Humberto

I would like to say a few words about Humberto Gomez, our Merlin guide through Mayaland.

Humberto is a man in his early seventies who looks to be about sixty. He is a short, very slight man with an aristocratic mien and bearing, like the Spanish hidalgos of his heritage.

For the first two days of our trip, he was quiet—polite, charming, extremely helpful but low key and unassuming.

On the way to Balancanche, however, Humberto could not maintain his silence. I knew that he had a degree in archeology. Now, however, I learned not only that he was an extremely erudite man with a vast knowledge of the archeology of his homeland, but also that it had been he, Humberto Gomez, who as a young man had actually discovered the Caves of Balancanche! As we drove into the parking lot at Balancanche, I realized that Humberto knew more about this site than any other person alive.

Although we'd been up for hours that day, it was still early when we arrived at the Balancanche museum. The caves were not yet open. So while we were waiting, I invited Humberto to tell us all about his discovery.

We gathered around, excited to hear what he had to say. And at first apologetically, but soon with great verve and color, Humberto made his incredible long-ago experience come alive for us. It was to be the first of many stories with which Humberto would regale us on our spiral trip through the Yucatan. What an incredible storyteller he was!

Humberto was a student of archeology in his early twenties when he happened one day upon a small, dirt-walled cave near his home. Telling no one about it, he made the cave his very own hideout. He used to go there to meditate or just to be by himself.

The cave was a magical place for Humberto, but there was really nothing special about it, he told us—certainly nothing that suggested it might have ancient Mayan roots. It was just a cave. But it was his cave, and he continued to visit it for many years.

Then one day, in 1959, Humberto had the urge to begin tapping upon a specific portion of the cave's side. This tapping produced a kind of hollow sound.

The wall was glazed over by the same natural chemicals that had been oozing out of the earth there for millions of years. It looked like any other part of the cave. But as Humberto dug through the earthen cave side, he found, hidden behind it, the familiar brick-and-mortar remains of an ancient Mayan wall! Imagine his excitement as he carefully removed a few stones from that wall, enough to climb through into the vast, hitherto-unknown underground cavern that was concealed on the other side.

All alone, Humberto made his way through seemingly endless corridors and pathways in the rock. There he found something unheard of and unduplicated anywhere in Mayaland. Scattered throughout the caves were altars made of natural stalagmite and stalactite columns. And around these altars were offerings that had been made perhaps a thousand years before, untouched in all that time. Each of the hundreds of clay pots, implements, images, and querns that had been offered up to the rain god, Chac, rested just where it had been placed by ancient Mayan hands in some long-ago ceremony. Nothing within had ever been seen or touched in all the years since the cave was sealed from human view.

Humberto immediately sought out government officials to tell them of this archeological discovery, in order to ensure that all it contained would be protected from disruption or vandalism.

Normally, when a site is found in Mexico, the government takes everything it can find and removes it to a museum. But in this most unusual instance, the scientists and officials who first entered the cave realized the importance of preserving what Humberto had found. They immediately shut up the entrance and set a guard to protect it.

And so it remains, untouched to this day. Nothing has been moved except to make a small path through the complex so that visitors can experience the cave as it was first discovered.

After the government came, however, word got around, and the next day, a group of Mayan elders and shamans appeared and announced that they were going inside to perform a ceremony. Humberto told us this with an amused smile. The Mayans did not, he emphasized, ask whether or not it would be all right for them to enter the cave and conduct this ceremony. They said, "We are going to do this." The government said, "But you can't!"

The argument and debate went on for a while, until the government finally said the Mayans could do their ceremony—but only if officials were allowed to attend and take photographs!

More argument and debate. Finally, the Mayans gave in, on two conditions: Everyone who went into the cave must be sworn to secrecy. And no one could leave until it was over, which meant twenty-four hours without food or water. If anyone left before it was over, the Mayans warned, they could not take responsibility for the awful consequences that would ensue.

And so it was agreed. The Mayans and the Mexicans went down into the darkness of the earth to perform the ceremony—and emerged, twenty-four hours later, into a torrential rainstorm. This was the sign that the Mayans were looking for. They knew then that Chac, the rain god, had accepted their prayers.

Humberto was one of the participants in that ceremony to Chac and has never forgotten its power.

After Balancanche, Humberto turned out to be an entertaining treasure chest of beautiful stories and information about the sites we visited and the history of the Yucatan. I asked him once if he would tell me about that Mayan ceremony at Balancanche, but he said no. He had promised. It was the only time he ever refused to answer a question.

Inside the Caves of Balancanche

I had never been inside the Caves of Balancanche; they were unknown for me. So neither I nor anyone else in our group could have expected or imagined the experience we were about to have.

To begin with, we were expecting that we would have to remain at Balancanche most of the day. This is because, to protect the cave, the guards would allow only ten people to go through at one time. Only in these numbers was it possible for the guards to watch closely enough to make sure that nothing was taken or even touched.

But Humberto had participated in our first ceremonies and could see the reverence we had for the sites and the Mayan people. He knew that we had permission from the Ancient Ones to be there. And since he had discovered this site, he used his power to make an exception. We would be allowed to go in, we were informed, in groups of twenty.

This was a great honor and trust. But as we started to divide into three groups, Humberto convinced the guards to grant us a further concession. We would be allowed, he said, to go in two groups of thirty!

I was the last person in the first group. With great reverence, we wound our way through the jungle pathway to the mouth of the cave, which was a huge hole that spiraled into the Earth. The birds flying out of the cave and the flowers hanging from all of the walls, all seemed to be bowing their heads. The hair on the back of my neck was standing straight up.

Entering that cave felt like entering the womb of the Mother. Immediately, my heart began to open. It was a completely involuntary response to the energies present.

We continued into the depths of the Earth, deeper and deeper into the darkness. I could feel that this was one of the most sacred places I had ever been in. My heart kept opening more and more. I couldn't help it. I could see and feel that the same thing was happening to all of the others in front of me.

I found myself chanting softly.

Then I heard a sound behind me. Turning to see who was there, I saw our second group rapidly approaching. Had they made a mistake? Were they not following instructions?

The first person of this second group approached me, smiling, feeling the sacredness.

"What are you doing here?" I asked.

"Humberto decided to let us all go in as one group," she said.

"Of course," I said to myself. It felt right having us all there together. My heart was already bursting with the sacredness and beauty of this place. This unexpected change just about put me over the edge.

And so we went on, a group of sixty people where normally only ten were permitted, united in a feeling of love and spiritual awe unlike anything any of us had ever felt before. And I am not saying these words lightly.

Then we entered the main part of the cave, where an enormous stalagmite had millions of years ago joined as one with an equally enormous stalactite, creating a giant pillar at least twenty meters high. Around the pillar were the offerings that had been left there by the Mayans long ago. Prayer pottery and vessels were arranged on the ground all around this central column, just as they had been for hundreds and thousands of years.

The feeling of holiness was overwhelming. My heart could not hold in the tears. I began to cry. With tears blurring my vision, I looked around and saw that all of the people near me also were in tears.

We had come to Mayaland to experience the Sacred Space of the Heart. And here we were, in an actual physical space that was alive with the heart's living vibration—and all of our beings were in tune with this space, together. My whole being was vibrating!

As we continued to wind through these caverns, there were two more, somewhat smaller, stalagmite-stalactite altars, with their ancient offerings. And the feeling of holiness kept building.

The Cenote of Balancanche

The Sacred Space of the Heart is always associated with water, and I finally came to another chamber in that cave where a pool of water pulled me toward it. The water in that pool was so clear, I could barely see it as it emerged out of an adjacent cave. This water was alive. Really alive.

When I looked into this cenote, it was as though I was seeing into another world.

Three people from our group stood there staring into the pool crying, and as I approached, we fell into each other's arms.

At that moment, I knew that I was with my tribe. And with our tears and our open hearts, we were praying for ourselves, the Mayan people, and Mother Earth.

I knew this place. I had felt it before, within my own heart. Can you imagine what it was like to be in this space physically, with other physical beings, all experiencing the same thing? It was like nothing that had ever happened to me before.

The cave guards, who had remained invisible, signaled to us with their lights. Our time there was over.

As I turned to leave, I couldn't speak. I barely remember walking out of the cave. It seemed like a dream.

The next thing I knew, I was out of the cave, approaching the museum. I sat down by myself and closed my eyes. I was still vibrating in my heart. It took a good half hour before the experience of what just happened was grounded enough so that I could stand and begin walking back to the bus.

I will never forget this experience, or the Mayans whose prayers still resonate in this sacred space, or the beautiful people who entered into the Mother with me.

Sitting under a tree waiting for the rest of the group to come, I remembered the prayer of my most intimate teacher, Cradle Flower, of the Taos Pueblo:

> Beauty before me
> Beauty behind me
> Beauty on my left
> Beauty on my right
> Beauty above me
> Beauty below me
> Beauty is love
> Love is God.

CHAPTER FOURTEEN

PURIFICATION OF MAYALAND

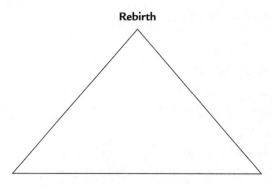

Rebirth

Figure 7: The Great Maya Heart Ceremony

The Temple of Chichen Itza

The elegant Mayaland Hotel is nestled in the Yucatan jungle, on the edge of the Chichen Itza temple site. We went straight there from Balancanche, arriving much earlier than we had expected because of our ease in visiting the caves.

That night, before dinner, I was asked to instruct our two groups, the Europeans with Carolina Hehenkamp and our own group, in the Living in the Heart Meditation. It was new only to a few of the participants. Many had already learned the meditation in a former workshop. With our powerful experiences of that afternoon, even those who had never breathed this heart meditation before were able to easily understand what this was all about—the need to move our consciousness out of the brain and into the physical heart—and how that is accomplished: the remembering of Unity Consciousness.

It takes a bit to understand and then actually make the inner change to begin living not from the mind, but from your heart. It is the way we used to live before the fall from One consciousness to good-and-evil consciousness 13,000 years ago. We began to judge every situation and every image that life gave to us.

Really, to return to the heart is so simple that most people find it a little difficult at first to have the experience. We have learned to believe that the more complex or complicated something is, the more important it is. But that doesn't apply to our original consciousness.

I believe that it is because I have learned to live within my heart that the indigenous peoples of the world have asked me to be part of their ceremonies. They can "see" that I am in my heart, not my mind, which is their way, and this is the primary aspect of the human soul that is important to them. We both know we can trust each other, and, as the Maya say when they greet each other, "*In Lak'esh*," "You are another me." When you are living in your heart, "*In Lak'esh*," has a meaning that only the heart truly understands, for the spirit that is within you is the same spirit that is within me.

If you want to know more, I have written a book called *Living in the Heart*, which not only explains all of this in much more detail, but also gives you the instructions so you can try it and decide for yourself if living in your heart feels better than living in your mind.

After dinner, under the stars, in this beautiful place with the heart-chakra pyramid of Chichen Itza close by, we all entered the Sacred Space of the Heart together and breathed as One.

And Now, the Dark Side: Only an Illusion

With everyone else going off to rest up for the great equinox ceremony and celebration, it was time for me to deal with the entity problem we had become aware of in the first ceremony at Labna and that morning with the crystal skull at Dzibilchaltun. This had to be attended to before we would be clear to participate in tomorrow's ceremony at Chichen Itza. If not, this energy would be able to interfere with everything all of us were attempting to achieve. We could not ignore it.

My estimation of what was going on was that this woman, a member of our group on this trip, had been attacked by a spirit or spirits whose intention it was to disrupt what we were doing in any way possible.

So the leaders—Diane Cooper; Lionfire; our tour guide, Mr. Humberto; and I—met and agreed that the situation had to be handled before we went to bed that night, since we were going to start out so early the next day.

But where to do the healing? I knew from experience that the woman possibly could be screaming when the entity left her body, and you can't have a woman screaming in a hotel. Someone would call the police. What should we do?

We asked Humberto where we could go, and he suggested an area near the hotel parking lot. It wasn't private, but we decided that we could put our van there and do the healing inside the van. If she screamed, the sound would be muffled.

Finally, everything was arranged. The woman voluntarily lay down across the van's middle seat. Two people from our group remained outside, in case someone approached. Two others were inside the van, in case help was needed.

The Shadow of Ancient Sacrifice

As I began to connect telepathically with the entities inside this woman, I realized that there were several, but that two of them were really one, and that this two-in-one entity was extremely powerful. It was connected to the Mayan world and to the ancient sacrificial ceremonies. In fact, this two-in-one entity and its desire to create chaos had actually been the force behind the Mayan practice of human sacrifice!

This double entity lived not only in this woman before me, but also in about sixty other people in Mayaland, mostly Mayans. It was interwoven and integrated into the land itself. It knew why we had come, and it was there to stop us from freeing the Mayan people who lived in the inner Earth. Its intent was to prevent us from creating balance.

I called in Archangel Michael and constructed the golden octahedron pyramid around the woman's body, which would contain the departing entities and serve as a dimensional window for sending them back to the world for which God originally created them.

For me, removing an entity is not about force, but about compassion and communication. In all of my experience, once spirits realize that we are returning them to their home world, where they can fulfill their own sacred purpose, they cooperate. Certainly, they do not do battle. In fact, they usually seem to me more like lost children than like devils seeking destruction.

But that was the past. I had a lesson to learn.

The smaller spirits were, in fact, grateful for the opportunity to go home, and as with my previous experiences, they left without a problem. But the last two, the double entity, refused to leave. The woman's entire body was distorting and bulging from their resistance. They could not give up. Their part in the ancient Mayan sacrificial ceremonies and their attachment to the land and to the Mayan people were too strong and all encompassing for them to relinquish. For centuries, they had been causing the Mayan people to do things that the Mayans themselves knew in their hearts were wrong.

Finally, I had no choice but to be more forceful. It was a role I had never taken before.

Using my Mer-Ka-Ba, my human light body, and the power and strength of Archangel Michael, together we began a series of waves of energy that would focus this dual entity's energies into the dimensional window of the octahedron, which would take them out of this world and into their own, home world, wherever that was.

Even though they resisted, if we succeeded, it would be for them like going to heaven!

First, the weaker part of the two was sucked into the vortex, with tremendous obstruction. This left the other, stronger part of this spirit still to be removed.

But finally, with even greater application of power and strength, this spirit, still resisting, emerged from the woman's stomach and slowly began to enter the dimensional window.

At the precise moment that the entity left her body, the Outer World responded from the sheer power of this spirit and its connection to the land. About a hundred feet on either side of us, two things happened simultaneously. The trees on the woman's right, in a small circular area of about twenty feet, began to shake wildly. A huge branch actually broke off and struck the ground.

On the left side, the same distance away, another circular group of trees, with trunks of about ten inches in diameter, also began to shake wildly. It was as if a bulldozer were at their bases trying to dig them out of the ground. Impossibly (there was no wind) most of them broke off at the base and crashed down on top of an old Volkswagen, completely crushing the roof and trunk.

In the instant that the spirit left this woman, I "saw" that the other Maya who were connected to these spirits, and the Mayaland itself for hundreds of miles around, suddenly cleared. It was as though a huge hurricane had instantly disappeared.

It was over. It was quiet.

Mayaland was now free. And this woman, once again, was alone in her body.

Our group now was truly prepared for tomorrow's Ceremony of the Heart at Chichen Itza—a ceremony long predicted by the Mayan people and their calendar, a group of indigenous elders, along with people from the four corners of the Earth, all praying together as One for the world to find peace.

Fulfilling an Ancient Prophecy

The sound of tropical birds pierced the wooden shutters as I woke from one beautiful dream into another one that for the moment seemed remote. Then I remembered. This was the day I had been awaiting for over two and a half years. Hunbatz Men had e-mailed me long ago to invite me to a ceremony that had been predicted by the Mayan calendar. Now that day had arrived.

I jumped out of bed, got dressed, and hurried downstairs, knowing that we had a tight schedule and that it was important not to be late or make mistakes. Too many people were waiting for this moment with great anticipation. If our group were late, I was thinking, they would have to go on without us.

In the lobby were sixty people, dressed all in dazzling white, as Hunbatz had requested. Their smiles and exuberant energy said everything. We were ready for whatever life had to offer and ready to give of our hearts and prayers. After the Caves of Balancanche, our hearts were wide open, and our group was One Heart. Life was ready to unfold another chapter of its mystery. Who knew what was about to happen? Not me, for sure.

We were lined up two by two so that we could enter the ticket gate, and we proceeded in this manner into the Chichen Itza complex, winding our way through the tropical trees until we came to the base of the Castle Pyramid on the east side. The sun was intense, so we moved under the trees to find shade.

Hunbatz was due to arrive with his expected entourage of more than 250 indigenous elders and shamans around 10 a.m. And so, gathered in little groups on the pyramid grounds, talking amongst ourselves, we simply waited.

And we waited and waited. The European group was also with us, and a few people started learning songs from others of different nations. The singing went on for a while, then faded away. And still we waited. Where were the elders? No one knew.

Late in the morning, the priest and priestess of the Uxmal temple walked up to me and introduced themselves. They were in full ceremonial dress, beautiful and full of energy. Their relaxed smiles and comfortable demeanor spoke of their great inner spiritual Light. They thanked us for being there and for taking part in these ceremonies. On behalf of our group, I extended our love and respect and any support that we could give to them.

Soon, another man—an Incan priest from Peru, also in full ceremonial dress—arrived and began to speak with a group who stood next to us under a great tree. His energy was robust. He was there, it seemed, to inspire the people for the great ceremony that was about to take place.

But where was Hunbatz Men? There was no sign of him.

It was now almost noon, and the sun was high in the sky. Finally, word came to us that Hunbatz and the elders had been delayed. The police had shut off the roads about a mile and a half away from the temple, and the elders had to walk.

So we waited a while longer, but then learned of still another problem. The ceremonial place, it seemed, had been changed to an area behind the Castle Pyramid, way back in the trees. And despite the absence of Hunbatz Men and the elders, the ceremony was going to begin.

I didn't know what had happened with Hunbatz, but my inner guidance clearly told me to go with this new ceremony.

Our Rainbow Circle

Our group walked a short distance and emerged into a large clearing in the jungle where the energy felt perfect for what we were about to do. We were with Carolina Hehenkamp's group now, and others joined us as we formed a great circle. A circle made up of people of every color and race.

The Uxmal priest and priestess who were to lead this ceremony laid special cloths on the ground to form an altar. Many crystals and ceremonial objects were arranged on the altar. Finally, first one, then two, and eventually, thirteen Mayan crystal skulls were laid out on the altar in a tight circle. And then a Mayan weaving was placed over them, hiding them from view, for it was not quite time yet for their "special" ceremony. The skulls seemed to me to be chanting, and I found myself once again entering into meditation with them.

To my surprise, the priestess, who clearly seemed to be leading the ceremony, asked me to enter the inner circle. She asked if there was anyone else from my group who belonged there, and so I asked for Lionfire. Truly, this Mayan world seemed to be his much more than mine.

About fifteen or so other elders and indigenous people were asked to join the inner circle. Some were Mexican, some were American, but most, including the Incan priest, were from indigenous cultures. I especially remember a group of three Incan shamans from South America who were so beautiful—that I felt the purity of Mother Earth coming from their hearts in ripples of pure joy.

The Mayan priestess lit ceremonial herbs and incense in a small, ancient Mayan cauldron, filling the air with a pungent scent. Then she raised her arms as her male companion blew the sound of the conch and opened the ceremony with prayers to the four directions.

Keeping the ceremony itself hidden, the priestess and priest prayed in the Mayan language. Their prayers rose, interwoven with the smoke of the cauldron. Then each one of us in the inner circle spoke and prayed in turn, asking from our hearts for what our hearts most wanted—the healing of the Earth and her people.

There was a beauty, power, and precision to what we were doing. It felt as though this ceremony had been planned eons ago. Everything seemed to be unfolding as though it had been carefully rehearsed.

But there was something else—an aspect I was not aware of because I was so deeply involved. And this had to do with the people in the outer circle.

As those of us conducting the ceremony, each in his or her own language, uttered the words we wished to send up to Spirit, our messages were being translated into several languages. One after another, the ceremonial prayers and sentiments wafted over that huge clearing in Mayan, Spanish, English, German, Russian, French—carried on the wind to this incredible group of individuals who had come from all over the world to help the world become One.

A woman said to me later, "I felt, all through that ceremony, that the Tower of Babel was slowly crumbling. That our world would never again be the same."

So perhaps, in coming together in this way with the Mayans in this ancient ceremony, we were symbolically ending the divisions among countries, cultures, and races. In time it will be real.

As the last smoke of the cauldron drifted over the crowd and the ceremony ended, we all rushed together like old friends from long-lost tribes, hugging and sharing not only love but also phone numbers and addresses—ways of communicating in order to keep together this energy we all felt. We were a rainbow of One Spirit.

Humbatz Men and the Elders

As I was leaving to head back toward the pyramid, a runner approached to tell me what had happened with Hunbatz Men and the elders. It seemed almost like a nightmare to hear this after the beauty of what had just transpired.

They all had eventually made their way to Chichen Itza and prepared to do their ceremony at the original site. They put a cauldron on the ground with herbs and incense. And when all the elders were ready, they began the ceremony by lighting the incense in this cauldron.

At that moment, police rushed in with a fire extinguisher and put out the fire.

The elders were enraged and began to argue with the police—although Hunbatz kept quiet, for he had been expecting this and had even warned of it.

In the end, the police broke up that ceremony and even arrested about eight of the South American elders. So before the ceremony even began, it was over.

Hunbatz told me later he then came to find our group. We were already in deep prayer in our own ceremony, and in accordance with his beliefs, he could not join us at that time. Instead, he walked two times around our prayer circle, blessing us.

He told me that if we had not come there, from all these other lands, and performed our own ceremony led by the two Mayan priests, the Mayan calendar would not have been fulfilled. He thanked us with tears in his eyes.

We felt into each other's hearts and were thankful, knowing that Great Spirit works in ways that are not always comprehensible.

The Coming of the Snake

With the ceremony concluded, our little international group of souls was free to join the huge crowd that had gathered to watch the "snake" come down the Castle Pyramid, just as Ken and I had done long ago, in 1985.

Now, on March 21, 2003, an estimated crowd of more than 80,000 people were there—so many that one could not even walk across the huge, grassy field in front of the steps where the snake was to make his portentous descent.

But, alas, the morning sun had turned to clouds. And the afternoon sky was gray. There was no sun to cast a shadow. Eighty thousand people—people who had come from all over Mexico, South America, and the world—sat or stood, with their picnic lunches and their families, all waiting for a shadow that might never appear.

And then, quite late in the afternoon, the clouds suddenly parted, and the sun struck through in a blaze of glory to light up the pyramid, casting its shadow at the side of the pyramid steps. The gathered crowd, in one thrilling voice, uttered a cry of pure joy, then fell silent as they watched the mystical moving shadow of the "snake."

Looking over that vast, rapt multitude, I was reminded of the rock concert crowds of the sixties. But it seemed that the Ancient Ones and the Grateful Dead had changed places. Instead of listening to a charismatic band whose exciting music exploded onstage, we were enthralled—each and every one of us—by a slow, silent shadow inching its way down the side of a mythic pyramid, in renewed affirmation of the Sacred Spiral of Life.

The Two Cenotes

As I moved away from the shadow finale, I remembered part of a conversation I'd had with Hunbatz Men, when he had unexpectedly explained to me about the two cenotes at Chichen Itza and how they were linked. He said that an underground river connected the two cenotes and that the Castle Pyramid had been purposely built directly over this river. It was this flowing underground water that charged the pyramid with its energy. Ken and I had known nothing of this second cenote when we were there.

Hunbatz Men looked me in the eyes and said, "Drunvalo, the other cenote also needs to be 'recharged' with a crystal. This would connect the energies of the two cenotes together."

And so, as I left the ceremony of the "snake" descending the pyramid, I headed in the direction of the other cenote to fulfill Hunbatz's request.

Crystal Completion

A few other people from the group followed me, probably thinking they wanted to see what I was doing. To me, of course, whoever was there was supposed to be there. There are no accidents, no mistakes.

Within a few minutes, I found the second cenote and noted that there were exactly fourteen people, including myself. I explained to them the story of Ken and me and the other cenote in 1985 and the present request of Hunbatz Men, and it was as if everyone had been to psychic school. They seemed to know exactly what to do.

We held hands and passed the crystal so that each person could pray into it. Their prayers were for the Mayan people and for Mother Earth to be healthy again. Then the last person threw the crystal into the deep, mysterious water.

I could feel the connection being made. I felt an energy emerge. And I could see in my inner vision the two cenotes interconnecting and the Castle Pyramid lighting up with a new/old energy form. I understood in that moment the importance of what Thoth and

Hunbatz Men were trying to communicate to me. It felt complete for the first time.

The Call of the Sun

Back at the hotel, Hunbatz Men left me a note suggesting that he would like to talk with my group. He had promised to be with us, and it had not happened—not yet. Although he was extremely busy now, he wanted to keep that promise.

We all assembled in a semicircle by the Mayaland swimming pool and waited for Hunbatz. It was dark now. Stars shown, and from the hotel there was an ambiance of soft lights all around us.

Hunbatz arrived and explained what had happened that day. He apologized to us and thanked us for performing the ceremony. Without our participation, he said, the Work would not have been completed. He told us we were all teachers of the new world and spoke to us of our responsibilities in this role.

And then he taught us a sacred chant to the Mayan sun god, Kin (pronounced *keen*). And because so many of our group were already "remembering" their Mayan heritage of the past, singing this chant awoke an incredible feeling of being in both places at once—the ancient, ancient past, and the now.

Our day at Chichen Itza ended with us all together under the stars, chanting and remembering our ancient connections.

We were so filled with emotion and the sense of mystery, it seemed as though we could contain no more.

If we had known how much awaited us, it would have been difficult for us to believe it. In truth, we had scarcely begun.

CHAPTER FIFTEEN

THE CIRCULAR
RAINBOW

The day after the equinox celebration at Chichen Itza—and with the ceremonies and prayers still lingering in our hearts—we left the Mayaland Hotel and turned our faces toward Quintana Roo.

On this day, we would journey toward the fifth-chakra Mayan site at Tulum. On the way to our hotel, a resort on the Mexican Caribbean, we would visit Coba—perhaps the largest site in the Yucatan, although much of it remains to be excavated. Later in the afternoon, we would make the trek to one of Quintana Roo's hundreds of cenotes, on private land, hidden deep in the jungles near Tulum.

As we slowly made the long drive to Coba, we had—after so many surprises—given up our expectations. Childlike, we brought with us now only open hearts and open eyes. We were simply waiting for God to show us our next responsibility.

The Ancient City of Coba

At Coba we found a compound surrounded by small, palm-thatched, open-air eating places, where we had lunch. One of the specialties served there was fresh coconut milk, which was sipped through a straw straight from the coconut itself. After lunch, we entered the temple site of Coba.

Coba covers nearly fifty square miles and was once home to an estimated population of 40,000 Mayans. The ancient city that originally surrounded Coba was so big that if we could see it as it was just over a thousand years ago, we would probably change our concepts of who the Mayans were. Looking out from the top of Coba's Great Pyramid—Nohoch Mul—we could see evidence of an extremely advanced civilization.

Our guide, Humberto, told us that Coba was the hub of a system of sophisticated ancient roads, called Sacbe (pronounced *sock*-bay). These were stone roadways built to a height of one or two meters and covered with mortar. Most of the mortar is gone now, but many of the Sacbe stones remain in place. Humberto had been pointing them out to us along our journey. In truth, at the height of Mayan civilization, all Sacbe led to Coba.

The existence of these roads, Humberto noted, was puzzling in that the Mayans had no form of wheeled travel or even horses. Perhaps the roads were used for religious processions. Most certainly, according to Humberto, the road's patterns are related to the Mayan calendar. They seem to be parts of a huge astronomical "time machine," but it was never made clear as to exactly how Humberto thought this all functioned. It's one of those things that someone should explore.

One of the delights at Coba was the bicycle cars. Those visitors who do not wish to make the long trek from the gates of Coba to the Great Pyramid may ride in these cars. Propelled by human effort, they are very much like four-wheeled rickshaws, except that the driver pedals them rather than pulling them on foot. We did not see these anywhere else in the Yucatan.

As I approached the Great Pyramid, Nohoch Mul, I wondered if it could be anything like what Ken and I had seen there many years before. In 1985, it had been nothing more than a small stone house on top of a large hill. Today, completely revealed, it is the tallest pyramid in the Yucatan.

Many more of Coba's estimated 6,500 pyramids, temples, and other structures had been excavated since my previous visit. Now, the Great Pyramid, despite its size, seems almost unimportant among so many others in this vast complex. It was surprising to see so much exposed and mapped out that had previously been hidden.

The energy of the place was fantastic.

We would not be doing ceremony at Coba, only sensing and communing. Hence, everyone in our group was free to explore, and like water evaporating, they quickly disappeared into the trees, exploring all parts of the site. Then, like fog separating and coming back together, we would find each other, discovering intriguing places, meditating. I had so much fun here. It all felt so good.

Tulum: the Circular Rainbow

In the eighteen years since I had walked upon the grass of Tulum, the government had built up the area in order to more easily control the tourists—and on this weekend day, there were a lot of them.

None of this mattered to me, though—not the crowds of people, not the changes. I could feel that what was about to happen here would be meaningful—and important to the balancing of the Mayan energies.

At first we all went in different directions, exploring, while I tried to remember where we had placed the original crystal. That had been so long ago. But after maybe twenty minutes, I found it. I knew right away that this was the right place when I looked inside and saw the frescoes.

Standing at this temple, I scanned the area of Tulum, looking for a place to do our ceremony. In a few moments, I saw, out in the expanse of grass that surrounds the temples of Tulum, one area that seemed to glow more than any other. I walked directly to it. By now, our group had collected, and so everyone followed.

The location was perfect. What it was, or why, I don't know, but it was perfect.

I then selected the spot that would mark the center of our circle, set a piece of cloth on the ground to form the altar, and marked the four directions. Someone in our group gave me a large crystal, and I placed it in the middle of this altar. Then others in the group added their own articles and crystals. Soon, everything was ready for our ceremony.

From those who volunteered, I chose four people—two males and two females—to hold the positions of the four directions. These four stood at the directions they represented, facing in toward the center of the circle. In turn, they each said prayers and "became" that direction, providing protection to the inner circle.

I then knelt in the center of the circle, representing the directions of above and below, and said prayers to seal this inner space.

I am now going to describe things that happened in this very powerful ceremony, on the "inner planes."

Within minutes of the opening of this ceremony, some of the Mayans living in the inner Earth made contact with me and asked permission to be part of this ceremony. Three very old Mayans literally appeared in front of me; their bodies were translucent, yet I could see them clearly. They looked into my eyes and, with great respect, telepathically asked if they could enter into this ceremony. They joined us, and there were more to come.

To help those in the group who could not "see," I began to speak and describe what was occurring in one of the invisible overtones of the third dimension all around us.

First, the three Mayan elders, who had just asked for permission, entered our circle from the north and stood in front of the altar. It was obvious that the oldest of these three, who was in the center, was their leader. He began to speak in Mayan, asking other members of his tribe to emerge.

Then four Mayans—two male and two female—came and stood behind our people in each of the four directions, sealing off the inner space even more with their knowledge and understanding. There followed about thirty other Mayans, who dispersed themselves around our circle.

Once this had happened, an interplay between our group and theirs commenced. Their primary interest was in gaining control of the environment and especially the rain, to bring balance to the Outer World and the Inner Worlds, both of which were out of balance. In fact, the Yucatan Peninsula was experiencing a period of severe drought. It had not rained for many months.

The Mayans began by "constructing" a huge energetic pyramid that extended into the four directions. They started small, making it about the size and area the group was standing in, and then enlarged it with their minds to be about two miles or so on each side. They did this in exactly the same manner as I was taught with the Taos Pueblo in New Mexico. They "saw" or envisioned this pyramid existing in space in the third dimension (our world) and, with their intention, made it real. They also breathed into it to give the pyramid life force energy, which is what really makes the environment react as though it is a real three-dimensional pyramid.

A normal person could not see this pyramid, but the environment doesn't know the difference. And a pyramid acts exactly like a mountain in nature. It draws in the clouds and the rain. Small ones don't have too much effect, but big ones, especially when they reach the size of about two miles, engage the environment just like huge mountains.

This pyramid became the centermost "mountain" to bring in rain. The inner Earth Mayans could control the mountain's height and thereby control the amount of rain that came to this area of the peninsula. To increase this pyramid's area of influence even more, the Mayans made more pyramids, all running together like a mountain range extending for many miles toward the north.

When this was complete, the central Mayan elder announced that it would now rain before tomorrow, and the drought would be over.

To end the ceremony, the Mayan elder asked that we chant to the sun with its name, Kin. Everyone, both spectral Mayans and our group, sang the sound of the name of the sun several times. On the last note, we raised our hands into the air and opened our eyes to the sky to end this powerful ceremony.

As we opened our eyes on the last note of the holy Mayan name of the sun, we peered into the heavens and witnessed a deliberate sacred sign that we had performed the ceremony correctly. Around the sun, on this clear and cloudless day, was a perfect, brilliant, circular rainbow, so bright that every color stood out like electric light.

In that moment, we knew that what we had just done and what we were doing on this journey was so blessed by Great Spirit. My heart opened so wide, I thought I might melt into the Earth along with the Mayan people who were now returning to their Inner Worlds. It was beautiful.

I wonder now what the hundreds of tourists and their children must have thought of us, all hugging and crying and grinning from ear to ear and speaking to each other in four or five different languages. At the time, though, I wasn't even aware that there were other people there.

Most of us ran down to the ocean and jumped into the gorgeous turquoise waves that threw us around like corks on a fishing line. Those who hadn't brought swimsuits just jumped in with their clothes, and we all splashed around and laughed and played. This was great! Life was great!

And still, in the sky above us, that magical rainbow circled the bright sun. It lasted a long, long time.

Another Crystal Skull Emerges

Eventually, it was time to head back to the bus—or so we thought. As God would have it, however, we were not yet done for this day. As I trekked out of the Tulum temple grounds on the way to the parking area, I was stopped by the Mexican man who had brought me the white skull at Dzibilchaltun. He was holding yet another ancient Mayan crystal skull. It pulled me to it like a moth to a flame. This one was green, like jade, and slightly transparent.

As I connected with this crystal, I was introduced to a single male who lived inside it. He demonstrated to me yet again how the ancient Mayans were using these crystals.

An individual was chosen to die, he affirmed. Then the spirit of this individual would enter the crystal and reside there until the crystal's purpose was complete. In the milky white crystal at Dzbilchaltun, the residents of the skull were a couple—a man and woman—and a grandmother. But if there was a grandmother inside this one, I didn't see her. Perhaps she was there but would not allow herself to be seen.

Always, it seems, the crystals' purposes are related to holding and maintaining the ancient Mayan knowledge and memories until the End Times—this time that we live in now.

I didn't know what it meant to have so many crystal skulls entering into the energies of our little group. A crystal skull would appear, as it did at Dzbilchaltun, and once it had revealed what it wanted to reveal, would disappear back into the jungle. Then another one would appear, let itself interact with our group, and disappear never to be seen again. This just kept happening, just as Hunbatz Men, in his Mayan wisdom, had predicted it would when we sat together in Merida having tea.

That night, shortly after we returned to our beautiful hotel, the sky opened up and the rain began to pour down in a veritable deluge, answering the Mayan elder's announcement that it would "rain before tomorrow." I looked to the heavens, closed my eyes, and thanked God for this blessing and this second acknowledgment of our prayers and ceremony. I couldn't help but feel again, as I had before, that this was the "right" group for what we were doing.

We had two more specific ceremonies to perform before returning to Uxmal and Merida. But first, there were two processes that needed to happen in order for us to prepare ourselves, and perhaps the world, by releasing our negative male and female energies of the past thousands of years. These two "processes" were to be very much like ceremonies, but were, in fact, probably more akin to modern-day therapy. Each member of this group came to the Yucatan with internal emotional disturbances associated with their sexual energies. This is true with almost every person alive.

In a nutshell, the sexual chakra, the heart chakra, and the pineal chakra, in the center of the head, all function together as one when they are aligned. Lack of alignment causes emotional disturbances, and emotional disturbances causes lack of alignment. These disturbances would have to be balanced in our group before the last two ceremonies could be completed or we would not be able to finish our work.

For many, these two processes, which were to take place after we completed our work at Kohunlich, the third-eye temple, were the most deeply felt of any experiences we had on our journey.

The energy in Tulum had built up in such a manner that we all knew our journey would continue to unfold in miraculous ways that were out of our hands. Only Mother Earth and the ancient Maya knew what was about to happen or where this all was leading.

And this is exactly what the present-day Maya have since said to all of us. In cryptic words, last August 2003, they told us that by December 15, 2003, we would enter a new world. And that in the interim, there would perhaps be chaos all around us.

I feel that our journey in Mayaland was demonstrating the nature of this shift that is about to come for us all. For truly, our world is a dream—and its dream nature is becoming more obvious. In fact, the Dreamer is about to wake up and realize that it is dreaming. Even more importantly, the Dream itself of living on this planet can now be changed. This is the key!

After November 8, 2003, when there was a total lunar eclipse and a Grand Sextile of planets—the astrological event that was called the Harmonic Concordance—we will all eventually begin to realize that the Dream is really "only light and intention." This is my belief, though I know it will still take a little more time. The portal to the fourth dimension will begin to open wide for those who know.

What does this mean? It means that we are out of time. We must really take responsibility for our thoughts, feelings, and emotions now. For each one of us is the Dreamer. And what we dream will become real in this world. This is the Mayan belief: that as we move closer to December 21, 2012, and February 19, 2013, the power of the Dreamer becomes stronger and stronger.

The Inner Worlds and the Outer World will begin to merge into one. This is the belief of not only the Maya but many other indigenous groups and prophets as well. And in creating this oneness, we must first burn away the dross of duality, the negativity with which we have lived for so long.

And so, appropriately, the next phase of our sacred journey in Mayaland seemed to present a pattern for this preparation that we are all going through now. In the two days of our trip from Tulum to Palenque, we all experienced a cohesive series of experiences and ceremonies that seemed designed to take us all to the next level of being.

CHAPTER SIXTEEN

KOHUNLICH AND THE THIRD EYE

THE INTEGRATION OF MALE AND FEMALE

As our group arrived at Kohunlich, the memories of my earlier trip with Ken were vivid. Questions raced through my mind. Would it be the same? Were the staircase and the triangular hole still there? I had not yet told our group about the past events.

We started out by trekking to the primary pyramid—the one with the huge human faces on the surface. At this point, we were all just being tourists, exploring and feeling the energies of this sacred site. Then I told everyone the story about the strange hole and the tree with the tiny hole. And, finally, we set off looking for the marble stairway.

But Kohunlich had changed. I had hoped to find the pyramid where I had placed the crystal with Ken years before and revisit those memories, but it was not meant to be.

There were trails all through the site now, which had expanded to many miles around, and maps at various locations. We followed these trails for a while, going off in one direction, then returning and trying another trail, but we couldn't find the special pyramid or the little hole in front of it that I had dropped the crystal into years before.

Finally, we came to a wide, ancient stone staircase built into a fairly steep hill. It was nothing like the marble steps Ken and I had found before, but the place called to me. We all felt pulled to whatever was at the top of those stone stairs.

As we reached the top, I could see that rather than being a pyramid or a sacred building, this area had actually been a residence for the ancient Maya. There were tiny rooms everywhere, in a most beautiful arrangement, and wide-open courtyards where people could congregate. And it seemed the perfect place for what we had come to do.

So I let go of the pyramid idea and the triangular hole, and we found our perfect spot under some trees that offered shade from the blistering sun. We laid a "cloth of the sun" on the ground, a center point was chosen, and our altar began to take shape as different people added crystals and sacred objects to it.

The group gathered in a circle around the altar, and again four people—two males and two females—were chosen to seal off the four directions.

As at Tulum, the head Mayan priest appeared out of the Earth in front of me, raising his arms to the sky, and placed four of his own people behind our keepers of the four directions. But then, many, many Mayans began to come out of the ground, forming a circle slightly wider than our own. At first, only their heads appeared out of the earth, spiraling around the circle. Then, slowly, as they kept circling, their bodies began to emerge from Mother Earth. Finally, the Mayans were on the surface of the Earth in our world. For every person in our group, the Mayans had assigned one of their own to stay with that person throughout the ceremony.

They were dressed in brightly colored robes, with geometric designs painted on their faces and feathers in their hair. Their energy was electric. I could sense that this ceremony was something they had predicted long ago and that it was of great importance to them. They were very serious.

The actual unfolding of the ceremony was very different than at Tulum. In Tulum, many energetic pyramids had been created over a great distance to bring balance back to the land and bring in the rain. This time, only one huge pyramid was created. And its purpose, I understood telepathically from the chief, had to do with the psychic awakening of the Mayan people.

I don't really understand all that transpired with these ancient Mayans during that ceremony. I do know that my heart kept getting lighter and lighter. Lionfire says that the Maya here at Kohunlich, when they left, took with them all the negative energy that we had been dealing with in our group up to that time and buried it deep, deep in Mother Earth. Whatever happened, it made us all very happy. I remember looking up, directly after the ceremony, and noticing that as I looked around, every last person was smiling and filled with light.

What happened then was a reflection of what had gone before—so perhaps Lionfire is right about the cleansing effect. People began to hug each other and play. There was a tremendous sense of well-being in all of us. Watching, I realized how perfect it was for us to be doing this in the actual living quarters of the ancient Maya, their homes.

But it was clear to me that, though the Maya helped clear out the negative energy of our group, they had not reached the deepest part of our psychic and emotional body—our sexual disturbances. Resolving these was something we had to do ourselves. This required deep forgiveness.

So the next day, with this newfound lightness, we were going to be plunging back into difficult inner work. But for today, our work was done. Joyfully, we all headed back to the bus.

Yes, I was still looking around for that pyramid with the marble staircase and the triangular hole. But somehow, I knew I was not going to find it. It had to remain secret.

The Temples of Forgiveness

The next day of our journey in the Yucatan was unique for me. I had never seen the temple sites we were going to. These temples represented the dark side of the male and female energies. There we would be doing two incredible ceremonies or processes there to release forever from our beingness the male-female polarities—leaving us free, with all of our divine strength.

Our purpose in visiting these sites was wholly concerned with the Now—with the End of Time, as the Maya call it—and the corrections that needed to be made within our polarity consciousness in order for us to move to a higher level of awareness. This simply had to be completed, or we could not go on. This balanced state would not last forever, for whenever we breathe and act we create more karma, but it would last long enough for us to complete our work.

Before this journey to Mayaland, we had no inkling that this kind of ceremonial balancing therapy was going to be part of our experience. It just unfolded before our eyes and hearts. This phase of our sacred journey in Mayaland seemed to present a pattern for preparation that we all are going through on Earth. In the two days of our trip from Tulum to Palenque, we all had a cohesive series of experiences and ceremonies that felt specifically designed by the Maya to accelerate us out of polarity and into Oneness, almost whether we wanted to or not.

Preparation: Beginning at Becan

As we headed out from our hotel that morning, there was not one of our entire group, except perhaps Lionfire, who knew how totally life-changing this day was to be for many of us. It was he who had chosen these three temples, and he alone of our group seemed to have a premonition of what was to come.

Lionfire had been deeply connected with the huge energetic events that were happening within our group concerning the dark side of male-female energies. He carries in his own shamanic being an energetic manifestation of the dual energies, a kind of kachina that is wholly dark on one side and wholly light on the other. It is part of his journey in this lifetime to harmonize and balance these two sides, and his presence helped to coalesce this energy in our group to the place where the negative aspects could be released.

Our beginning at Becan had within it the spirit of fun and play. It was a perfect preparation for the ceremonies we would do later.

Becan itself was a regional capital of the ancient Mayan empire, first built around 600 B.C. but most active between A.D. 600 and 1000. It is one of the most important architectural sites in Campeche.

This ancient city is surrounded by a ditch that is unique in the Mayan area. In fact, the word *becan* in Mayan means "ravine formed by water." It is believed by some that the ravine served as protection in the event of war. Others feel that it represented a social class division: The elite built their monumental structures within the area encompassed by the ditch, and the lower classes lived outside.

A surface tunnel, made of stone, links the two main plazas of the ancient city, and in one place there are amazing painted masks. Standing on one altar, we could "feel" that it had once been used for human sacrifice. Whether that's true or not I don't know, but it is true that the Mayan culture was led astray at one point into this horrific practice.

For us, Becan was the temple site of male-female integration, a place of balancing. In Lionfire's words:

As many of us talked to Drunvalo at the male-female integration altar, others went off to play and dance with the pyramids. Earlier in the trip, at Coba, I had talked about how each pyramid was like a musical instrument, and that they were meant to be "played" in different ways, depending on how you "danced" them. When we left the altar and wandered through the courts, to my amazement, most of the group were dancing up, down, around, and on top of the pyramids.

What a joy! This was exactly what we needed: the fun, the child. This was the preparation. The group had walked through fear. Atop the acropolis of Becan, we could clearly see in the distance the temples of Xpuhil and Chicanna, the sites where we would perform the ceremonies honoring the blending of the masculine and feminine energies within ourselves.

Xpuhil: Ceremony of Male Integration

From Becan, we drove the short trip to Xpuhil. There we all walked quickly along a rocky path through a forest, finally coming out in a grassy compound at the temple of three towers, where we would do our ceremony.

Xpuhil means the "place of cattail reeds." Its stunning towers depict Itzamna—Creator God and first shaman—as a celestial serpent. The main building in Xpuhil has twelve rooms and platforms, with three enormous towers reaching to the sky. In the center is a recess surrounded by the head of a serpent. This complex integrates low, middle, and high masculine energies, focusing on cosmic sex and love.

The male-energy integration ceremony we were about to do, like the female-energy integration ceremony that would follow later, was something I had never experienced before. I didn't know how it was going to work or what would happen. I was just allowing myself to feel what needed to be done and said so, with no preconceived ideas.

First, I found a spot out in the grassy field in front of the temple of Xpuhil, and there I asked all of the men to get together in a group and sit down on the grass, while the women formed a standing circle around them. The women held hands and set the energy of the group.

I then felt guided to construct sacred geometry forms around the men, specifically the Platonic octahedron in a golden light; the apex was connected into Father Sky, the bottom half completely inside Mother Earth, and the bottom apex connected energetically to Mother Earth herself. In so doing, I felt these forms come alive with prana, life-force energy.

I asked the men to release all of the negative side of their masculine energy into these two poles, and to visualize this energy leaving out of their mental, emotional, and physical bodies and flowing out like water through these two apexes. The mental energies would go up through the top and be released to Father Sky. The more physical and emotional energies would go deep into Mother Earth.

And just so you know, this negative energy is no problem for our Divine Mother and Father. It is simply rebalanced and reused back into Life.

I just became silent then and let it begin.

It was very hot in Xpuhil that day, and we were standing in the sun. Before the ceremony, we were very much aware of the heat, and afterwards it came back to assault us with its almost tangible presence. But while this ceremony was happening, I don't think a single member of our group was aware of anything but the spiritual energies that were moving and changing.

We could all feel what was happening as the men let go of the negative masculine aspects from all of our history, represented in their own bodies and energy fields in the here and now.

At first, it went slowly, but as the men got into the flow of what was happening to them, the release became easier and faster.

For me, I am able to see these kinds of energies moving, and it was both beautiful and chilling at the same time. Spiraling out of the men were energy patterns mostly of red, black, and a kind of yellow-green, but really everything was happening at once.

I could see on their faces the pain of letting go of something they had been holding onto for thousands of years, lifetime after life-time—energy that had been severely affecting their own relationships with wives, daughters, and female friends in ways they could not control, all of it ancient and beneath their conscious awareness. All the rapes and violence and murder and pain that collective man has inflicted upon innocent women and children—all of it was revealed and moved into the hearts of our Divine Mother and Father, who, with their divine compassion, were healing these men's souls.

At one point, there was a shift. You could almost hear a kind of collective sigh going up from the group as a whole. And soon after that, it was done.

I would like to say here that this was as strong a group of men as I have ever been with. There was a larger proportion of men to women in this group than was usual, and the men themselves were extremely powerful, many of them being high-level shamans and healers in their own right.

Because of their spiritual level, these incredible men were extremely open. They had not only the insight but also the capacity to actually do what I had asked. When I said, "It is finished," most of these men, sitting in the center of the circle of women, were crying.

I asked the women to hug the men, and this hugging went on for a long time. The men went to one woman after another, tears in their eyes, embracing. Silently thanking Woman for the love she still holds despite the gulf between the sexes that has existed for so many millennia. Silently asking forgiveness. Allowing themselves to feel vulnerable. Allowing themselves to be nurtured. Letting go of the core of rigidity and aloneness that has been the masculine burden down through the centuries.

We all spoke of feeling that this release had been done not only for ourselves, but for the entire Earth. That we had in some way created a pathway for others to follow, in a process that would continue to grow over the coming days, months, and years, until the integration was truly complete for all mankind.

As we walked back to the bus, we were all very quiet. No one could have predicted how powerful the integration ceremony was going to be. And everyone seemed to know that coming to this experience had been one of our major missions in this lifetime. Every single person belonged there. Every one was unique and precious and necessary to the whole.

In this atmosphere of silent Oneness, we drove to the temples at Chicanna, not even dimly realizing the explosion that was in store.

Chicanna: Ceremony of Female Integration

Still on a tight schedule—we needed to reach Palenque that evening—and still feeling the residue of emotion from the ceremony at Xpuhil, we all walked the rocky, leaf-strewn paths at Chicanna in search of a place to do our next ceremony. It was even hotter now, and so we looked for shade.

Lionfire told us that Chicanna was very different than other Mayan sites, featuring an elaborate, baroque style of architecture. As we saw, the buildings are small, with doorways portraying the mouth of Itzamna, this time in the form of the Earth monster, whose gaping mouth represents the gateway to Xibalba, the Mayan underworld.

It is said that initiates often feel dimensional shifts here and the sensation of walking among the stars. It is a place of intense dark feminine magic. Chicanna balances and integrates the feminine and masculine energies within women. It was here that we would do the female-energy integration ceremony.

We came to a small pyramid with a courtyard in front of it and a low, hemispherical stone wall near the forest's edge. It was thus shaded by trees.

I asked the women to gather in the area along and in front of the wall and to sit comfortably there in a slight semicircle. Then I asked the men to stand in front of the women in a straight line, from edge to edge of the wall. We were now arranged in the shape of a long, shallow, lidded bowl, with the women inside the bowl and the men forming the lid.

The men held hands, and we sealed off the energy of the space. I constructed the same sacred geometry Platonic octahedrons but with a soft pink light around the women, so that they also could release their energies upwards into the heavens, or Father Sky, and downward into the heart of Mother Earth.

And then I began to speak. I did not know what I was going to say. At first, my directions to the women were pretty much the same as those I had given to the men. And then it came to me to ask the women to use this opportunity to let go of all of the unspeakable things that had been done to women down through the ages of civilization, to release and forgive.

As I said those words, there was a gasp from many of the women. Something changed in our energy field, as though there had been a kind of crack in this human bowl we had made. And then I became silent and let the process begin.

It was quite different than what had happened for the men. The women were trying to allow themselves to contact pain and horror that they had never before been able to look at or feel. One by one, they entered into the reality of what life had been like for womankind in the ages when she was treated as chattel—and worse. So much worse.

The women needed help to continue. So I intervened, asking the men to go to the women, caress their faces, look into their eyes, and give them the tenderness and love and understanding that they were needing at this time. I joined with the men, as we went from woman to woman, comforting them, helping them to get through the huge assaults of emotional pain and grief that they were experiencing and trying to release.

This went on for a long time. Women were screaming, sobbing, with the kind of deep, soul-wrenching grief that they had never before been able to look at. And the men were holding them, consoling them, loving them. A couple of the women went into a fetal position, and they were held and comforted with unbelievable tenderness, like little babies.

One woman told me afterward that she spent the first ten minutes of this process wanting to throw up. This was a new experience for her, she said. She had never understood why people in books talked about feeling nauseous at the sight of desecrations of the human body, but now she realized her lack of understanding had been because she had never, ever been able to "go there" before.

On this day, with the amazing support of the others—the women who had the courage to make first contact with their true feelings and the men of our group who had just come into their own strength—she had finally allowed herself to face and experience feelings that had been shoved aside for lifetime after lifetime. When the full emotional contact finally happened, she was doubled up with it, overwhelmed. And then, as she received comfort from the men, the grief was released, and she felt whole—for the first time in thousands of years.

In Conclusion

Silently and with red eyes from crying, emotionally exhausted, we eased our way into our old familiar bus and headed southwest to Palenque and the final ceremony our group would perform along the spiral of temple sites that had been given to me by Thoth.

I feel that the integration we performed on that day is still happening. I feel that our allowing of the full experience of male and female energy, the release of all the anger, fear, and hatred, is still going on. But on that day in Campeche, I truly do believe we created a pathway for others to follow—a pathway that eventually leads to a new way of being for men and women on Mother Earth.

CHAPTER SEVENTEEN

PALENQUE AND THE LIGHT SHOW AT UXMAL

After the two ceremonies integrating the Divine Masculine and the Divine Feminine, we boarded our bus for the long trip to Palenque. We would spend three nights there. And the next day, although we still had other sites to visit, we would perform our final crystal ceremony at the pyramid site of Palenque.

As we traveled, some of our group expressed concern about the location of our next hotel, for it lay on the outskirts of the city and in order to get there we would have to pass a military inspection point. We'd learned that the delay could take hours. But Divine Spirit was apparently with us, for we were not stopped, and we arrived on time at our hotel.

It was a beautiful resort, with low buildings surrounding a grassy compound, whose walkways were bordered in palm trees and flowering bushes. As we had been so many times before in our visit to Mexico, our group was greeted at the hotel with festive fruit drinks and flowers.

The next morning, after a beautiful breakfast in the resort's large dining hall, we headed for Palenque.

The Palenque Temple Site

Lionfire, in our itinerary, wrote of this site that, besides being the capital of the pineal chakra, Palenque is where the active arteries and ley lines of the Feathered Serpent cross.

A most elegant city, Palenque sits at the edge of the Peten Jungle in the state of Chiapas, a huge area southwest of the Yucatan. It is many things: the Pleiadian Hall of Records, a mystery school of sacred geometry, a major archaeo-astronomical center, and the initiation vortex of the inland West.

Palenque integrates the Kundalini energy throughout all the chakra centers and spirit bodies of the initiate, and because of this the Serpent of Light uses this temple complex to bring in the new Kundalini energy from Chile to the Mayan people, much like a magnifying glass focuses the light of the sun. Therefore, this temple site was of great importance for all that we were doing.

For me, Palenque has a unique mystery among the Mayan temple sites. With exquisite balance, Palenque focuses the energies of the pineal in a way that surpasses that of all other sacred sites on Earth. I was honored to be back within this beautiful, ancient world of such deep psychic understanding.

Once we were admitted, everyone in our group went off exploring this huge site with its many pyramids and stone platforms, while I tried to find the place where Ken and I had put the first crystal. Only after I knew where that crystal was buried could I determine the appropriate spot for our ceremony.

Finding the spot was not easy. Much of what I could see now had been buried under sod when I first visited Palenque. I remembered that, eighteen years before, Ken and I had placed our crystal between a pyramid and a small hill. But the "little hill," as I soon realized, had been excavated. Now it was a little pyramid! As soon as I realized this was where we'd put the crystal, I headed in that direction.

When I got to the little pyramid, I saw that one of our group was sitting on top of it, so I climbed up to talk with him. By the time I got there, he was in meditation, so I left him alone and also began to meditate.

In doing so, I saw that the energy coming off of this pyramid was extremely powerful, moving outward in a spiral that extended for miles. I understood now, as I had not before, why we had placed the crystal in this spot. Clearly, the crystal had been programmed to make use of the site as an antenna to spread its message to the world—especially to the Mayan world.

When I opened my eyes, my friend also opened his. "Do you feel this spiraling energy coming off this little pyramid?" he asked. "I can't believe how immense it is, and yet no one would know just by looking at it."

A Strange Visitor

For the ceremony, I picked a site that was in alignment with this little pyramid and this enormous vortex and the slightly larger pyramid nearby.

As I laid down the altar cloth, oriented to the four directions, and placed a crystal at its center, a few members of our group started to congregate. So I left one of them to watch the altar while I went off to gather up the rest of our wandering pilgrims, scattered in small groups throughout this vast site.

Then I returned and sat down under a tree to wait for everyone to get the message.

I was thinking about the nearby Temple of Inscriptions, where many feel that a Mayan astronaut is depicted on a large interior burial stone. I was actually sitting near the base of this temple, under an old leafy shade tree, remembering that Khan Kha was the architect of this building and how similar it was to his other work of art in Chichen Itza, when an older woman approached me.

She had traveled all the way from South America, she said, in order to be at a ceremony. She didn't know who I was, but she thought I might know where this ceremony was going to be held.

Amazed, I pointed in the direction of the altar. And as she turned to go, I stopped her and asked why she had come all this way.

"I am a shaman," she answered me. "I know that this ceremony is of great importance. This ceremony is known all over Central and South America. Many people are praying for its completion."

I told her who I was, and she came over to me and gave me a long, heartfelt hug. She asked permission to be part of our ceremony, and of course this was granted.

I'd had no idea that anyone except God, our group, and a few Mayan elders knew what we were doing. But I might have known, for word travels from jungle to jungle like a condor in full flight.

The Ceremony of Light

The ceremony began like the others. But very soon after we started, an ancient Mayan elder appeared from within Mother Earth and raised his hands. As he did, a strong energy began to rise up out of the earth.

The energy kept rising until it was the only thing I could feel. It was all around me and within me. And the only thing I could see was white light.

I know something must have been going on in the third-dimensional world, but I can't describe the rest of the ceremony in those terms. I don't even know how long it lasted. I knew nothing beyond this amazing energy of white light. I can't even tell you what the ultimate purpose was!

Perhaps it was my inexperience on these levels that kept me from seeing the greater picture. But what I was left with was a sense that this ceremony had been planned for over a thousand years and that by its completion life was going to be better for the Maya and for the world.

Despite how little I understood of what had actually taken place, I rose up from the ground with a hugely happy heart. Love was in the eyes of all the people. I knew that whatever had happened, it had happened "right." And I also knew that before this trip was over, our little group was going to be shown how much Mother Earth and the Maya appreciated our love and support for them.

How this would happen remained a mystery, but I knew that it would. I walked away from the ceremony at Palenque in deep meditation, my hand over my heart.

Descending into Pacal's Tomb

Meanwhile, a group of us had been extended a privilege, usually given only to the indigenous Mayans, of viewing the ancient tomb of the eighth-century king Pacal. It was important that members of our group take advantage of this privilege, for soon after we left Palenque, Pacal's tomb was to be closed up for all time.

Pacal had been the last of the great Mayan kings and is looked upon as a god. The Mayans believe that after his death—when he had been placed within the sarcophagus that he himself had designed, and covered over with jade—Pacal ascended to divinity, transcending death and becoming reborn within the Mayan pantheon.

Since only a small number would be admitted, I stayed behind, for I had been allowed long ago to be within this tomb for as long as I wished. Here's a description of Pacal's tomb from someone who was there on this journey. They don't discuss the incredible imagery on the surface of the lid of this Mayan king's tomb, but at least one book has been written about it, as it is so mysterious and filled with secret knowledge. I suggest you study it.

> The entryway to Pacal's tomb was by way of a stone stairway that descended into the depths of the Temple of Inscriptions. To get to this stairway, we first had to climb all the way to the top of that pyramid.
>
> Our permit was checked very carefully by a government official, who counted carefully to make sure that only the number specified would be allowed in.
>
> At the entrance to the central stairway, we were met by an old Mayan who, as we learned from Lionfire, had been the guardian of this tomb since long before Mexico began

The lid to Pacal's tomb

protecting the Mayan sites. The government, of course, believed that this man was in their employ—but truly, he had been standing guard there for most of his life, and he served only the gods.

To reach the tomb, we climbed carefully down the inner stairwell, which was dark, narrow, and steep, going down and down and down, all the way to the level of the earth and beyond. The steps were of a pink, marbled stone and had been made utterly smooth by the passing of hundreds upon thousands of devotional feet over the twelve centuries since Pacal's death.

The sarcophagus itself was in a little stone room, protected by an iron grille. We sat there in the stairwell—just a few of us at a time, for the space was tiny—communing respectfully and prayerfully with this great king. The sanctity of Pacal's tomb was palpable.

Then, feeling gratitude and a sense of great peace, we toiled back up the steep, dark stairwell and into the light of day.

Dancing in the Dream

Before I tell you about our next miraculous-seeming experience, I need to say something about the Mayan site known as Tikal.

To all of the Maya, Tikal represents the eighth chakra, the one that's one hand length above the crown. This chakra holds our mystical connection with All That Is and is the opening to the higher levels of consciousness. Ken and I had placed a crystal there, and I felt the energy of Tikal to be higher than any other Mayan site I'd visited, even Palenque.

But Tikal was in Guatemala, and our group could not go there. Instead, Spirit had provided us with Nadia and Adam, two beautiful beings who lived in Guatemala and who, like the lady from South America, had felt called to be with us on our sacred journey. Although they had not signed up for the tour, Adam and Nadia were a part of us. And they knew the moment I asked them that it was their task to place a last crystal at Tikal, which would transmit our intentions and prayers to that final temple.

Strangely, we had not seen Nadia and Adam for the past couple of days. Then they showed up at the ceremony in Palenque, and we found out why they'd been gone. They had actually traveled all the way home to Guatemala in order to bring back for us a group of musicians whose playing was as much sacred rite as it was entertainment. The group was called Kan Nal, and they were there to play for us that night under the stars.

We all gathered outside after dinner, at a place in the resort that had been set aside for us. And as the torches were lit, the music started, slowly, softly, one rustic instrument sounding a call, another joining in, the toc-toc of a wooden drum, the haunting trill of a flute, the occasional shrill sound of a jungle bird.

As the music grew in volume and complexity, a priestess passed banana leaves to each of us. Upon these leaves she laid kernels of corn, crystals, and other natural objects sacred to the Mayans. Choosing our own time, we each brought this bounty as a sacrifice to the fire.

Now the music took on a hypnotic beat, and a member of our group, one of the many gifted shamans who were with us, took up some of the lighted torches and began a fire dance, moving with the music, twirling the lighted torches like batons.

We all began to move upon the gravel "dance floor," swaying ecstatically to the haunting, organic sounds of Kan Nal.

The dancing went on into the night. I am told that I danced barefoot for an hour on that gravel. I suppose I did, but I might as well have been dancing on clouds!

We needed this celebration. And it was given to us. All in perfect time.

We're All in the Same Boat

The next day, we traveled southeast to the border with Guatemala. We would return that night to our hotel in Palenque.

Along the way, we visited Bonampak, where there are astounding ancient murals depicting Mayan life and ceremonies in great detail.

But our major destination was the Jaguar Temple at Yaxchilan. It is a fantastic temple built on both sides of the river. One side is in Mexico and the other side is in Guatemala. The Mexicans have excavated their side of the site, while the Guatemalans have not allowed anyone to touch their side of the temple complex.

We went there knowing that a dam was scheduled to be built along the river where these temples were situated and that very soon this precious site, along with all the others along that river, would disappear forever beneath the waters.

The Final Sign

On the last day of our Mayan journey, we would visit Uxmal one more time. We needed to be there at a certain time, in order to view the light show that Uxmal puts on each evening. We would end our journey on that note. It was supposed to be a beautiful presentation, and Uxmal was on our way back to Merida, completing the enormous circle of temples we had been visiting.

But there was grumbling from the group saying "Why are we ending our journey at some hokey, touristy, technological exposition?" Basically, they thought it was a stupid idea.

I couldn't answer their question, as I only knew that we were "supposed" to view the light show at Uxmal and that it was really important for us to be there. So against the rebellion, we continued.

At Uxmal, there are restaurants and shops, and no one is allowed to visit the pyramids until the light show is over, so we just waited and shopped or had a bite to eat. Everyone was still wondering why we had to end our incredible journey at a tacky little light show in Uxmal.

At exactly the time when the Uxmal light show would have started, as we all stood waiting for it to begin—*it* began. First a drizzle of rain, then the sky opened up with a downpour that quickly turned into a torrent. Lightning streaked across the sky and thunder crashed all around us for two hours. This was a serious storm. Mother Earth had decided to put on her own light show where we could watch it under the cover of the outdoor building complex at Uxmal.

We had arrived in the Yucatan in the midst of a long, long drought. Already, we'd seen rain—a short storm on the Caribbean after Tulum and a slight spattering on the way south—but nothing like this. The Mayan god Chac was honoring us, and from our way of seeing, Chac was telling us that our ceremonial work was accepted into the Maya world.

I can still see us there, soaked to the skin by slashing rain that came right in under the outdoor roof—all of us knowing finally why we were there in Uxmal, laughing, dancing, hugging each other, tears of joy on every face, as we watched and listened to our own personal light show brought to us by Mother Earth and Father Sky.

As we entered Merida on our way to the hotel, the streets ran ten inches deep with water, and our bus appeared like a ship in the night, waves plowing off the bow, heading home from a long voyage at sea.

Our hearts were wide open and again, one more time, we were of One Heart and the grids around the Earth were closer to perfect balance.

CHAPTER EIGHTEEN

THE INCAN INVITATION TO PERU

The angels told me before these journeys began that Peru and the Inca Empire would be one of the places where ceremony would be needed to bring balance to the world. When I was in the Yucatan directly after the ceremony at Chichen Itza, an Incan priest and shaman approached me and asked to speak.

He was a young man in his late 30s, dressed in full ceremonial Incan robes, with feathers in his hair and a beautiful smile. His father, also an Incan shaman, had sent him to talk with me. The young shaman told me that his people had a prophecy that a group of people—he called it a "world circle"—would come to Peru from all over the world and heal his people of something they had done in ancient times.

He was emphatic that his father was the one asking me to assemble this "world circle" and that he wanted me to come to Peru to perform ceremony with him and other shamans. But he also said that his father was not sure if the group I would bring to Peru would actually be the one in their prophecy. He said that would have to be determined by the Incan elders once the circle arrived in Peru.

Incan Shaman at Chichen Itza

I told him I would meditate about what he had to say, and if it was in Divine Order, we would arrive sometime in 2004. We gave each other a big hug, connecting our hearts, both knowing it was now all up to Great Spirit.

Back home in the States, the two angels spoke to me at length about how important this journey would be. They said the Inca had also left many of their people inside the Earth as they came into the Fourth World, and that this division within their culture had to be healed to balance the Unity Consciousness Grid. The Inca could not perform this healing without external assistance anymore than the Anasazi or Maya could.

The angels also said that this imbalance within the Unity Consciousness Grid was more severe than anything we had been witness to before. Further, they said that with the successful completion of this journey, the Serpent of Light's Kundalini energy would, for the first time, really be able to move into the hearts of the world's females, especially in the areas of Chile and Peru. It would align the females in almost perfect position to begin their teaching of mankind (womankind) in the ways of the Light, even while mankind (womankind) continued to live in the darkest part of the darkest cycle, named Kali Yuga by the Hindus.

The angels told me that the final ceremony in Peru would be for the Inca to remember their knowledge, memories, and wisdom—something the angels said was essential if humanity were to continue into higher consciousness. According to the Inca priest, it was prophesied that their knowledge, memories, and wisdom would return to them at the moment when this world circle came to their land.

The angels also spoke about a ceremony that we had to perform on the Island of the Sun in Bolivia on Lake Titicaca. In it, the power of the old cycle of 13,000 years, led by the male, would be transferred to the female so that she could complete her work on Earth and lead the world back into the Light.

In chapter ten I spoke about a similar ceremony on the island of Kauai. That ceremony was the true and actual transference of power from the male to the female on the fourth dimension. Now it had to be performed on Earth as it was in heaven.

This was the only information I was given about the three ceremonies. I knew the first ceremony had to take place at Machu Picchu and the second had to be performed at the Island of the Sun, but I had no idea where the third ceremony was to take place. I knew at all times I had to be surrounded by Trust and the absolute knowing that Great Spirit lived all around me and within me.

So I told Diane Cooper, my manager, to make sure that the first place we went to was Machu Picchu and that somehow we ended up on the Island of the Sun. Other that that, I left her free to make up the itinerary in any way she wanted. On July 24, 2004, the journey began.

Machu Picchu

This journey was called the Call of the Condor, the bird that represents South American consciousness. Our group assembled in Lima, Peru, from twenty-two nations around the world, and amazingly enough, everyone arrived on time. This was a first.

As I had witnessed in previous groups, these were not ordinary people. They had been meditating and studying esoteric teachings from almost every tradition in the world and were well prepared to be of service to Mother Earth, or as they say in South America, *Pachamama*.

By the second day, we were on the road, traveling into the Urubamba Valley and heading for the Andean village of Ollantaytambo, where we were going to catch a two-hour train to Machu Picchu.

I had taken this train in the mid-1980s when I was studying with the Egyptian guide Thoth. He had led me to a Quechuan Indian named Narciso, who was the individual to find the Inca Trail that ran roughly forty miles from outside the beautiful city of Cusco to Machu Picchu. Narciso became our guide to take my small group of ten people over this grueling trail over 14,000 foot-high mountain passes, dropping down to Machu Picchu at about 9,000 feet. It was so great!

At that time the Inca Trail had only just been discovered, and tourists hadn't found it yet. The train that we were about to board now had a stopping place for people to get off who wanted to make the journey on foot, but in the 1980s, there was nothing. We had to talk the conductor into stopping in an undefined patch of railway high up in the mountains. He had said okay, but that no matter what, he would take off again in exactly sixty seconds. Back then, the train was filled with people, singing songs at the top of their voices and playing instruments. Chickens, dogs, and goats were traveling first class along with their human friends. The train was so filled with living things, one could hardly move. We all had to throw our backpacks out the window and jump out after them just as the train took off again.

Things have changed considerably in the last twenty years. With hoards of tourists arriving every day, the money that flows in changes everything.

We arrived at Aguas Calientes to discover this tiny village transformed into a tropical fiesta village with hot springs and quaint tourist shops. Whatever you wanted, the natives could get it for you. I have to admit, it was beautiful, even delightful.

And, looming 2,000 feet above this little village, almost straight up, Machu Picchu floated majestically in the clouds.

The Incan priesthood was waiting for us and had prepared themselves for three days before we arrived. They had positioned themselves in the surrounding mountains where they could observe us without our knowing. They had been in meditation without food or water, praying that our group was the one that would fulfill their prophecy.

The Incan shamans listen to their inner guidance, but it is their tradition that anything of this magnitude must be proven by signs that are outside of human control. They needed three signs before they could accept us.

All I knew was that we had to begin at Machu Picchu and that the first ceremony had to take place there. After the long winding bus ride to the top of the mountain, we assembled near the opening to Machu Picchu. After a simple opening prayer to bless our beginning, I stepped through the archway along with our humble group of consciousness explorers.

As we entered this sacred space, an enormous condor flew directly above us. One of the shamans later told me this was an incredible sign to the Inca priesthood. They had not seen a condor over Machu Picchu in more than twenty years. But this sign was not enough. There had to be three.

When we entered the grounds, we went in different directions, each following our heart. But we agreed we would all meet back together at a certain time to fulfill the healing ceremony for the Incan land and people.

Many of the group decided to climb Waina Picchu, a phallic mountain towering another 2,000 feet above the primary site. From the top of this sacred site, you appear to be sitting in the middle of a perfect circle of mountains, and if you're sensitive, you can feel the intense energy flowing out of the mountain's crest and spreading over the entire area. I remember when I first climbed this mountain years ago I found it difficult to leave, as the energy supercharged my body and spirit.

There are two places in Machu Picchu where the ancient libraries and records are kept, sitting right out in plain sight. All over Peru are temples, and in the middle of most of these temples will be a rock that has been carved into what looks like a stone sculpture. But these rocks are much more than that. With a bit of sensitivity, you can sit next to one of these "record keepers" and, by running your hand over a particular curve on the rock, the detailed images placed there hundreds or thousands of years before will appear in your inner vision. You will know by seeing in detailed images what the person who carved that part of the rock had placed into the records.

It is for this reason that the floor of the Inca observatory is also a rock "sculpture." In order for the Inca to perceive such astronomical changes as the Precession of the Equinox, they had to record phenomena and changes in the night sky over hundreds and thousands of years, far beyond the life of a single human being. What the Inca created with these rock record keepers equals the accuracy achieved by our modern computers.

A predetermined area was chosen for our first ceremony, and as the time approached, people from our group began to arrive. Finally, the whole group was assembled.

I laid a Peruvian woven cloth—bright red and thin strips of black—on the ground and placed four crystals in the four directions. I brought a special crystal for the centerpiece and then opened up the ceremony for the participants to place on the altar whatever objects they had brought. Soon the cloth was filled with sacred objects. Though this is very much in the tradition of the Inca, the objects they use are programmed in ways most people are unaware of.

Once the altar was ready, we began the ceremony. And at the very second that we began to set the energies of the four directions, again a giant condor flew over our group. In fact, it hovered directly above the altar for a full minute before flying on.

The Incan shamans observed this sign with great joy, for this was the third sign they were looking for to prove to themselves that we were the international group they had prophesized to come and save their people. What was the second sign? I don't know, the shamans would not tell us except to say that it was observed.

One of the group took this photo of the condor as is flew over us.

We finished this ceremony by creating an enormous energy vortex that allowed the Inca trapped inside the Earth to come onto the

The condor flew over as a sign.

surface of the planet, giving them the opportunity to be born into today's world. It also gave them the opportunity to move with the rest of the human population into the higher consciousness of ascension that is about to take place. And most importantly, it geometrically altered the Unity Grid above the Earth, so that it can be a more perfect vessel for the transformation of human consciousness. This, in turn, allows the Serpent of Light's Kundalini energy to be utilized by humanity on a higher level. All things are connected.

Soon after this ceremony, one of the Inca shamans appeared to us and said that the three signs had materialized. He then asked us if we would come with him to be part of an Incan ceremony involving the eagle and the condor. Of course, we gave him our permission.

The shaman led us down the side of the mountain that Machu Picchu perches on to a secret crystal cave, where he asked us to move in close to him as he performed this ceremony. At one point I found myself in front of this shaman; he gave me a condor feather, and I gave him an eagle feather. The eagle feather represented the consciousness of North America.

After this ceremony, word spread throughout the indigenous Peruvian world and farther. It seemed that everywhere we went, Peruvian shamans, both male and female, came out of the jungle to ask us to be part of their ceremonies. This happened seven unbelievable times. Though these ceremonies were important in themselves, they belong to the Inca, so I am going to keep them secret—with the exception of one of them.

CHAPTER NINETEEN

THE ISLAND OF THE MOON AND THE ISLAND OF THE SUN

Life truly is amazing! What happened on the small island in the middle of Lake Titicaca could never have been planned, as it was perfectly timed and performed with the precision of a surgeon's knife. We were merely witnesses.

Our great silver bird landed in La Paz, Bolivia, and we slowly made our way to a village with a European feel called Copacabana, on the edge of Lake Titicaca. The Island of the Sun, where I knew our second ceremony had to take place, was within reach, but Diane had arranged for us to go to the Island of the Moon first. This seemed logical to me, since the islands were only perhaps six or seven kilometers apart.

I didn't expect that anything would happen on the Island of the Moon, though I knew there was a sacred site there called the Temple of the Priestesses. It was said to be one of the most powerful centers of feminine energy on Earth, and we had been asked to participate in a native ceremony called the Offering to the Mother. Even so, my thoughts remained on the ceremony that I knew was to take place on the Island of the Sun.

We were greeted by the oldest woman on the island, Grandmother Mamani, who set up to perform her ceremony in a small house on the edge of a cliff overlooking this incredible lake that feels more like an ocean. Only a few could be inside this one-room house at a time, so most of us waited outside, taking turns entering into the ceremonial area. We were told that the reason she was doing this in an enclosed space was because she was afraid of what the other elders would think if they knew she was performing such a sacred ceremony with non-natives.

This was a long ceremony lasting over two hours, and I didn't understand what its purpose was until just before we left, when she told me. This was a ceremony held only every 13,000 years, for the purpose of transferring power from the male to the female!

The truth of the moment was that here we were on the Island of the Moon, the female island, transferring power from the male to the female, and immediately afterward, we were going to perform the same ceremony on the Island of the Sun, the male island.

Wow! Pachamama is alive!

As our small band of boats carried us to the Island of the Sun, I remembered the events of the Peruvian woman on the island of Kauai who received the skeletal crystal from the Polynesian male who had guarded the Earth for the previous 13,000 years. When she left that fourth-dimensional ceremony, she traveled here, to Lake Titicaca, where she placed the crystal exactly equidistant between the Island of the Moon and the Island of the Sun, deep in the water.

And there, directly in front of us now, was the beam of ultraviolet light coming out of the lake. Without saying a word to the boat driver, we passed directly through this beam of light, and again, I realized the truth of Universal Consciousness. Everything is alive. Everything is conscious. There are no accidents. We are living the unfoldment of the cosmic DNA that slowly reveals the intentions of Great Spirit. There is nothing to do but to be in the moment.

I was brought back to this reality by the boat driver saying, "Where do you want to land on the island?"

I hadn't thought of this, so I said, "Where are all the people?"

He pointed to the right side of the island.

I yelled out, "Okay, then go to the left side of the island."

We moved around a huge rock in the water that technically was an island in itself. There were no houses or signs of life anywhere.

"Over there!" I pointed to a jagged rocky point.

Our five boats crept up to the land, and we found a way to anchor to the rocks. As we carefully disembarked onto the land, we found human-made steps emerging from deep below the water, leading up the side of this hill. We followed the steps to see where they would lead.

At the top of the steps we found a round, flat area providing an awesome view of the lake. There were no signs of humans or human activity to interfere with what we were about to do. It seemed a perfect place to perform our second ceremony, so without further ado, we prepared ourselves.

Just as we were about to begin, two young women, perhaps in their twenties, appeared out of nowhere and approached us.

"I am from England, and my friend here is from Scotland," one said. "And we knew in our meditations that you were going to give this ceremony today on this island. We traveled all the way to be here. Would you allow us to join your group?"

What could I say? Not even I had known where this ceremony was going to take place until perhaps thirty minutes before. The Island of the Sun was a big place. How could they have found us so precisely? I figured anyone who could do what they had done was supposed to be there.

"Please, take your place in the circle with the women," I said.

The four oldest grandmothers were chosen to sit in the four directions, with the oldest grandmother to the east. The rest of the females were to sit around them, enclosing the altar. Around them was a standing circle of the men, holding hands, protecting the inner female energy. With the blessing of the four directions, the ceremony began.

The angels had instructed me earlier that morning to bring my drum, which I had used in ceremonies for over twenty years. I began to burn cedar and sage and walked around the outside of the group in a clockwise direction, purifying the people and the energies of the land. On my second time around the heartbeat drumming began to bring everyone's breathing into sync.

At one point in the ceremony, I asked the men to surrender their spiritual power to the inner circle of the women, for now they were to lead us for the next 13,000 years. A few men found it hard to do this. It was a struggle of a kind they had not experienced, but eventually all the men allowed the women to lead.

When the last man turned over his power to the women, the angels appeared to me and said, "Now it is your turn. Give your drum to the Grandmother of the East as an outward sign of the release of male power."

Without hesitation, I went to the Grandmother of the East. "With this male drum as a symbol," I said to her, "we ask you to finish this ceremony, and from now on, you are to lead this group in ceremony." She took the drum, began a slow even beat, and continued the ceremony to completion.

I wish I could remember her words. I cannot. They went into my heart to be secretly remembered at another time, perhaps. I knew that history was being lived as the waves of the lake sang their millions-of-years-old song of beauty, the wind surrounding and caressing each of us. We could all feel the blessing of the Mother with each breath of life. And then it was complete.

CHAPTER TWENTY

THE HIDDEN CITY OF CAHUA CHI

In South America you always must expect the unexpected. The last time I was there, back in the 1980s, when I'd been led to find Naciso, the Shining Path rebels had taken over most of Peru, and we were constantly being stopped, our lives being threatened. But once inside the country, there is not much you can do.

On this journey we were supposed to fly out of La Paz to visit the mysterious Nasca lines, but the entire airport in La Paz was shut down because of some political dispute. We had no choice but to hire a bus to drive us to the coast.

What we didn't realize at the time was that we were going to have to pass over the Andes Mountains at altitudes of 15,000 feet and more. This can be a problem with elderly people because of low oxygen. As it turned out, that was not a problem for our group, but another problem did become apparent. Many people lost their hearing for one to three days. I never heard the phrase, "What did ya say?" so much in my life.

But life goes on. After a long, but beautiful trip through the Peruvian landscape, we found our hotel and had time to rest up for the evening. Our group met in a native restaurant where we had to wait for our tables to be free. I was sitting at the bar drinking some coffee in an effort to wake myself up a little, when an Inca shaman entered the room. His attire attracted the attention of almost everyone, with the two feathers jutting out of his hair straight to the sky, the tan leather tunic to his knees, and the massive necklaces around his neck made of bones and crystals. He appeared to be lost or looking for someone by the way he kept searching the room.

Beside him was his son, a young man about ten years old and obviously following his father's path. He looked like a smaller version of his dad, wide-eyed, but strong and no fear.

Without any prompting, his father zeroed in on me, walked up and sat down. He offered me his hand, said his name, said that he knew we were going to perform ceremony tomorrow at Cahua Chi, and asked to be part of this ceremony.

I asked him how he knew we were going to give a ceremony at Cahua Chi, because at that moment I didn't know.

"Everyone knows you are going to give a ceremony at Cahua Chi," he said. "It is our prophecy."

"Do you understand the history of Cahua Chi?" he asked.

I shook my head no. Actually, I had never even heard of Cahua Chi before and had no idea what it represented.

He slid his chair closer to me and began to speak. "Long ago, more than 500 years, Cahua Chi was a huge city with many, many pyramids and temples. It was a modern, powerful city that held great respect in the whole region.

"But the Spanish conquistadors were about to find this city, and the people knew that Cahua Chi would be lost to them. So the shamans and priests all came together to find a way to save their city. It was decided that it could not be saved at that time, so the holy ones prayed to the wind to help them. They asked the wind to completely bury Cahua Chi in sand so that the conquistadors would not find their beautiful city.

"Now, Drunvalo, you must understand that only 100 meters away on the other side of the river are the Nasca lines. They are the reason that Cahua Chi was built in this location. Cahua Chi was a place where people would come from everywhere to be in the energy of the Nasca lines. It was considered a holy city.

"And the Nasca lines were created by removing rocks from the topsoil leaving a slightly different color surface exposed to the air. So, all of these patterns that are found in this desert are only a centimeter deep. But because it never rains here, these patterns have been preserved for thousands of years.

"So when the shamans and priests prayed to the wind, they asked the wind not to touch the Nasca lines or the other side of the river. And then they prayed that long in the future this city would be reopened at the right moment in history to bring back the Inca's knowledge, wisdom, and experience to the Inca that would be alive at that time. They knew then that this city would reveal special knowledge that would help the entire world.

"The shamans and priests then set up the altars in the temples and pyramids with sacred objects in patterns in such a way that when the city was rediscovered in the future, their future Incan brothers and sisters would know by seeing and holding the objects that were left for them, and they would remember their ancient knowledge, wisdom, and understanding.

"And then the wind began to blow and with it the sand was carried. The storm lasted for weeks, and in the end the entire city of Cahua Chi was completely buried with sand to a depth of more than sixty feet above the highest pyramid. But on the other side of the river, no more than 100 meters from one of the pyramids, not one grain of sand landed on the Nasca lines. To this day, they are untouched and perfect, but the city itself was lost to human memory. The Spanish conquistadors knew that Cahua Chi existed, but they were never able to find it.

"And so it was decided 500 years ago that the rediscovery and opening of this ancient city would align with a ceremony that would be performed by a circle of people that were coming from all over the world. Drunvalo, we believe this group is the one."

Once more he asked, "Can my son and I have permission to be present in the ceremony that you will perform?"

I turned to face him fully and said, "My friend, I am not the one who will perform this ceremony. It will be the oldest grandmother within this group. But I know that she will allow you and your son to be present. After all, the city of Cahua Chi belongs to you, not us."

Early the next morning we all boarded the bus, along with our two new friends, and we headed out into the desert. The bus only had room for one more person, so the shaman's son decided to sit on my lap for the ride. He just cuddled in, and I felt like we had known each other all our lives.

We drove along endless sand dunes that were a hundred or more feet high. The sand appeared to be getting deeper as we moved farther into the desert. In my mind I knew that under this sand was a gleaming city of great power for this time we live. It was a strange feeling knowing something almost no one else in the world knew.

Without the river to our right-hand side and the trees and growth that clung to the water, there would have been nothing but sand on the horizon. This young man and I kind of fell into a trance watching the sand continuously pass our view. We both became very quiet.

After perhaps twenty miles, at what seemed like any other place in the sand, the bus pulled over to the side and shut down its motors. We were there, I guessed. Once out of the bus, I looked up to the apex of a huge sand dune. It had been cleared by perhaps thirty feet or so, revealing the very top of an ancient stone pyramid. This was no small pyramid. The sand was deep here, and if this pyramid went down to ground level, it must have been a couple of hundred feet high.

This pyramid was just the beginning of the exploration and exposing of the city of Cahua Chi. According to the archeologists there, this was the tip of the iceberg. The city stretched as far as one could see away from the river. We were standing there at the very moment this lost Incan city was being reborn.

We climbed a long time, up the hot sand, past the pyramid that had been exposed, to another pyramid-shaped sand dune. We knew what lay beneath the sand. The wind had blown a flat place on top of this dune, and it was there that the grandmother decided to perform this last ceremony, a ceremony that the angels had told me was for the Incans to remember their knowledge, wisdom, and experience. It was so perfect I couldn't speak. Obviously, Mother Earth was leading this group, not me.

The grandmother laid the Peruvian cloth on the ground directly on top of this enormous ancient pyramid and began to lay out the power objects in the four directions. The women were in the center around the altar, and the men stood on the outside, protecting the women. The Incan shaman stood with us in the outer circle, but his son was asked to come into the inner circle with the women. While the grandmother prepared for the ceremony, the shaman lit herbs in a seashell and walked around our group, blessing us and purifying the energies.

The women had practiced a ceremony for this place with songs and words to be used. As the ceremony began, I realized that this was the first ceremony to be given by women in the energy of the new cycle that would continue for the next 13,000 years. I was witnessing the prophecy being fulfilled.

And then again, the miracle happened. In the middle of the ceremony, a condor flew over the altar, circled back, and hovered above us for several minutes, just as the one had done in Machu Picchu. We pointed our cameras to the sky.

As the grandmother finished the ceremony, completion on many levels of life was achieved, even as a new cycle began. The women of the Earth were beginning to lead, to take us all to a new height of consciousness, just as the prophecies had predicted.

Finally, as we slowly made our way back to the bus, the shaman and his son came over, and both of them gave me a big hug. They said thank you to me, but really to the group. At that moment, once again, the condor flew over the circle, and this time released a single feather from his body. It began to float to Earth.

The feather circled in the sky for several minutes with the three of us following its pathway, wondering where it would land. And where it landed was yet another demonstration of the consciousness of the Earth. The feather touched ground directly in front of the shaman.

He carefully picked up the condor feather, looked at me, then turned to his son and gave it to him with these words: "Son, this is

Incan Shaman and his son in Peru

yours. You are the future and the condor will help guide you all of your life. When you see this feather, remember me, but also remember all of your ancestors who have given you life. They are inside of you."

I walked down the hill with them by my side, feeling such gratitude for being in the presence of the living magical history of this third planet from the sun. May Great Spirit bless this Incan empire, and may it some day live again its once great glory.

CHAPTER TWENTY-ONE

THE WAITAHA AND THE MAORI OF AOTEAROA (NEW ZEALAND)

Long ago a Native American friend, Mary Thunder, called and asked if she had permission to bring a Maori by the name of Mac Ruka to my house. He wanted to speak with me. She said he was considered the spiritual head of the Maori and that he had journeyed all the way from New Zealand to invite me to his land, which he called Aotearoa.

I told the story in my last book, *Living in the Heart*, but didn't give it as much attention as it deserved. I didn't realize at the time who this man was, and how important his lineage was to the ascension of the human race. Mac asked that I visit New Zealand, saying that more would be revealed then. But the trip proved impossible as life unfolded, until 2007. Unfortunately, Mac died in the late 90s, and I never was able to meet with him again.

Mac was involved in the creation of the book *The Song of the Waitaha* and other books about the Waitaha. It is my understanding that he was also behind the writing of the movie *The Whale Rider*, which won so many international awards.

I met Mac in 1994, but now, thirteen years later, I decided that I should go to New Zealand to make good on my agreement to someday visit his tribe. Diane and I planned to go there with another world circle, this time of fifty-five people from nineteen countries.

The way it came into my consciousness to actually make this trip was interesting. A copy of *The Song of the Waitaha* by Barry Brailsford of New Zealand had been given to me. While reading this book, I realized that the Waitaha were speaking about the very way of Dreaming from the Heart that I was experiencing in my life and that I had written about in *Living in the Heart*. It was a way of dreaming that actually changed the outer world that we walk around within.

I discovered while researching my book that almost nothing was written about the Dreaming from the Heart or the Sacred Space of the Heart, except the Upanishads from ancient India and the small book connected to the Jewish Torah called *The Secret Cavern of the Heart*. Other than these two books, all teachings that I am aware of on this subject have always been contained in oral traditions. Both books were ancient, but here from New Zealand was a new book describing this experience in detail and from an ancient native tribe called the Waitaha, the Water Bearers.

In their own words, the Waitaha were native people that are considered Maori, but from their way of seeing, they were actually much older—reaching back into the time of Mu or Lemuria 60,000 plus years ago. Actually, I believe that 60,000 years ago was the end of Lemuria and that the beginning of the Waitaha lineage could be extended to 130,000 years ago. They realize that they cannot prove this statement with science, but within their own oral stories and songs, this knowing is alive.

I was intrigued. And, as the angels guide my life, a few years ago, right after reading *The Song of the Waitaha*, I traveled to Switzerland to visit with a man named Shin Shiva, a guru teaching Kundalini. While eating lunch with him in his home, I mentioned the Waitaha, as the content of this book was still moving through my mind.

Shin looked at me with surprise and then told one of his disciples to bring Ojasvin to the room. A few minutes later, a young handsome man with dark skin and black hair quietly entered the room. His presence was elegant.

"You mentioned the Waitaha, and here standing in your presence, I introduce to you Ojasvin," Shin said. "He is Waitaha."

Ojasvin gave me a warm, slow hug, and we began to converse. Within minutes he was crying, saying to me, "I haven't found anyone outside my tribe that understands the Dreaming of the Heart. It is so good to know you."

We talked for some time, and then I left for France where I was to give a workshop. But I never forgot this man. This I remember to be 2003.

As this journey to Aotearoa began to take shape, the angels said that I would learn much on this journey and that what I would learn must be part of this book I am writing. In fact, to leave it out would be to never disclose the whole truth about the Serpent of Light, for the Waitaha hold the secret piece to the world ascension process. They hold it in their DNA.

I invited Ojasvin—his Waitaha name is Kingi—to come with us, as the angels said he would be "invaluable to bridge across the world of the heart to the world of the mind." Kingi accepted his Waitaha name for this journey and did become an invaluable light to this whole group.

The Queen of the Maori

Though we were invited to New Zealand by Mac Ruka, we received another invitation, which erased all doubt that we were meant to be there and involved in traditional ceremony. The queen of the Maori, Teahairangi Ka-ahu, which means "the Dawn Light who Opens the Way to the Heavens," personally invited us to her beautiful islands, which all Maoris know as Aotearoa.

Only two weeks later, she died. But her son took over and allowed our group to continue.

The burial of Queen Teahairangi Ka-ahu became a national event televised throughout New Zealand. Her holy passing brought the nation together as one. Befitting her status, her traditional burial included moving her by a boat, called a "Waka"—a handmade, hand-carved boat capable of traversing the Pacific Ocean at speeds of up to thirty-five knots—slowly downstream to her resting place on the side of a sacred mountain by this river.

I would like to bless her in these writings with the love in our hearts, and I wish her a safe passage into the higher worlds.

The Journey Begins

We all first met each other in Auckland, as the silver birds from the four winds slowly delivered each of us to this one location. Such beautiful faces, open and ready for whatever may come! And such courage! We looked into each other's eyes and knew that something incredible was about to happen, but I don't think any of us knew just how deep this experience was going to be.

Besides the people on the journey, there were many authors, spiritual investigators, archeologists, and tour leaders working behind the scenes helping to bring this world group into the remote world of the native peoples. Most people on this journey had no idea what kind of planning it took to arrange this, and for that matter neither did I. But I knew that without the help of the New Zealand community, our journey would have been only an ordinary tourist trip.

Two Maori were assigned to be our guides and to stay with us as we moved about the country. Little did we know who they really were. One was a Maori grandmother named Makuini Ruth Tai. She asked us to call her Ruth, and we all very quickly brought her into our hearts. The other guide was a Maori man named Herini. He embodied the male Maori principles that have thrived on the islands for thousands of years, and his guidance into the Maori world was impeccable and necessary.

By the time our journey was complete, these two Maori had shown us the heart of the Maori pathway, as they helped us to understand and live an ancient way that is a long lost memory to most of the world's population.

Thank you both for being alive.

Carving that shows traditional
tattoo patterns

The Waitaha

On the second night, we arrived in the heart of a green, hilly valley. It was warm and inviting, as children, dogs, and young men ran to our bus to see who had come from all over the world to this tiny isolated spot deep within a small island separating Antarctica from the rest of the Pacific Ocean.

We were as curious as they were as to what was about to happen. They told us later they had never seen so many people, especially from so many different countries. And we had never seen anyone that looked like them. From ancient times, the Waitaha have tattooed their faces and bodies, creating images of both beauty and fear. To meet them on the street would cause most people to try to protect themselves, but if you meet them in the heart, theirs is a beauty that rivals even the lotus flowers.

We unloaded our pretentious and never-ending baggage beside the bus and removed the bus from the holy ground. Within minutes the sacred ceremony began.

Ruth asked all of the oldest women to line up with her in the front, with the younger females behind them, and finally the men behind them in the last row. We waited in silence.

Six grandmothers dressed in waterlike blue shawls made a straight line on the steps of the long-house, the traditional place where the Waitaha and the Maori would sleep and dream together. Whenever two or more tribes came together, they would meet each other in strict protocol based on thousands of years of tradition. The entire ceremony would continue under these laws until the different tribes were merged and they became one. At that moment, we all would become Waitaha.

The grandmothers began to sing in Waitaha a song of welcome, their voices loud and reaching the hills behind us. Then the Maori grandmother Ruth and the women of our group sang back to them in Maori the response that is necessary to fulfill the tradition. We had been trained by Ruth on the bus as we drove to this valley. The singing would move back and forth between the grandmothers as they slowly moved closer and closer to each other.

With this part of the tradition complete, we flowed like water into the long-house for the next stage of the ceremony. The Waitaha carefully placed us in specific prearranged places within the long-house. Then the Waitaha men spoke to us first, mostly in Waitaha but sometimes in English, speaking from their hearts. After each man spoke, he would sing us a song or play music from one of their instruments. It was their way. When someone spoke from their mind, they rephrased what was said by putting their intensions into music from their heart. It was beautiful.

Since I was considered the chief of my "tribe from nineteen countries," I was asked to speak to the elders and the group. But before I did, I asked permission for Kingi to be by my side. I would speak to them, but I wanted him to sing to them in Waitaha to more deeply reach their hearts.

I remember saying to them that they were the original people of planet Earth, coming from Lemuria, and that within their memories, knowledge, and ancient DNA, were the secrets to healing the Earth and enabling mankind to continue to higher levels of consciousness. I knew also that the Dreaming from the Heart was the true secret to man's ascension, and no one alive understood this better than the Waitaha, not even the Kogi Mamos of Columbia.

Unknowing, modern man is walking around "inside" of his mind, thinking that the stars and planets are "outside" of himself. But this is all an illusion. In truth, according to the Waitaha and the Kogi, there is nothing in the external world whatsoever. It is all simply a hologram that our mind is creating. After all, any scientist knows that our only proof that the stars and the planets actually exist is based upon the electrical impulses within our brain and body, our five senses. But sensing does not prove that anything exists; it actually proves nothing.

The Waitaha believe—and so do many other indigenous races, including the ancient Hindus, who call the reality "Maya," meaning illusion or "not true"—that the outer reality is not real. Reality to them exists only within the heart and specifically within a sacred space within the heart, not the mind. I realize this is very hard to believe, let alone understand, but if the Waitaha are right, soon we will know the truth.

I was beginning to realize that the Serpent of Light that was beaming its powerful rays out from Chile over South America was also beaming out from high in the Andes Mountains across the Pacific Ocean to these original people. I realized this as I spoke to them, looking into their eyes, and it took my breath away. It completely changed my understanding of what was happening in the world with this powerful Earth Kundalini energy.

Mother Earth is so intelligent. She placed her spiritually awaking energy in exactly the right location to have maximum effect on all of her people.

When I finished talking, Kingi sang to the Waitaha in their own language with the intention that I had spoken. Kingi is a master translator and one beautiful singer.

This way of being and perceiving began little by little to change our Western mind-sets and soften our hearts to experience another culture in a direct and intimate manner. We began to melt and turn into little children.

With the words exchanged, we moved to the next part of the ceremony, where each person in our group (or tribe, as the Waitaha saw us) greeted each person in their tribe—men, women, and children—with the Maori greeting of touching their foreheads and noses together and breathing together. It is called the Hongi.

After each person of each tribe has greeted the other, it is traditional to eat a meal together as one big family. So we moved to a kitchen area, where the Waitaha had created a beautiful meal for us. We all shuffled ourselves up to meet each other, pray, eat our meal, and, in Waitaha style, sing songs, play music, and dance throughout the meal. It was more like a party than a ceremony.

Drunvalo and Kingi performing hongi

As the day was quickly fading, we set up beds, about eighty of them in straight lines against the walls, and prepared to go to sleep. It is Waitaha tradition that after two tribes meet, they sleep together. They also *dream* together, which is the key to the ceremony. Dreaming to the Waitaha is more that just a vision one has at night. It is the future reality, if it is dreamed in ceremony.

After two tribes have performed their ceremony, exchanged words, breathed together, and slept and dreamed together, they are one family. The Waitaha Ruka family accepted us as an intimate part of their family, and from that moment on, we were all Waitaha. It was beautiful, and it was a high honor.

I have to admit that I had expectations about what was going to happen in the collective dream state. I was very excited to go to sleep thinking that something incredible was going to happen. But it didn't happen that way, at least not for me. It felt like I laid my head down on the pillow and woke up only a few minutes later.

It was not until much later that day, when I was speaking with Mac's older brother Barney, that I realized the collective dream was manifesting. Wait a little and you will understand.

As the morning sun took us all out of the internal dreaming into the dreaming we call reality, bodies slowly began to emerge from under blankets and sleeping bags. Children ran through the house, men and women began their dance of life, and grandmothers and grandfathers set the energy for the day. This was to be a day of sharing knowledge and experience.

Grandfather Barney Ruka asked me to come with him alone into an open field. He wanted to speak to me in private. For almost an hour Barney gave me secret knowledge of the Waitaha that when (and if, of course) the Waitaha prophecy manifests, it will change the world forever.

Mac had given me some of this information when we had met years before. Now it was vastly expanded, and I realized that what was to unfold on this journey was of great relevance to the Serpent of Light and its Kundalini energy radiating out into the world. While Grandfather Barney didn't know what was being written in these pages, his words revealed great knowledge of the original histories and of the Precession of the Equinox. He filled in the missing pieces with precision. And at that moment, Grandfather Barney asked me to swear to secrecy my knowledge of the Waitaha prophecy until the right time.

Suddenly, everything began to click into place. I could see the bigger picture, and yet I am not allowed to speak about everything quite yet. I will tell you what I can, but according to Grandfather Barney, the Waitaha prophecy predicts a pivotal moment in history on August 15, 2009. This event may or may not be known publicly, but it will be the beginning of a new human dream, a dream almost identical to the Mayan belief that the heavens will open and our brothers and sisters of the universe will reveal themselves.

As Barney spoke, I felt the dreamlike state that was being created by his words. These were concepts and understandings that no modern man has believed in or even considered in thousands and thousands of years. If he is right, the world is in for a grand surprise, a glorious surprise, an awakening into a new world of light and ease.

As newly born Waitaha brothers and sisters, we left this beautiful green, hilly world and began to travel into many worlds of giant trees, enormous rocks, awesome beaches, and places where one could easily spend the rest of one's life. These pages are not the place to go into all of the beautiful experiences we had with each other and with the land itself. But these experiences slowly opened our hearts, and this opening was vastly important in order for us to continue on this spiritual journey, for the Waitaha/Maori would not have taken us deeper into their world if we had been unable to open our hearts. This was paramount to the fulfillment of their prophecy.

Secretly they appeared. In the disguise of feeling the energy of an enormous sacred tree that is about 2,000 years old, a small group of Maori stepped out of an old car near our bus. Before I even exited our bus, I could see from the windows a man that I knew well but had never met in the physical. His name is Walisi. He had brown skin and long, long white-gold hair tied into a single braid. He was one of the people who were in the background at the ceremony in

Kauai. Remember, the fourth-dimensional ceremony of the transfer of power from the male to the female? (See Chapter Ten.)

I approached him, and he wrapped his arms around me in a slow and heart-felt embrace. He knew me, I knew him, and we both knew exactly from where. He wanted me to understand how the Pacific Ocean culture, one of the oldest cultures alive, was an intimate part of the Serpent of Light and the New Dream. His words reached inside of me, for I was already becoming aware of the significance of how the new Earth's Kundalini was reaching into Aotearoa.

Walisi began to weave in and out of our journey until he had relayed the information to me about the coming changes in humanity. It was an honor for him to share this secret knowledge with me. I know I will see him again.

Another woman was introduced to me by Walisi. Her name was Loma Allen, and she was a grandmother from a Maori tribe who would play a central role in revealing even more of the secret knowledge of the Maori to us. But we didn't know who she was as we sat nonchalantly with her, drinking our tea and making small talk.

We continued to move through this ancient land from one amazing place to another, with continuous Maori/Waitaha teachings being revealed by different native teachers who materialized along the way.

The Ceremony of the Releasing of the Fragrance of the Flowers

On February 20, 2007, we were asked to be part of a ceremony called the Ceremony of the Releasing of the Fragrance of the Flowers that the Maori said only takes place every 13,000 years. We were asked to walk barefooted for roughly three kilometers along a quiet rural dirt road that leads to one of the most sacred sights in Aotearoa, the Crosshouse of Miringa Te Kakara.

When we reached this holy land, the gatekeeper held us back until final arrangements could be made to receive us. Then, walking in slow motion, we approached this place out in the middle of an open grassy field, where the grandfathers and grandmothers were sitting waiting for us to appear. We didn't know it at that moment, but we were only perhaps fifteen meters from the center of this ancient holy site.

As with the Waitaha, the oldest women led us to this point, with the younger females behind them, and the men behind the younger women. But as we came within a few meters of the Maori elders, the men were asked to circle to the front to face the elders, for they were to speak to the elders first.

The ceremony proceeded in a similar way; the men spoke first back and forth, and then the women spoke as they wished. Again, we all came into a line where each of us in our group performed the Hongi with each member of this Maori tribe. Only this time after we had breathed with each Maori, we were asked to move directly to the area next to the elders, where there was a cross cut about a foot deep into the ground.

As we waited for the group to finish the Hongi, we were told some of the history of where we were sitting. Even though the Maori believed this location to be extremely important to Maori/Waitaha knowledge of the universe, it outwardly appeared as nothing special, just a pattern etched into the ground and surrounded by green rolling hills.

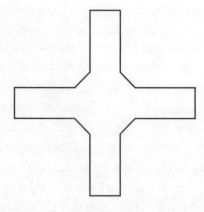

Figure 8: Cross

SERPENT OF LIGHT

We were told that there used to be an old wooden building enclosing this cross and that the building held a secret knowledge, but that it had been burned down deliberately in about 1985. They also told us that it had burned down four times before, that each time it was rebuilt, and that it was going to be rebuilt again in the future. Why they kept burning down this building and then rebuilding it was never explained to us.

By now the group was assembled. The men sat on the ground on the edges of the cross, and the women stood outside the cross in a group, waiting for the grandmothers to give the signal to emerge into the cross area and sit with the men. As the women began to approach the cross, the men, lead by Kingi, stood up and began a dance symbolic of the male phallic power to receive the women with great energy. It must have been amazing to watch the strength of these men as they created an envelope of energy, based on Waitaha tradition, for the women to enter into.

The women chanted secret songs in Maori to the men, as the men's arms went from high above their heads to their knees and they sang back from their hearts in Maori to the women. It was beautiful both to be part of this ceremony and to witness it. And this was just the beginning.

Eventually, we ended up standing in a large circle with the cross in the center. I was asked to hold the hand of the Maori chief on my right to complete the circle. Beginning with me, we all spoke, one by one, from our hearts to the ceremonial participants, a vision or dream of the future for all mankind. Moving clockwise around the circle, the last to speak was the chief whose hand I was holding.

The dreams we spoke about were to become reality in the future, as we were dreaming from the "center of the world." But what this meant only slowly began to unfold for us, as almost nothing was told to us about this sacred sight until after the ceremony and really not completely until the next day. Had I known where we were performing this ceremony, it would have changed my whole being for what was transpiring.

A drum that came from the Netherlands was handed to me; it appeared Native American in design. This peace drum was moving around the world to different circles, like our own—circles of people with inner dreams of world peace.

I began to drum, slowing dancing around the outer edge of the circle clockwise as my tradition had instructed me. When I completed the circle, I lead the group in a long line to the kitchen where the meal part of the ceremony was to take place.

The Maori had built a beautiful wooden hogan to fulfill this part of the ceremony. A fantastic array of colorful food and plants with intricate designs carved into their surfaces was displayed on the surrounding tables. I peered into these designs and wondered who would want to eat these works of art and destroy their beauty. The flowers placed around the room had their leaves woven into incredible patterns that I'm sure held significance to Maori/Waitaha eyes, but to me, they were principally things of beauty to behold.

After the meal, the chief brought out a photo album and began to tell us the history of this sacred site. He said that long ago a group of extraterrestrials from Sirius had hovered about the exact spot where the cross is in the ground, and they placed a huge crystal into the Earth in the very center of that cross.

This crystal was the reason the Maori held this spot sacred. It was this crystal that gave this place the power to become the Maori University. He told us that when the wooden house is placed over the cross and the crystal, the Maori University is complete, but he never completely explained what that meant.

He talked about a Maori man who had studied in this old wooden house for fourteen years, and then put on a suit and went to England to become a great professor in one of the universities even though he never went to formal school. I never learned his name. Somehow, by studying in only this old simple wooden building, the man had come to understand the universe.

As interesting as this was, I really couldn't understand what he was talking about. So much was being kept secret that I could only "feel" why the Maori felt this place to be sacred. Was it only because of the E.T. crystal, or was there something else? My spiritual curiosity was on end.

Finishing the ceremony with long hugs and special gifts coming from both tribes, we knew it would be another 13,000 years before this ceremony would be performed again.

One of the grandmothers gave me a large piece of cartilage that fits between the vertebrae of a whale. Almost the shape of a heart, this part of the whale had been on her altar, and the energy coming off it was extraordinary. "This is a gift from our ancestors," she said. Both the Maori and the Waitaha believe that the whales and the dolphins are their ancestors, that the cetaceans actually created humankind. (This is also the belief of the oldest human culture in the world, the Sumerians.) By looking at the Waitaha/Maori's ancient wood carvings, which are seen at the opening of most of their sacred buildings, you will see their human ancestors depicted with webbed hands and feet, indicating at least that they spent a great deal of time in the ocean, perhaps gazing directly into the eyes of those who they consider their ancestors.

A wood carving over the doorway of a Waitaha/Maori temple. Notice the webbed feet of their ancestors.

Two days later, as we were about to have our closing circle for this journey, one of the local women showed me the sacred geometry of the old wooden house that covered the sacred cross in the field. In minutes I realized how a little wooden shack could be a university and how a man could sit in this building and understand the entire universe.

Here is some of what she showed me. All of this information (and much more) can be found in the book *Ancient Celtic New Zealand* by Martin Doutré. You can purchase this book at *www.celticnz.co.nz* if you wish to go deeper into the ancient understandings of the Wait-aha maori.

This is a drawing by W. A. Taylor of how the cruciform building looked when in pristine condition.

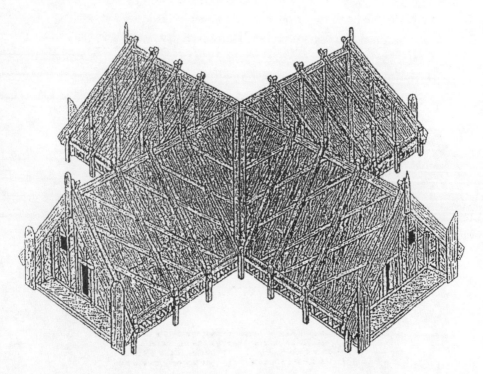

Drawing by W. A. Taylor of the cruciform building

This is the plan of C. G. Hunt of the Crosshouse building, with the cross inside of the building.

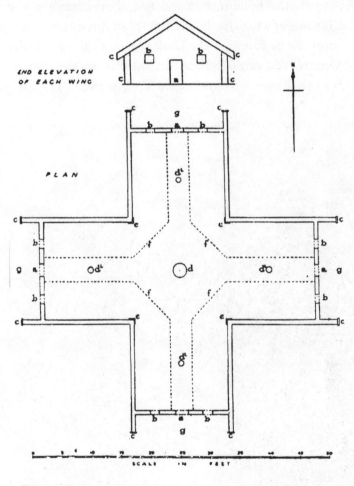

CRUCIFORM BUILDING, MARINGA TE KAKARA

Key:
a: sliding wood doors 4 x 2 ft.
b: sliding wood ports 18 ins. square
c: wood facings 12 x 2 ins.
d: centre upright 6 ft. circumference
d¹: small uprights 18 ins. circum.
e: L-shaped corner pieces
f: foot boards 12 x 2 ins.
g: porches open on one side

Plan of the Crosshouse building by C. G. Hunt

And this is one of the sacred geometrical drawings showing the relationship of the circle and the square to the building structure. The Phi ratio geometrical progressions of the circle and the square are obvious. These reducing circles and squares define significant positions within the physical Crosshouse. It is rotated to north to align with the Earth and the stars.

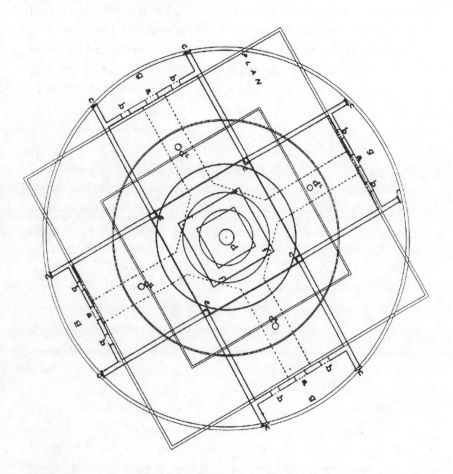

Figure 9: Phi ratio circle and square drawing

This is only one drawing obtainable from the geometries of this building, and as you study the relationships more and more, the knowledge of the universe begins to appear, just as it does in the Great Pyramid in Egypt.

But what was not apparent to the modern Maori/Waitaha was a secret code hidden within the building shape. I say "not apparent" because no one brought up this possibility. I don't mean to say that no one knows, only that it was not talked about with our group.

This secret, for those of you who wish to explore, can be found within chapter nine of my second book, *The Ancient Secret of the Flower of Life, Volume II*. The Maringa Te Kakara could very well be used as the "Center of Creation," from which all sacred sites within the island complex of Aotearoa could be precisely located, above or below ground.

This same building shape was used in ancient Egypt for the very same purpose. What became clear to me as I examined the sacred geometry of the Maringa Te Kakara is that the Waitaha/Maori have an understanding of the universe that parallels all of the great ancient cultures that have ever existed on Earth. And with the same precision of the ancient Egyptians, they are able to predict the future with amazing accuracy.

The Waitaha have remained hidden with their intimate knowledge of the creation process until now. This knowledge is only partially contained within a building. The crucial secret is contained within their DNA. The Waitaha are the first people to come out of Gondwanaland to live free in Mu or Lemuria, and within their DNA is the original secret from God of how to use their dreams to create or to alter reality in this universe of the stars and planets.

Without this secret knowledge of the Dreaming from the Heart, mankind would never be able to transcend this world and ascend into the higher levels of consciousness. But, thank God, the Waitaha are still living and breathing this way of being, and because they are, all of mankind will be able to move to the next level of life.

The Serpent of Life and its transforming power is radiating out into the Pacific Ocean, awaking the Waitaha and, along with them, the Maori. It is this Earth Kundalini energy coming from Chile that is accelerating their awaking. With their special understanding of Life, they will be a catalyst to the world to move human consciousness into the next level of existence. The Waitaha know that the time is now, and it is now that they are calling the world to their doorstep.

The Peruvians and Chileans will be the teachers of the new female way, but the Waitaha and the Maori will be the examples of the pure vibration contained within every cell of their bodies. One learns from the Waitaha simply by being in their vibration and dreaming with them.

CHAPTER TWENTY-TWO

UNCONDITIONAL LOVE
IMAGES WITHIN THE HEART

The Serpent of Light is in its geographical location for the next 13,000 years and is functioning perfectly. The Unity Grid above the Earth, which holds and focuses human consciousness and allows it to move into higher consciousness, will be finally completely adjusted by the middle of 2008. There is still a little bit more that must be done, but not much. On my end, there must be a trip to Easter Island to heal a certain aspect of the Maori, and one last ceremony on the island of Moorea to complete the Unity Grid and actually turn it on in a way the world has not seen yet.

The year 2009 will bring the first real connection with life from other worlds, which could not have occurred before the Unity Grid was functioning in a specific manner. This is a prophecy coming from several indigenous people, including the Maya and the Waitaha.

By December 21, 2012, the Precession of the Equinox will complete itself, and the beginning of a new cycle of another 13,000 years will be initiated. By this time the old cycle and the old male ways of controlling human life will be in disarray.

By that time, the female will be in control of leading humankind back into the Light. And on February 18–19, 2013, the Maya will perform the first ceremony of the new cycle, which will trigger the opening of all life everywhere to begin interchange with humanity in a "personal" manner, and humanity will begin a rapid healing of the remaining people on Earth. By that time, February 19, 2013, Earth's human population is more than likely going to have been reduced dramatically, but those that are still here on Earth will truly begin to show love and caring as the new way of the world.

What I am saying is that the next few years will be the most important years in human history. We will survive these vast changes in human understanding with the help of Mother Earth and her Serpent of Light, as we have many times before, but never before has the universe opened to us as it will in the coming years.

The secret is Unconditional Love, which will present itself through human beings who will change life of Earth forever. Most of these human beings will be children or young adults who have found their way into their hearts. And it will be the women who will understand and follow the children into their hearts and take this new way of being to the world. Finally, probably with great trepidation, the men will make the transformation that will truly complete the cycle. It is almost always this way.

It is the images or dreams that come from the hearts of these children that will be the power that actually makes these changes. The children and the women will be the first to enter into the act of creation and change the world from within.

Let me explain more deeply, using ceremony as the example.

Ceremony is the result of the ancient understanding and wisdom that the outer world of the stars, planets, and everything on the planets was created by the inner human world of images within the heart and the interaction with Great Spirit. Almost all indigenous people know this as a fact of life.

Much of modern man thinks that God is unattainable. He thinks that possibly God is in nature somewhere or somehow or perhaps even beyond nature, but definitely, for most people, God is not "intimately inside of us." And, for most people, God and man are definitely not the same consciousness. And yet, paradoxically, the source of this thinking also says we are "made in the image of God"!

Inside the human heart is a special place where all of creation is conceived. This was the primary teaching of Jesus, though it was discarded by the Greek and Roman church leaders for political reasons, and this understanding extends back even further, at least three thousand years before Christ, into ancient India and Egypt through the writing of the Upanishads and the oral teaching of Egyptian tantra.

When we humans begin to realize who we really are, truly the Sons and Daughters of God, the consciousness that created everything in existence, then and only then will humankind and God be one in mind, heart, and body and the veil of slumber be lifted.

The original people of this planet can help us so much, as they know so much and remember their eternal connection to Mother Earth and Father Sky. How else could they have lived on Earth for so long with so little imbalance?

The Serpent of Light has now moved to a new geographical location, and with this movement, a new vibration is being emitted on Earth. This vibration is drastically different than what was emitted for the last 13,000 years. The cycle is not a circle, but a spiral. Each time it goes around, it does not return to the same place, but a new part of the spiral, just like the DNA molecule. And, like the DNA molecule, the codes are released in new patterns. From this comes a new way, a new world, and a new interpretation of the One Reality for humanity to behold and eventually live.

You ask what you can do? Easy—leave your mind and your constant thoughts and return to your heart. Inside your heart is a tiny place where all knowledge and wisdom resides. Whatever you need on all levels of your existence is there for you.

And, in the human and earthly changes that we are surrounded by, and the incredible changes that are about to permeate our everyday lives, if you are living in your heart, Mother Earth will take care of you with her soft magical love, the same magical love that created this entire physical planet in the first place.

Remember who you really are, trust yourself, and open your eyes to the new beauty of a new Earth unfolding before you as we breathe. Peer past the darkness and destruction of the ending of this old male cycle. Do not look into Kali's eyes. But put your attention on the budding life and light in the center of the vortex.

Like a seed, your future is only beginning to emerge out of the darkness, but someday you will look back and realize that all the fear and distress was only a dream created from the confusion of the ending of one cycle and the beginning of another. Death and life are part of the same circle.

Now, look into the Light and breathe deeply the joy of life. Eternal Life without suffering was yours all along. Never were you ever separated from the Source. Live your life without fear. Live your life with open eyes and an open heart from the jewel within your heart, and you will extend yourself into the next 13,000 years here on Earth and far, far beyond.

OM MANI PADME HUM
OM MANI PADME HUM
OM MANI PADME HUM
Behold! The Jewel in the Lotus!

ABOUT THE AUTHOR

 Drunvalo Melchizedek's love for all life everywhere is immediately felt by anyone who meets him. For more three decades he has been bringing his vast vision to the world through the Flower of Life Program and the Mer-Ka-Ba meditation. He is the author of three previous books, *The Ancient Secrets of the Flower of Life, Volumes I and II* and *Living in the Heart*. These books have been published in 29 languages and reach out to over one hundred countries throughout the world. Drunvalo is the Editor-in-Chief of the international Internet magazine, Spirit of Ma'at, *www.spiritofmaat.com* with over 1 million viewers each year.

A child of the sixties, formed in the campus turmoil, counter-cultural revolution, and spiritual questing of the time, Drunvalo is a world traveler, a spiritual ambassador to and from many of the world's indigenous peoples who have information to share for the good of the planet. He has given workshops, seminars and lectures on sacred geometry, human energy fields, spirituality, meditation and living in the heart in countries around the world. The stories of many of his healing ceremonies and travels in the service of Mother Earth are recounted in this book.

His meditation with the angels and his work with prana and energy healing has helped tens of thousands of people. Drunvalo has expressed that healing in these areas are of extreme importance, for the difficulties with one's own body often stops us from continuing on our spiritual path. His research in the third dimension with natural products and methods to help heal Mother Earth and all life forms is also a major focus in his life.

He lives in Arizona. Visit him at *www.spiritofmaat.com* or *www.drunvalo.net*.

TO OUR READERS

Weiser Books, an imprint of Red Wheel/Weiser, publishes books across the entire spectrum of occult and esoteric subjects. Our mission is to publish quality books that will make a difference in people's lives without advocating any one particular path or field of study. We value the integrity, originality, and depth of knowledge of our authors.

Our readers are our most important resource, and we appreciate your input, suggestions, and ideas about what you would like to see published. Please feel free to contact us, to request our latest book catalog, or to be added to our mailing list.

Red Wheel/Weiser, LLC
500 Third Street, Suite 230
San Francisco, CA 94107
www.redwheelweiser.com